PRESENCE OF MIND

Literary and Philosophical Roots of a Wise Psychotherapy

STEPHEN SCHOEN, M.D.

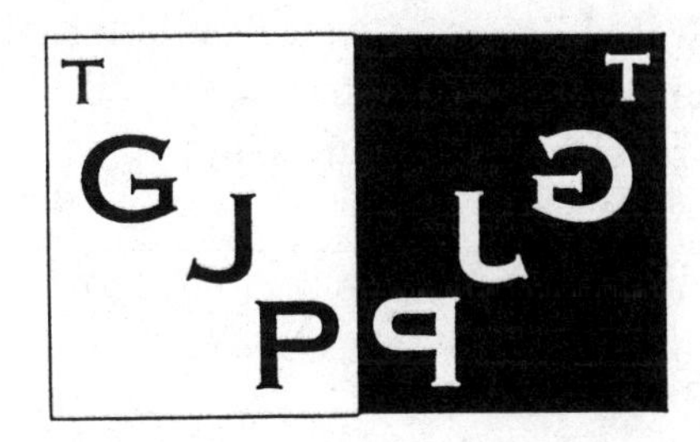

Published by:
The Gestalt Journal Press, Inc.
A Division of:
The Center for Gestalt Development, Inc.
P. O. Box 990
Highland, NY 12528-0990

ISBN #0-939266-19-9

FOR MARGOT

"That alone is true which is fruitful."

Goethe

Contents

1 To Throw Your Heart Over the Fence 7

2 William Blake: Right Knowing 23

3 Rainer Maria Rilke: When What is Near You is Far 47

4 Franz Kafka: Holy Fire 69

5 Martin Buber: We Together 91

6 Lao-Tzu: Things As They Are 121

7 Gregory Bateson: Metadiscourse 145

8 Jiddu Krishnamurti: The Unconditioned 179

9 Contextual Therapy 211

10 Toward a New Paradigm of Therapy 239

Notes 257

Bibliography 286

Name Index 298

Subject Index 301

Chapter 1

TO THROW YOUR HEART OVER THE FENCE

This book is about values in psychotherapy — for the reader who is in search of his own values. That aim, of course, includes professionals whose work is the practice of psychotherapy. But I am appealing to the ardor and the seeker in the specialist, a quest which knows no bounds of career. It is a general human calling.

And yet the field of therapy itself has grown so thick with subdivisions that it is hard to pose any questions about values without at once being assigned a cubbyhole. What is it, I am asking, that a client and a therapist can expect to cure? A specific behavior or specific feeling? Or a total state of mind? What is incurable? What is the illness needing cure? "So this book is concerned with significance in life. That's the branch of 'existential psychology,'" the informed reader may think. But this thought raises new questions. Can *existence* be a "branch"? Can we avoid values in any action? The way I greet you, or ignore you, on the street; the letter I consider writing to a half-forgotten friend, and then altogether forget about; the newspaper I pick up in the morning, or disregard — all these actions or nonactions carry a flag of values. "So this book is concerned with the messages in behavior," the attentive reader may now reflect. "That's the school of communications theory." Well, yes, I am speaking about the messages in behavior. But can *communication* be one of several "schools" — as though, for instance, we also had a "school of noncommunication"? What behavior is not a message? — though messages *inadequately received*, perhaps a screaming child's longing for love, may be one good way to define a psychological problem. Yes, we are all message-bearers: messengers of ourselves. With messages of what? Of the values we live by. When the therapist puts down, or disregards, his morning newspaper and walks into his consulting room, he continues to transmit the values by which he lives. And so the behavior therapist who cures a woman's phobia about leaving her home by progressive desensitization: first she opens a window, then she goes and fetches a rake from her backyard, etc.; the systems therapist who sees in her phobia her way of keeping her husband at home, and suggests other ways of her making the request, and of the husband responding to it; the psychoanalyst who understands her phobia as a continued anxious clinging that was repressed in childhood, and encourages her to feel fully her old need to be secure — all these reveal their own quite different, though perhaps related, values. Psychotherapy, of whatever branch or school, is inseparably about values; and my concern here is to present the values in it which I find most valuable.

I shall do so through a series of text commentaries. And the first thing to be said about the texts themselves is that none of them is by a professional therapist. They are from William Blake, Rainer Maria Rilke, Franz Kafka, Martin Buber, Lao-Tzu, Gregory Bateson, and Jiddu Krishnamurti. That is, from poets, story writers, and speculative thinkers. Now, there are many contrasts as well as likenesses between these writers, but they have one fundamental communality: a religious purview, the sense that life is spiritual life. "Ah! Finally!" the alert reader may now observe. "So this book deals with *transpersonal* psychology. That explains a certain protest on the author's part to being pinned down. You often find it in the transpersonal approach: 'I don't mean this.' Or, 'That word won't do.'" Well, I shall confirm the reader's rule by agreeing: "Transpersonal" won't do, either. We shall hear Blake say that his specific concern is the ordinary "Minute Particulars" of life — there's nothing "trans" about that. Krishnamurti will implore us just to pay attention to "what is actually happening." Buber will tell us that it's exactly the *personal* which counts. I shall return to the "transpersonal" in my last chapter. But my suggestion now is that we drop, for a while, all concern with psychological classification, and open ourselves to another question: Is there a special relevance, for psychotherapy today, to the encompassing values of meaning in life which are expressed by my non-psychiatric sources? I believe that there is.

By the mid-years of our century, psychology, as the science of personal development, had made crucial contributions. Freud had documented the formative psychic influence of family life in childhood. Jung had pointed to the continued integration of the psyche in adult years. Some of the great literature in the first half of the century — for instance, James Joyce's *Ulysses* and Thomas Mann's *Joseph* books — bears witness to the impact of scientific psychology: Joyce's use of the free-associational structure of consciousness, and both writers' themes of the search for personal identity and family ties, of blood and of the spirit. Popular culture, into our own day, is full of true stories of "finding oneself," from *I Never Promised You a Rose Garden* some thirty years ago, to the latest account of psychic breakdown and reintegration. Psychotherapists are featured in films with an international audience: "A Single Woman," "Ordinary People," "Zelig."[1] Today the basic assumptions of psychiatry are common coin: that we have unconscious depths and personalities which were shaped in childhood; that we are destabilized by outward stress and inward anxiety; that we cope with both kinds of tension with the best psychological defenses that we know; that drugs exist to lull excessive tension; that therapists exist to teach us better ways to cope.

But just after the mid-century, a shock wave ran through psychological consciousness. It came, in part, from clinical dissatisfaction with the prolonged course and often meager results of analytic therapy, and also with a new burst of theorizing: that life exists fully in the present; that the slow excavation of the soul's archaeology is not needed. Gestalt therapy, distilled from the emotionally expressive side of psychoanalysis and from Gestalt psychology;[2] new ideas in communication that looked on human problems as a current network;[3] somatic tension-release therapies;[4] experiments with human potentiality in direct interpersonal encounter;[5] and hypnotic appeals to the unconscious,[6] all shared the credo: "Everything to be expressed is here at hand, unified. It is happening now."

And, in fact, the dissatisfaction within psychotherapy was part of a larger *Kulturgeist* of inward release. Among the American "Beat" writers of the 1950s, freedom meant, very simply, no restraints. Strip the soul naked, and the body too. Tell, show everything, right now, though madness itself be the price; and often it is. And so swarming, surreal madmen are the people Allen Ginsberg celebrates in *Howl*:

> who lounged hungry and lonesome through Houston
> seeking jazz or sex or soup, and followed the brilliant
> Spaniard to converse about America and Eternity,
> a hopeless task, and so took ship to Africa...

In this new poetic voice, the howling voice, it is as though Milton had got very drunk, read Rimbaud, and then poured out his own updated pastiche of him. And the drunkenness was essential. It made for the abandon, for the cult of insanity as enchantment. Thus Jack Kerouac, in *On the Road*:

> ...the only people for me are the mad ones, the ones who are mad to live, mad to talk, mad to be saved, desirous of everything at the same time, the ones who never yawn or say commonplace things, but burn, burn, burn, like fabulous roman candles exploding like spiders across the stars...

So falls his grand Niagara of rhetoric. And, indeed, "never to yawn or say commonplace things" takes special supplies: not only alcohol, but drugs — and not the ameliorative ones of conventional psychiatry, but the psychedelic expanders of mind: LSD-25, mescaline, psilocybin; these were getting writers, and many psychotherapists and their clients, drunk. The psychologist from Harvard, Richard Alpert, discovered LSD and "everything at the same time." From *Be Here Now*:

> YEAH! I'M GOING TO DIE WOW! I'M GOING TO LIVE WOW! DIG THAT! GARBAGE WOW! NEW BLOSSOMS ON THE TREE WOW! PATTERNS OF ENERGY...YOU'RE PART OF IT ALL!

And yet in the patterns of energy there is the morning after, too, without capital letters and exclamations; and it brings up new questions. If consciousness-expanding drugs *enforce* liberation, where is the freedom in that? And is life ever just naked, in soul or body? Isn't flesh itself a mask of spirit? — as Karen Blixen, in her tale, "The Deluge at Nordeney," has Miss Malin reflect: "The Lord himself...seems to me to have been masquerading pretty freely at the time when he took on flesh and dwelt among us."[7] The pure and eternal embodied in the frail, mortal, murdered man: here is a paradoxical reality which we cannot make simple. Facing these facts in the bones, the experimenters of the 1950s and 1960s began to reconsider; the first shock wave settled into second thoughts. For clearly the trip back from psychedelic high seas, over the next weeks or months, kept foundering on the shoals of one's lifelong character. Inhibitions, depressions, anxieties, reasserted themselves. One's continuous life outfaced the revelations, or burned out.

Among the writers, Kerouac died of booze; Ginsberg became a Buddhist. In psychology, Alpert transformed into a Hindu yogi with the name Ram Dass; and many other clinicians, of diverse backgrounds, became interested in the relevance of Indian religious thought to psychotherapy. A fresh wave of interest also developed in short-term strategic therapies, largely influenced by the brilliant intuitive work of Milton Erickson, and by the eternal wish of the heart, as brochures put it, for "quick, deep, lasting results." But many avant-garde therapists of the 1960s and early 1970s took a conservative turn: with a new respect for the deep roots of character, they began to study the characterological coping styles — schizoid, narcissistic, and borderline-psychotic — that psychoanalysts for many years have been exploring. In the bookstores, Kerouac's novel, *The Dharma Bums* ("Dharma" is the Pali word for "cosmic law") was replaced by essays of a young couple titled *Dharma and Marriage*. We have returned from the Bohemians to the good burghers.

But this new turn is not only conservative. There is a renewed wish, in psychological thought of the last twenty years, to appraise the whole range of experience, and to balance values: to accommodate both peak events and "commonplace things"; above all, to find the ways in which the big and little realities interpenetrate. We have heard Miss Malin's view: that big and little interplay in masquerade. And responding to her in the story, the actor Kasperson talks of the truth which a mask "ingeniously reveals...[For] so speaketh the Arbiter of the masquerade: 'By thy mask I shall know thee.'" So, it seems, reality stands; it is by our masks that we are revealed. The identification of the undisguised person in his disguise of character is the subtle and full task of self-discovery; and between people, of true relationship.

This identification is the domain of psychotherapy. And, equally, it is the domain of religion — not as regards any one sect or school, though of course it doesn't exclude the explicit interests of some therapists today in religions East or West. But I am speaking in a larger sense: of a universal potency of human life, wherein our personal moments, personal masks, intersect with a kind of experiencing to which we make no personal claim at all; in which, while still entirely myself, I enter naturally into a state that feels clearly "more than myself" or "no longer myself." The house, the garden, the other person, certainly the sky, are not "mine," and yet I am "at one with them." This is the domain, too, both supernal and everyday, in which the texts that I shall discuss make their profound and varied statements.

The question of the disguised and the undisguised presents itself to us initially in the very medium of our material. All our authorities write; all of them will give us their sense of the truth in words. Here, at once, is a catch. For while we think of language as a basic tool, a basic gift, of human communication, strictly it is only a marker of what is meant, a system of signs which codes or clothes meaning.[8] And we know quite well that it can be used in a variety of socially acceptable lies: that journalists in the news media falsify blatantly, with omissions and misquotations; that words can be cleverly warped, like the Newspeak of Orwell's *1984*; that even their factual truth can be made impotent, as in those profitable ads of our free culture which show radiantly healthy men and women lighting up, just above the government statement that cigarettes kill. And so about language itself, and the uses of language, we face fresh questions. For the truth of the soul, is the clothing of words ever apt? Is the disguise ever transparent enough? What, perhaps, may words *not* be able to say?

The questions are important not because we can expect a single conclusive answer to them, but precisely because we cannot. In one moment, my own words — the very words of the sentences I am writing here — seem to be the direct bequest of truth. In the next moment, they are ashes in the mouth. And, in fact, throughout literate culture, testimony both for and against language is eloquent, even, one might wryly say, decisive. I shall give a tribute — a little cloudburst of quotations from each side which seem to freshen the spirit in quite different ways. First, the advocates:

"In the beginning," St. John himself begins, "was the Word, and the Word was with God, and the Word was God." All creation, here, is word; the emblem is at the core. And the first man of Western myth was brought the birds and the beasts for naming: "and whatsoever Adam called every living creature, that was the name thereof." Language, therefore, as our measure of clarity and order. In ancient China, too, Confucius insisted on the fundamental need for correct discourse. For, he taught,

> If what is said is not what is meant, then what ought to be done remains undone...morals and art will decay...justice will go astray, [and] the people will stand about in helpless confusion. Hence language must not be allowed to deteriorate. This matters above everything.[9]

In India, the Buddha listed as a primary virtue Right Speech: honest talk, at the same time without abuse or slander.[10]

Where there is conflict between people, for instance, Right Speech will mean openness about hurt, promoting an open response, rather than abusive anger, which evokes defense and abuse from the other. Thus language as exemplar of the soul, boon of the spirit. And after this fashion, over the centuries, have come to it the widest cultural praise and power. For the good Ali Baba, "who eked out a scanty livelihood" selling fuel, the two words, *Open Sesame*[11] were sheer magic, revealing to him, within a rock, a treasure of hidden wealth. Coleridge, in his *Biographia Literaria*, tells us that imaginative writing repeats "in the finite mind...the eternal act of creation" — words, again, as the coinage of truth. In *A Midsummer's Night Dream*, Shakespeare salutes them in a light vein, as the gift to poetic nature; they give

> to airy nothing
> A local habitation and a name.

While in the despairing love-mood of his "Marienbad Elegy," the aging poet Goethe finds in them the great consoler: instead of mute pain,

> God gave me the gift to say what I suffer...

Among the writers in this book, we shall be hearing Martin Buber, of our time, speak in the manner of St. John about Primary Words as acts of fundamental creation. And the novelist Hermann Broch, concluding his *Death of Virgil*, has the dying poet rhapsodize in diapason on the archetypal word:

> ...consummating and initiating, mighty and commanding, inspiring and protecting, gracious and thundering, the word of discrimination, the word of the pledge, the pure word...the word beyond speech.

So much, then, for language as glory, adorning the soul it covers, expressing all that needs to be expressed.

But to its adversaries, quite the reverse: language is the most ill-fitting garment of the soul. In our book, we shall hear the ancient Chinese sage Lao-Tzu note dryly:

He who knows does not speak;
He who speaks does not know.

And, in Western religious tradition, the 14th century mystic Jon of Ruysbroeck refers to the "imageless Nudity"[12] of the divine; while the anonymous author of *The Cloud of Unknowing,* from the same period, tells us of the quest for God: "When you begin, you find only darkness...[and] if you are to feel him or touch him in this life, it must always be...in this darkness." To this view, the hard brightness of words can be only a barrier, not the gift but the bane of God; striving to be clear and fluent, the soul speaks with speech only broken speech. To be clear, it must speak in silence — as the old hag proclaims in Karen Blixen's story, "The Blank Page," "Who then...tells a finer story than any of us? Silence does."[13] And many other eloquent writers have not said less. "What do you read, my lord?" Polonius asks Hamlet. He answers, "Words, words, words," to make light of them three times. "Human speech," Flaubert sighs to us in *Madame Bovary,* "is like a cracked kettle on which we tap crude rhythms for bears to dance to, while we long to make music that will melt the stars." And Nabokov, going to meet a lover of his youth, on a rainy evening, at his uncle's manor house in the country south of St. Petersburg, muses in his autobiography on all the sensations and feelings of that remote time "that one always hopes might survive captivity in the zoo of words"[14] — and do not. Within the dialectic of words and the wordless, at best we can know what Broch's Virgil has known, "The word that always returns to silence." Or, with still greater austerity, Wittgenstein concludes his *Tractatus Logico-Philosophica,* "What we cannot speak about we must consign to silence."

Thus the evidence, pro and contra. How can the written word honor both sides?

Perhaps in the manner that this review of the evidence itself makes plain: I mean, by the capacity of words to move us. In his essay on Pope, De Quincey writes:

> There is...the literature of *knowledge*; and...the literature of *power*. The function of the first is to *teach*; of the second, to *move*. The first speaks to the *mere* discoursive understanding; the second...to the higher understanding, but always through the affections of pleasure and sympathy...There is a rarer thing than truth, namely *power* or deep sympathy with truth.

The "language of knowledge" occurs in psychological theory, which describes mental life, personal development, and social behavior in terms of "discursive understanding." De Quincey's "higher understanding" and "rarer truth" is language with the pulse of the soul. I shall have something to say, later on, about the overlap between these two. But haven't we clearly heard the pulse beating in Flaubert's lament about the limits of language? Don't we listen for it in all great writing, which combines, in Nabokov's trim phrase, "the precision of poetry and the intuition of science"?[15] For just as, earlier, I spoke of personal experience intersecting something vaster, no longer personal, so also words can be at times transfixed by a wordless vastness, can make the inexpressible expressive. Gide once commented on the worth of language: "It is not so much what you say in a book that constitutes its value...[but] all you would like to say, which nourishes it secretly."[16] Whether they are for words or against them, the writers we shall be discussing all let us share this secret.

It is perhaps time to take sides against this book. The Gestalt therapist, in this way, makes use of a voice of Loyal Opposition within the client, which lays siege to his own noblest plans, and which needs to be heard and answered. And so I summon up a reader with precise objections.

"All right," he says. "You want to give us great thoughts about life, its free and its restrictive function. But why, of all people, *these* writers? Why not the really great ones? Why not Tolstoy, Goethe, Emerson, Dante, Plato? And what about the other half of humanity? Why have you no great women? No

Simone Weil, Hannah Arendt, George Eliot, Emily Dickinson, Hildegard of Bingen, Lady Murasaki. One could find seven other people perhaps better than the ones you've chosen; or seven times seven. Let's go down your list. Two poets: Blake and Rilke. A schizophrenic who hallucinated and wrote in a private mythology; and a man so wrapped up in himself as to be well called, today, a narcissistic personality. Kafka, your main storyteller: one of the unhappiest men ever to survive without a suicide attempt. Writing so much about suicide forestalled that. With his nightmare sense of reality, he's surely borderline-schizophrenic. Buber, your religious philosopher: an arrogant dogmatist. Bateson: a cryptic logician — *why* Bateson, if you want a speculative thinker, and not the rounded, lucid, religious-minded philosopher Whitehead? As for Krishnamurti: an eccentric mystic, known for his *idée fixe* against all authority. Who else? Oh yes, I forgot Lao-Tzu. But he's the one who probably never existed. There you are: six strange men and one myth. And *these* are your authorities who are to give us — wisdom?"

Unsparing critic: well asked! But there are important facts that you ignore. Strike the crystal in any of the writers you mention, and it has the same ring as in these of my choosing; and these I know with a particular closeness and fondness. So I am most inclined to recommend them to you. You will feel my sympathy with them as with beloved friends; but I'm aware of and shall assess their shortcomings as well. And are limitations of character so special to these men? What else, *whom else*, do we find anywhere? The bland and the sunny of the world exist of course, who "go skimming over the years of existence,"[17] but they do not show us the waters more than a few feet down. We value a man after all not just for his talents and his freedom from difficulties, but for all that he has managed to make of his difficulties. The men I've chosen, we shall see, have mined their own difficulties well and found much gold. That is one way to describe their wisdom.[18] At the same time, I don't intend them to inaugurate a new "system of thought," nor to "outdo" other wisdom, nor to replace the science of developmental psychology; my writers contribute only sketchily to developmental thought, though in the cases of Buber and Bateson, the sketching is profound. And other people, of course, are as deep, or deeper in other ways. Certainly women would give the different perspective which comes with different sex; we feel it in the woman I've already quoted several times, Karen Blixen; and were I myself a woman, especially in our age I would gravitate to several women mentors more naturally. But, most of all, I present these writers to you in the conviction that they are, simply, among the best. They are all revolutionists and individualists of the spirit. They are all concerned with basic commitments: how to conceive of life, appraise life, engage in life; and they explore these commitments to the full. They all know love as a state of being, not of grasping. They experience a sacred world. They fulfill a mission in it.

Shall we go on with them?

(The critic grunts and shrugs. I take that as a nod. He continues to look over my shoulder as I write. So much the better for the book!)

The texts which I shall be discussing, in Chapters 2 through 8, are as follows:

William Blake, "Proverbs of Hell," from *The Marriage of Heaven and Hell.*

Rainer Maria Rilke, Letters 4, 7, and 8, from *Letters to a Young Poet.*

Franz Kafka, Aphorisms, entitled "Reflections on Sin, Death, Hope, and the True Way," printed in *The Great Wall of China, Stories and Reflections.*

Martin Buber, *I and Thou,* part 1.

Lao-Tzu, *Tao Te Ching.*

Gregory Bateson, Metalogues, 1 and 4-6 from *Steps to the Ecology of Mind* and the epilogue to *Mind and Nature.*

Jiddu Krishnamurti, *Freedom from the Known,* Chapters 4-5 and 10-12.

With the exception of the *Tao Te Ching,* which is almost immemorially old, and Blake's Proverbs, dating from England of the 1790s, the texts are from 20th century Europe and

America, and they are all readily available in print. They are all, also, short. The complete *Tao Te Ching* is often decked out with photographs and exegesis. By itself, it prints to 40 pages. The sections from Rilke, Buber, Bateson and Krishnamurti, and Kafka's series of aphorisms, fill about 25 pages each. Blake's Proverbs takes 3 pages. It has intrigued me to prove the point that Polonius skirts: the soul of wit is brief; wealth of wisdom condenses far.

Commentary, on the other hand, expands on meaning, and has required, for me, a book. My chapters on the texts divide into three parts: the first sets the scene, both from the writer's life and thought and in terms of associations that the reader today may bring to the work; the second confronts and discusses the text directly; the third rounds out the writer's sense of reality, and discusses its implications for psychotherapeutic work. By their nature, too, the texts bring many other texts to mind; they are full of echoes which my ears have listened for: Kafka's work and the devotional writing of Donne; Buber's and Hasidic tales; Bateson's and the conversation of Socrates. Beyond the writers' individual contributions, I develop, also, enhancements and contrasts which they bring to one another; and these ripen in the last two chapters, which center on therapy directly. The first of these presents my own work; the second, a significant schism in the field today between individual and system therapies, and also new pathways in the making. I find that our texts cast light on all these matters, and suggest how great differences may not be irreconcilable ones. While I save for the end current controversial questions in psychology, this is the time to state plainly that, as to therapeutic schools, my point of view is relativistic. My training has been diverse: private psychoanalysis; training and practice in family therapy, hypnotherapy, and Gestalt therapy.[19] The last of these I have also taught for 20 years. But while I have a personal affinity for the emphasis, in Gestalt work, on self-awareness and good contact with others, I assume that all the current schools of psychotherapy hold valid shares in the psychiatric corporation. Also, that none of them is clearly a majority stockholder. Do we not know enough about the limits of what we know, to be a little humble that the other fellow may know something too? The truth, I am sure, has not seen fit to grace some useful theories and not others.[20] To the extent that the foci of practitioners vary, of course, so do their assets. With each asset, in turn, goes an accompanying liability. To the extent, for instance, that you pay attention to the unconscious and the past, you tend to miss something in the present and the conscious. And conversely. That is the nature of things.

One other point: many talented therapists have written books illuminating psychotherapeutic process from literature. For example, Watzlawick, Bavelas, and Jackson have analyzed communicational patterns of the play, *Who's Afraid of Virginia Woolf?*, in *Pragmatics of Human Communication*. Freud confirmed the problem of Oedipal guilt in Hamlet's indecision. My method is the reverse. I give the literature or philosophy center stage, and illustrate psychological process from it. In my last chapters, too, although I focus on practice and theory, I use the texts for clarifications. All this, I trust, adds something new. But it is definitely not final answers. Those desiring a How-to-do-it book — the ten best ways to do therapy, or to live happily — must look elsewhere. Those interested in what "It" is may want to continue. And knowing "It" better, then "the thing to do," or at least an approach to take, may become self-evident.

Karen Blixen once observed to a young Danish admirer: "It takes terrible courage to create. A French officer who rode in the *concours hippique*...told me that one had to *jeter le coeur* over the fence first, and then it was easy to make the horse follow. Writing is the same."

"To throw the heart over the fence!" A total commitment, in writing — and first of all, in living — where courage is reckless and the quality of risk, a little crazy. And then the horse safely follows.

Strange if confident advice, and an essential paradox. Like Goethe's curious maxim: "For a man to do all that is demanded of him, he must regard himself as greater than he is."[21] What is *he* saying? From self-delusion arise the actual achievements of one's life — the achievements, even, that are "demanded," that one owes to life? From nothing less than his craziness can spring Don Quixote's intelligence, courage, ardor?

All this goes far. But we can take the paradox still farther. We can imagine a craziness still more refined: Don Quixote, with his fearlessness and all his uncompromising convictions, knowing too that he is plain Alonso Quijano, the good gentleman of La Mancha, "of a kindly and placid disposition," one ordinary mortal among other mortals.

This courage, this abandon, this clarity, all our writers share.

It is the last great bond of theirs, by way of introduction, that I want to point to. And it is the great force by which they lead us, too, over the fence, propelling us, in Walter Benjamin's fine phrase, to "the epic side of truth."[22] For that, I would say, is their province. From different eras, perspectives, and starting points, each of them takes us just there, to a fullness of vision and of communion with the world. And we arrive then — just where? Back home; with ourselves; more fully known to and generous with ourselves. That is the course before us. Let us begin.

Chapter 2

WILLIAM BLAKE: RIGHT KNOWING

The genial, original thinker Emanuel Swedenborg, who, after many years of scientific achievement in physics and metallurgy, had begun to have spiritual revelations, used to entertain visitors at his estate on the outskirts of Stockholm with a *trompe l'oeil* garden. From the real garden, you entered a structure through open double doors, and there it lay; reflected in a mirror covering the rear wall. He called it his second garden, and relishing the conceit, said it was much more beautiful than the first one. On his earnest and zealous side, Swedenborg had announced in his writings the occurrence of the Last Judgment of Christ. This had taken place in 1757, when he was himself 69, and it had bridled forever the forces of evil in the world, so that the life of the spirit could flourish. We miss here the leaven of his playfulness; what can be put on the calendar "forever"? But he had chosen, indeed, the year that William Blake was born, the most ardent champion of the inward eye in English letters. And we ourselves can go on to imagine the child Blake visiting the magic garden in Swedenborg's old age, and astonishing his host with the remark: "Yes, it is more beautiful than your other garden. But it is still just a replica. Let's see it when the doors are shut."

The "visit to Swedenborg" is my own fancy. But the "inward eye" is entirely serious, and so is the connection between the two writers: to the young poet the old philosopher's books were to be a mentor, spurring on the imagination which he held sovereign, and which led him to his boundless faith in the individual. "No bird soars too high if he soars with his own wings." Blake's vision came to take in clearly the vested interests of his era and the wholesale dehumanizing of the Industrial Revolution; he saw all the seams of the garment. "Prisons are built with the stones of Law, brothels with the bricks of Religion." The same vision swept through the natural world and went past it. "The roaring of lions, the howling of wolves, the raging of the stormy sea, and the destructive sword are portions of eternity too great for the eye of man." I quote from his Proverbs of Hell, which we shall be looking at in detail. But already we notice their great range, and we begin to feel that Swedenborg's announcement of the Day of Judgment, in Blake's visionary mind, is not so odd after all. It has an unexpected majesty. It speaks the advent of a worldly grasp and Biblical grandeur from a poet whom Swedenborg never knew. In integrative power, with Blake we begin at the top.

And yet, equally well, we could say that we begin at the bottom — with disorganization. For my fiction about the visit to Swedenborg's garden picks up on a fact: Blake hallucinated; this was a daily matter. And he was always wrapped up in his inner life to an extent that we call schizophrenic. What should his sensible father, a London clothes maker in factory-filling England, with its industrial mills and its mass labor — what should he do with a child who sees a tree filled with angels, and God himself peering at him through a window? The boy also showed that he could draw well. Faced with a misfit youngster who might have talent, the father fortunately gave him rein: he sent his ten-year-old son to Mr. Pars' school for drawing. Then, at 14, Blake was apprenticed to an engraver, with whom he stayed seven years. His life moved on with a rare simplicity. The young engraver and developing young poet, happily married at 25 to a devoted wife, began to print, from etched copper plates with his own drawings, his own idiosyncratic poetry, which kept the imaginativeness of an unafraid child. From *Songs of Experience*:

The modest Rose puts forth a thorn,
The humble sheep a threat'ning horn;
While the Lily white shall in love delight,
Nor a thorn, nor a threat, stain her beauty bright.

Thus the delicate lyricist. But many prose passages state his view of imagination with a trumpet blast. From *A Vision of the Last Judgment*: "'What,' it will be Question'd, 'When the Sun rises, do you not see a round disk of fire somewhat like a Guinea?' O no, no, I see an Innumerable company of the Heavenly host crying, 'Holy, Holy, Holy is the Lord God Almighty!'" And to make plain that he had not taken leave of his senses, indeed how well he partook of the senses, he goes on, "I Question Not my Corporeal...Eye any more than I would Question a Window concerning a Sight." And then comes his great, almost offhand equation of eye and window. "I look thro' it and not with it."

Marianne Moore's "imaginary gardens" of poetry, "with real toads in them,"[1] are clearly the gardens of Blake's real world. Or we can say that, for him, the poetically imaginative was not a profession, but a way of life. But also, like Hamlet, he knew a hawk from a handsaw. Is this schizophrenia? One of Blake's achievements is to defy our categories. For his is a clarity that comes dripping wet from the waters of hallucination; the clarity, in fact, takes in these waters many a refreshing dip:

For double vision my Eyes do see,
And a double vision is always with me.
With my inward Eye 'tis an Old Man grey;
With my outward, a Thistle across my way.[2]

And he was his own most sane-sounding defender. Early in his adult life he had sharpened his teeth on the mechanical cataloguing of experience he saw in Locke's philosophy: that the mind begins as a *tabula rasa* and constructs all its ideas from sense data. Well, but where then is the *fundamental reality* of imagination, its verve and glow? So, too, with the science of his day. "God forbid," he notes in the margins of Joshua Reynolds' *Discourses*, "that the truth should be confined to Mathematical

Demonstration." To be truly awake is to see with many levels of vision. It is, according to his well-known motto:

To see a World in a grain of sand,
And a Heaven in a wild flower,
Hold Infinity in the palm of your hand,
and Eternity in an hour.[3]

But at the same time that he opposes literalness, he repudiates all generality too. From his long poem *Jerusalem*:

He who would do good to another must do it in
Minute Particulars.
General Good is the plea of the scoundrel,
hypocrite, and flatterer.

"Minute Particulars" also distinguish his drawings: human forms, and physical nature too, that seem to pulsate, in subdued tempera colors from cloudy grays and browns to luminous silver, blue, and gold textured like old parchment; rapt figures and faces that are caught in an elemental ritual dance. But never, in their rhapsody, insubstantial. Each one retains its individuality with a clear bounding line. In art, one learns this specificity best by good copying; in fact, "Servile Copying," our apostle of Imagination notes, "is the Great Merit of Copying."[4] For thus art achieves the technical excellence and precision of nature, while it transmutes nature beyond the Guinea sun. And thus, too, the eye trained for detail shows another side of the poet, turned outward from his multiple vision into the town wit with a worldly eye:

A petty sneaking knave I knew —
O! Mr. Cromek, how do ye do?[5]

Three barbed words, then a ruse of polite surprise — and runty Mr. C. stands before us. But Blake's satire is also, after all, a child of Imagination, which always is called on to complete a thing — be it base or noble, desolating or sublime. Nor does Imagination lead only to something affirmative. It can raise an irreconcilable doubt, like the great question that Blake faced in the ferocity of the tiger:

> Did He who made the lamb make thee? [6]

For Blake's vision takes nothing away from life's anguish. Defying categories again, his confidence and assurance reflect William James' Religion of Healthy-Mindedness and its followers of mind-cure.[7] But unlike James' group, which cultivates an impregnability to the ills of living, Blake accepts them fully:

> Man was made for joy and woe;
> And when this we rightly know,
> Thro' the world we safely go.[8]

He was 36 when he composed *The Marriage of Heaven and Hell* and in the full swing of his productivity. *Songs of Innocence* had already been published; *Songs of Experience* was about to be. These are the volumes with his most famous lyrics, full of child-joy, child-sorrow, in awe equally of human beauty, cruelty, and deceit. He had begun working too on his notoriously obscure prophetic books, with their host of mythological characters and spellbinding, dithyrambic lines:

> I seized thee, beauteous Luvah; thou art faded
> like a flower,
> And like a lily thy wife Vala, wither'd by winds.[9]

The Marriage, a tract of 12 pages, is middling obscure. Blake's prose vignettes of vain Angels who spout Aristotle's Analytics (the scourge of Imagination) and of grand, Christ-loving Devils, his prophetic tone and occult visions, all bewilder us.

But the centerpiece of the work and our particular concern, "The Proverbs of Hell," are in a world of light — impassioned, psychologically subtle, taut, bright with gnomic wisdom.

And yet, accessible as they are, we do well to look first at the entrance ways Blake provides to beckon us on to them. For these Proverbs need to be prepared for. A tone of expectancy and intensity must be set, Blake's philosophy itself must be addressed, if the mind's eye will bring them properly into view.

He begins *The Marriage* with a verse that sounds like a drum roll:

> Rintrah roars, and shakes his fires in the burden'd air;
> Hungry clouds swag on the deep.

Rintrah, a Blakean demiurge, will figure as Wrath in several prophetic books to come; here he presages Revolution. The fiery air, the hungry clouds are ready to devour the old world order. We are in the early 1790s, with the soot of the Industrial Revolution in mouth and brain. It is the aftermath, too, of the French Revolution, and the second decade after the American Revolution —— and Blake wrote prophecies sympathetic to both. But we are also in the world era natural to the visionary. It is today; it is every day; it is the normal hypocritical society of man, in which

> ...the sneaking serpent walks
> In mild humility,

and it is time now — for this, especially, the drum rolls — to revive the eternal order: Adam in Paradise and all those who are, according to Isaiah, "ransomed of the Lord." A wedding is announced. And now, in detail, we learn just how joy and woe are "rightly known." It is in the welcome and the joining of life's Contraries. Blake writes: "Without Contraries is no progression. Attraction and Repulsion, Reason and Energy, Love and Hate, are necessary to Human existence." And again: "Good is the passive that obeys Reason. Evil is the active springing from Energy." These two are Heaven and Hell. Of course, Hell, with its relish of energy, stands opposed to the perfect concord of Heaven. But Blake, today, will marry them.

And with this singular covenant of his own, he finally defies Swedenborg too, his old friend of deep vision and direct illumination from God. For Swedenborg's was a static, spiritually balanced Heaven and Hell which remain separate and in fact had their particular points of correspondence in the human body: the open heart of Heaven, the gnashing teeth of Hell, and so on. But to Blake all this is too clockwork, like Newton's world. His own view is entirely different. Soul and body are indivisible. The body, all of it, is imbued with soul. It is, everywhere, the soul's energy and exaltation. Repulsion and Hate themselves, what we cannot abide and what we detest, tap an uncurbed energy which we have called Hell, but which is the real heart of life, which is "the only life." And of itself, "Energy is Eternal Delight." Swedenborg, turning his back on Hell, has only "written all the old falsehoods." The Marriage of Heaven and Hell is both requisite and indissoluble, because reason and energy are both part of the body: reason, Blake says, is the "outward circumference of energy." This marriage, to be sure, abounds in its own contraries: reason can usurp psychic energy; psychic energy can bend reason. But Blake's concern is to show the union in its strength. The Proverbs of Hell are its marriage vows.

He gives us one other point of entry to them: poetic vision. In an early tract he had written: "The Poetic Genius is the True Man."[10] And we have heard him say the same thing of imagination. It is clear that to him the reasonings of imagination are at one with this genius, and stand ordinary reason on its head. Thus, for instance, Milton thought he wrote *Paradise Lost* to justify the ways of God to man, but a "true Poet, [he was] of the Devil's party without knowing it." And how well indeed Blake's eye of the mind fits the poet of the Fall: blind Milton, with his luminous Satan! This Devil, Blake tells us further, is *really the Messiah*, who "formed a Heaven of what he stole from the Abyss," and who knows the *refreshment* of Hell, which is Desire. The Proverbs themselves are the progeny of Desire. Who knows their number? Why would it not be infinite? Blake himself has been walking among the fires of Hell, delighted with the enjoyments of Genius," and has collected for us sixty of the Proverbs, to "show the nature of Infernal wisdom," the signature of this new order.

And so we enter into their presence.

From his tone throughout these preliminaries, we sense that in him the new spiritual order has long been established. Since the days of his own childhood angels, the high magnification of his vision had been set. Experience seems to have filled it out like so many variations on a theme. There is a portrait of him by Thomas Phillips that shows him at about the age when he proclaimed the Proverbs. We see a genteel, neatly dressed man with a receding hairline, at once elfin and sturdy. There is nothing other-worldly about him, but the alert, clear eyes, turned away to the left, seem to be looking straight at the Heavenly Host. Or, perhaps, at the Hell he refashioned from the old one, swirling upward now to become, afresh, paradisal earth.

The sheer plenitude of the Proverbs — their number, variety, their recurring *message* of plenitude! "The road of excess leads to the palace of wisdom." "You never know what is enough unless you know what is more than enough." In their own abundance, these children of desire show, in a sense, an absence of desiring: everything is realized. But, also, the realization is not at all a finished thing, complete and done with. It is present music. And it is played, as it were, on a pipe, like the one the child speaks of in *Songs of Innocence*:

"Piper, pipe that song again"...

For the abundance that leads to wisdom is, in the cadence of the Proverbs, trim and lithe, like a single line of melody. Listen again: "He whose face gives no light, shall never become a star." Now we are hearing, in the rush of the words, the ardent, impetuous piper, but most concise. And once again (plenitude in the briefest form): "Exuberance" (the word rising like a dancer on her toes; then, in a downward relaxed curve) "is beauty." As we take in Blake's meaning through its expression, we learn, over and over, of excess, but as a kind of simplicity; of extravagance, but as a kind of restraint.

This sense of measure, fitted to the cycles of Nature, is explicit in several of the Proverbs — in fact, from the first of them: "In seed time learn, in harvest teach, in winter enjoy." Later in the series: "Think in the morning. Act in the noon. Eat in the evening. Sleep in the night." We are given the body's measure too: "The head Sublime, the heart Pathos, the genitals Beauty, the hands and feet Proportion." And also, the body and the natural elements mixed: "The eyes of fire, the nostrils of air, the mouth of water, the beard of earth." At the same time, all this charting of action and significance returns us to *the uncontrolled*; for the body is a supreme glory beyond our own power over it. "The lust of the goat is the bounty of God." "The nakedness of woman is the work of God." Consider, also, how these hymns to sex are uncontrolled beyond their era: it is the age of Joshua Reynolds' decorative portrait painting and Jane Austen's language of proprieties. And while Blake's feeling for measure leads to his practical instructions — what to do in the morning and the night — the larger truth is: "The hours of folly are measur'd by the clock; but of wisdom, no clock can measure."

We begin to see that Hell's wisdom is rich in opposites. And, indeed, how could this not be, with the psychological tensions of life as we know them — the Contraries that exist in each moment? But in the first place, always, Blake's is the wisdom of excess: not of "the cistern [that] contains," but of "the fountain [that] overflows"; and in the overflowing, the Contraries do a kind of mutual service; they circle back toward one another. Thus: "Excess of sorrow laughs. Excess of joy weeps."

Also, they work complementarily. We have already heard that

> Man was made for joy and woe...

But Hell's great gloss on this fact is: "Joys impregnate. Sorrows bring forth." How, beyond their circling together, this image gives to each of them a new fulfillment! Encompassed within sexual fecundity, joy and sorrow, each in its own right, serve together; and each in this way finds its own measure too.

The Proverbs continually surprise us with these many levels of balance — playing with opposites, so to speak, to reveal the dancer perfectly poised. "Damn braces. Bless relaxes." Here the opposites stay counterposed: the rigidity of the first; then, at once, the flow of the second. Again: "Shame is Pride's cloak." A constancy of opposites, of contrasts, once more, but in inverse order from our usual expectation. For when we are ashamed, ordinarily we assume that our pride is undone, our confidence *dismantled.* But no! In our depths, Blake declares, confidence always asserts itself; and so shame, when it occurs, shows confidence, but confidence that is cloaked, *mantled.* On the other hand, when we are open with our pride, we may feel royal even in adversity: thus emerges still another conventional pair of opposites counterposed, *fool* and *king*: "Listen to the fool's reproach! It is a kingly title." And facing the fool himself, we can envision the truth of psychic excess, the swing to the other side. Therefore: "If the fool would persist in his folly he would become wise."

A special expression of the opposites occurs in Blake's Christian Proverbs. His themes are familiar to us: humility, adoration, forgiveness, trust in God and thanksgiving to Him. But these themes, here, are apocalyptic. They have nothing in them of Sunday School, nothing of moralistic injunctions, and everything to do with Blake's dance of impulse.[11] One could imagine him with all his self-assertion, feeling a Nietzschean scorn for weakness. But his sense of power is of a power granted beyond himself, beyond his control, the power not of overcoming but of feeling overcome, and it leads naturally to his feeling humble. Therefore it is the one whose face gives light, who "soars...high...with his own wings," who would "sooner murder an infant in its cradle than nurse unacted desire" — just this one who puts himself forward is he who knows love as adoration. "The most sublime act," the Proverb exclaims, "is to set another before you." And again, as the fruit of yielding: "He who has suffered you to impose on him, knows you." Not resentment, as one might expect from being imposed on, but comprehension. Again, the sense of bounty which accompanies *gratitude* (usually we think that bounty accompanies acquisition): the Proverb says: "The thankful receiver bears a plentiful harvest." And once more, most terse, strangely matter-of-fact: "The cut worm forgives the plough." We hear this — what to all appearances is unforgivable — as simple declaration; and in Blake's realm of fertility, it sounds true: injury transfigured into new loam, for new harvesting. So Laertes and Hamlet "exchange forgiveness," after each is the cut worm to the other. And with their deaths in the play, a new reign of order begins.

Blake's "truth of the opposites" is borne along on his unusual sense of time. Wisdom, we have heard, does not go by the clock;

and certainly the Proverbs give no credence to the future. They all ring out with the sound: *Now and forever is this so.* But also they give the past its due. "If others had not been foolish, we should be so." Therefore we become free of outworn beliefs, like, "The world is flat." And we do not eat poisonous mushrooms because others, once, had eaten them. As to all achievement, in art, in science, "What is now proved was once only imagined." Therein lies the virtue of the past: thus it has nourished us. But neither shall we venerate it: in the harvesting of Hell, there will be no respectful pauses at old tombstones. Rather, "Drive your cart and your plough over the bones of the dead." They, too, are all meant for loam. Once more, also, we are given an image of fertility; for we can think of all the past as the great gestation of the present, and so hear in one exquisite Proverb a double-entendre: "To create a little flower is the labour of ages." And once more, too, we have imagery of lovemaking, where the bed is the heavens: "Eternity is in love with the productions of time."

Let us look round, now, at what time has produced. For Blake, humanity divides between the wise-and-free, and the foolish-and-caged. Not only do perspectives differ for the two; so do simple facts. "A fool sees not the same tree that a wise man sees." Fools, basically, are weak, but by no means unresourceful. "The weak in courage is strong in cunning." Courage itself soars, like the eagle. Cunning entraps, like flypaper. And Blake sees the upholders of Law and Right as the cunning makers of social traps. As we have heard: "Prisons are built with stones of Law, brothels with bricks of Religion." Also, the law-bound and the righteous are always conservative, and conservatism is always small-minded; it would paint over the world's diversity in its own color. "The crow wish'd everything was black, the owl that everything was white." One step further, and we slight or condemn whatever differs from us. This righteousness is clear depravity, and Blake's own thrust against it is razor-sharp: "As the air to a bird or the sea to a fish, so is contempt to the contemptible." The lowest of all is the greatest enemy of excess: that is, stagnation. Here we have Blake's definition of real Hell on earth: life with its breath held, unmoving. The Proverb says: "Expect poison from the standing water." All negativity breeds in it: backbiting, undermining, coldness of heart. But then, as we breathe, as we move, life returns; and moving freely, its own nobility begins again too and cuts a path that lowness does not want. "Always be ready to speak your mind, and a base man will avoid you."

On the side of passion, which is the side of wisdom, imprudence of course will reign: "The tigers of wrath are wiser than the horses of instruction." For life is essentially risk, and what may appear like a maze of uncertainties is just right for mankind. "Improvement makes straight roads, but the crooked roads without improvement are roads of Genius." Blake's own case confirms the point. And we can play with him ourselves as an expression of life's gross imprudence, in which it shows no mere branching off of straight roads. For he appeared among us, in a sense, with no right; he came from no direct gestation of the past. Rather, like Minerva out of the head of Jove, he arrived full-grown from a quite different body of thought. Or we can say, thinking in terms of the range of psychic experience, that the intensity of his presence revealed the intensity of what was absent from his era. Eighteenth-century England around him was imbued with a controlled, executive, ego-coping wisdom. On the subject of prudence itself, his fellow Londoner, Samuel Johnson, had noted during Blake's childhood: "Prudence is of more frequent use than any other intellectual quality; it is exerted on slight occasions, and called into act by the cursory business of common life."[12] This estimate is eloquent indeed on "common life." But Blake, the uncommon imp, will snap his fingers at it. His Proverb runs: "Prudence is a rich, ugly old maid courted by Incapacity."

His own view, capacious and inclusive, seeks in its very immoderation for what is real. "Everything possible to be believed" — simply nothing less — "is an image of truth." That will take care of exclusive system-makers, both in philosophy and in science. And, once more inclusively: because truth, beyond its images, is one truth; because imagination is the fundamental reality and is limitless; because the Eternal's love for the things of time is a constant love — therefore we have the Proverb: "One thought fills immensity." Blake calls it "thought," not "impulse" or "feeling"; and we remember how intellect, too, is a part of this world of energy; intellect is its "outward circumference." There is to be no diminution of thought in the honoring of emotions and the body, nor any division between these three. In a sense, for Blake, the psychic world surpasses the physical simply for its being without limit; in the physical, we see only "portions" of the larger truth. "When thou seest an eagle, thou seest a portion of Genius; lift up thy head!" And again: "The roaring of lions, the howling of wolves, the raging of the stormy sea, and the destructive sword are portions of eternity too great for the eye of man." But the main thrust of the Proverbs is not the measureless psyche but the soul commensurate with the body, soul and body as one, and therewith the fullness of physical being. We hear: "Where man is not, nature is barren." And so, in the fullness of physical action (which is action, too, of the soul): "The busy bee has no time for sorrow." And in physical daring (which is daring, too, of the soul): "No bird soars too high if he soars with his own wings." This fullness, we know, has the quality of overflow, in which everything — joy, sorrow — has its sufficiency. And thus the final summing-up Proverb, grandly, briefly: "Enough! or Too much."

So the piper pipes, and the Proverbs come to us as music. Elfin-light, too, they dance. But they are also — and here is a word of compliment after Blake's own heart — *full-bodied.* In them his imaginative vision sacrifices none of the hard facts of existence, its turmoil, deceptions, suffering. Rather, it presents the facts, as he might have said, unfractured. And this unfractured vision is his recovery of Eden.

Great wits are sure to madness near allied,
And thin partitions do their bounds divide.[13]

So Dryden, writing of clever schemers a century before Blake, announced the relation between the greatest and the least psychological order. Blake's wits, as near to madness as sanity can be, deepen the image, since they reveal artistic and literary genius. And yet what are we today to make of his Proverbs — we who do not deal with apocalypse, who face prosaic daily life ourselves, or who wish to help, with psychotherapy, those in trouble with daily life? How can we reckon with his Eternity and his Excess? Or are they right here? For we can think of Freud's own work, a century after Blake: his discovery of a timeless unconscious beneath our productions of time; of the passions that underlie and give shape to reasons; and of the "thin partitions" between dream insanity and wakeful sense. The steps from Dryden to Blake to Freud show the development of a single thought: this too, like Blake's flower, is "a labor of ages."

And may we not, today, develop the thought further?

The new thought turns on the validity we find in the subjective. Here Freud's views differ. For he wished to establish an objective science of the psyche, and he looked upon mental health as rational self-control, guided by outward reality. But, in the meantime, natural science itself has shifted its course. The picture of a mechanically regular, objective world — what Blake called "Newton's sleep"[14] — has given way to "Einstein awake," showing us that all physical movement exists only relative to the observer of it; that objectivity, in short, is always a standpoint. Not that outer reality doesn't exist, but that, inescapably, we know it only in our own shaping of it; we are all, in the word of the mathematician Heinz von Foerster, "constructivists."[15] And fullness of construction reasserts the subjective, the eye of the mind beyond the retina and the optic nerve. Here is the realm in which both the physicist produces his equations and the artist his achievements. And equally it is the realm where, as we say, we are "captured by imagination"; where children dream themselves heroes; where men and women in love see in the other person a rare treasure of beauty and virtue; where the largest ideals of social justice — in our age those of Gandhi's nonviolence and Martin Luther King's racial equality — are born and move forward, against ongoing obstacles, into the light of day.

When we look with this perspective at psychological distress, we see again the relevance of Blake's inward eye. For the imagination, clearly, is constricted in the monotony of psychic depression. It is specially fixated in hallucinations. It capsizes in self-doubt. It gnaws on itself in anxiety. Clinicians since Freud have often, in fact, used a kind of Blakean approach in healing. Jung literally speaks of Active Imagination[16] — imagining, say, a climb up a mountain, or down into a cave — as a way for us to reconnect with our unconscious sources of vitality. Hypnotherapists utilize trance, in which the client may imagine, and find, himself free of an obsession or a fear. And a wide variety of therapists today "reframe" perception and thought: the glass "half-empty" is also "half-full." Nor are these changes mere expedients to restore "an objective reality." They speak of an ultimately subjective truth. There is a famous anecdote of therapeutic reframing: Milton Erickson greeted a psychotic in a mental hospital who for years had done nothing but wear white sheets and proclaim himself Jesus. "I understand that you're a carpenter." The man, after a moment, acknowledged that he was. "I wonder if you would do me a favor." And the doctor respectfully asked to have a small bookcase built; he specified the measurements. The next day the man was busy at work in the carpenter's shop.[17] The story is one of permitting an *idée fixe* to grow mobile, of encouraging the patient's own fantasy of divinity to flower in a human action. For a *fixed* sense of things — and Blake would make the point as much of Newton's mechanical world as of the mental hospital Christ — is insane. The release of imagination, as in Erickson's masterful approach, restores sanity. It allies the wildest dreamings of the inner world to the sternest realities of the outer. That is how, so near to madness, great wits flourish.

Imagination, too, is always an event in the present: the spark which ignites it, and the landscape in which it flares, occur now. In our time, Gestalt therapy in particular has made much of the present moment as the actual arena of life. We do not breathe in the past or the future, and our mental and emotional experiences, too, have their full patterning, their *Gestalt*, only in the actual event now. But in two senses the present moment may not be enough. The first is the sheer weight of the past which the present can bear: those interpersonal realities of long ago, usually with parents — "how you betrayed me, engulfed me, bossed me" — all the still-painful and long-defended-against insults to emotional nurture. The second is a much more subtle learning from the past, which taught me to have experiences without registering them, so that I barely taste the food I eat, or feel no intimacy where intimacy exists. For all these burdens, the Proverbs give the moment new scope and power: both in their timeless-present tense and in their concern with the wholeness of each experience, their voice is a Gestalt voice. But with Blake's special inflections and amplifications. One reclaims the self which the past has betrayed or made shallow as, in the moment, one trusts desire, soars with one's own wings, knows the body as God's bounty, opens oneself to another. Above all, as one reclaims Imagination: from it is etched the vividness of the Proverbs which makes each feeling vivid, sun-flecked, loam for new harvest. Or to give them a spatial image: Blake has provided us with a cartography of affective states: joy, sorrow, cunning, contempt, enthusiasm, adoration, awe. We see them all as in a landscape. Each one (look again at "Exuberance is Beauty") is presented as statement — the fact about beauty; as interpretation — this is how beauty must be understood; and as oracle — "now and forever is this so." And these levels of meaning are superimposed one on another, like so many map transparencies, of which the total is Imagination Vision. Herein, each moment of experience finds its full depth.

Each moment, too, is needed. Blake speaks for joy *and* woe, not for a combing-out merely of pleasures. Our problem is not, as we usually think, "If only I could get rid of certain feelings!" but "How can I accept them all?" "Going safely through the world" depends on that. The same with physical weakness or defect. To quote from Erickson again: in a therapeutic *jeu d'esprit*, he taught a lonesome young woman, who considered herself particularly unattractive because her front teeth were spaced, how to squirt water between them. Then, using her "defect" at the drinking fountain in her office, she sprayed a young man who interested her — and so began a relationship which ended in their marriage.[18] Thus "good" and "bad" are joined in us, though we wish to sunder them, like Heaven and Hell. And thus Blake is led into wide shifts of imaging and tone on the subject of wisdom itself. At times, as the Proverb says, it is a "palace." But also, sings a voice in *The Four Zoas*:

> ...it is bought with the price
> Of all that a man hath — his house, his wife, his children,
> [It] is sold in the desolate market where none come to buy,
> And in the wither'd field where the farmer ploughs for
> bread in vain.

This cost, this lament is wisdom with its outcast face, yet no less a part of the psyche's flourishing. A little later in the same poem, another voice encourages the dejected soul:

Yon Sun shall wax old and decay, but thou
shall ever flourish.
The fruit shall ripen and fall down, and the
flowers consume away,
But thou shalt still survive.

So "Sorrows bring forth." And imaginative vision sustains the labor at its most trying.

But granting the power of this vision, the fullness and strength of this acceptance, we sense also that a problem lurks in it. For the imagination — that essential sanity of life, according to Blake — cannot be distinguished from psychological projections and what they ignore or distort. We have clear instances in Blake's own views. His idealized picture of the French Revolution left out the "Minute Particulars" of the Reign of Terror. The catalogue of Biblical atrocities never troubled his admiration of the Bible. He found Greek art uninspired and abstract; he simply did not see its sensuous beauty. We face, in all this, the great glaring blind spots of a visionary. And the energy he proclaims, imagination in its dance, does not *always*, as he tells us, change into its opposite. We have conscienceless killers. We have had hate-driven Hitler, persisting in folly, and the more committed to it as he persisted. Human truths tend to be not only one way, and the qualifying words absent from Blake's Proverbs are just what add worldly breadth to many of La Rochefoucauld's *Maxims*. "Our faults are *often* more attractive than our virtues." "We are *sometimes* as different from ourselves as from other people." (The italics are my own, to bring out a contrast to Blake. Reading the *Maxims*, we feel the weight of their adverbs.)

Looking back at Blake's Heaven and Hell, we can say that he doesn't altogether uphold his own view; he announces a marriage but doesn't quite present one. He is always an advocate of one side — call it the bride's side — of impulse, energy, beauty. The other side — reason, judgment, balance — gets short shrift. Near the beginning of *The Marriage*, we hear:

"Those who restrain Desire do so because theirs is weak enough to be restrained..."; we do *not* hear that Reason ever puts one desire to bed with a fever, and sends another out to play.[19] At the end, the conventional world is promised the Bible "in its infernal or diabolical sense" — in all its passion, that is — "if we behave well." Its celestial sense, apparently, is no reward.

And if we turn these ideas to the course of therapy, we may wonder how a patient's freedom of imagination and impulse, granting his need for it, is to be protected *from the therapist.* Here Freud's concern with rational self-control clearly bids for our attention. For he pointed out how the therapist can transfer his personal problems to his work. What if his anger at his patient[20] stems from his reactions to his own wife, or mother? What if his guidance comes from his wanting his own way? What if he remains confused out of sheer unawareness? His own therapy is supposed to free him from these problems, but who can say that they will not recur? Isn't further supervision, or a lot of self-monitoring, needed to control his conduct? — although control, we know, is far from Blake's infernal wisdom.

Two incidents come to my mind from the world of psychoanalysis. The first concerns a conscientious young psychiatrist in his first year of practice, who often doubted the value of what he offered his patients. Some got better, some did not; there was an unpredictable factor in it. He undertook analytic training and felt a new security. "The wonderful thing about this method," he told his supervisor, "is that, even if the patient doesn't improve, I know that I'm doing the right thing."

So much for an assured sense of control.

The second story is about the great psychoanalyst, Frieda Fromm-Reichmann, who worked with schizophrenics when they were considered, in their autistic isolation, "unanalyzable." Her dictum was: "There are no hopeless patients. There are only hopeless techniques."[21] And disobeying the rule that one mustn't at all regress to the level of the regressed patient, when a schizophrenic man sat naked on the hospital floor playing with his feces, she put on rubber gloves, sat down with him, and joined in the play. After a little while, the man stopped the activity, went with her to her office, and began talking about himself. What had happened? By daring to "suffer [him] to impose on [her]," had she given him courage to come out of his self-enclosure, and begin to open his soul?

These two incidents suggest a generalization: In seeking to promote psychic health, daring is better than caution. And the generalization is Blakean. Emotions, of course, can be problematic, and on that account champions of Blake are sometimes apologists. For instance, the poet Auden has observed that, if Blake lived in our time, he would likely have amended his Proverb, La Rochefoucauld-fashion: "The road of excess *sometimes* leads to the palace of wisdom.[22] I do not think so. Blake's language is absolute because it is the language of the unconscious, in any time. He takes his chances with it. And he would understand all distortions of reason and feeling, as we know them in therapy or in political and civic life, as a failure to let the unconscious be full. In this fullness, we see "through, not with" the eyes. Or, as a famous statement in *The Marriage* says: "if the doors of perception were cleansed everything would appear to man as it is, infinite." That is what dictators, hypocrites, and addicts of various kinds do not see — and the rest of us, when we become one of these. For then our eyes squint. But with our eyes open, all the myriad colors of life, and all its daily truths, happy or painful, are in clear view. The child sees the naked emperor whose pretended clothes are being admired by everyone else who has blinded himself. The professional fool calls Lear the natural fool. "All thy other titles thou has given away; that thou was born with."

With all his partialities, Blake's own range and balance amaze us. He will present us with spiced common sense, in the manner of *Poor Richard's Almanac*:

A truth that's told with bad intent
Beats all the lies you can invent.[23]

Then, quite beyond Poor Richard's morals, we have his wisdom of plenitude. This specifically includes sex. In the sparest language:

What is it men in women do require?
The lineaments of gratified desire.[24]

and the verse neatly goes on, like a tribute to sexual equality today:

> What is it women do in men require?
> The lineaments of gratified desire.

His vision of evil is precisely of desire's lineaments not gratified, but debased. Now the scene is social corruption, the tone oracular:

> But most thro' midnight streets I hear
> How the youthful harlot's curse
> Blasts the new-born infant's tear,
> And blights with plagues the marriage hearse.[25]

For desire bound is always desecration. Desire free is endless freedom. In the tone of the piper:

> He who bends to himself of Joy
> Doth the wingèd life destroy;
> But he who kisses the Joy as it flies
> Lives in Eternity's sunrise.[26]

The last words, *sub specie aeternitatis,* bring us back to his visionary landscape. But we see, too, that all these verses which I have gathered up, simple and lofty, earthly and aerial, lie in this landscape, and could well be called: Blake's Rhymed Proverbs of Hell.

A story is told about Blake himself. A friend came to visit and found him and his wife nude in the garden. "Come in," Blake urged hospitably. "It's only Adam and Eve in Paradise." The story was repeated often, though the friend who was its supposed source later denied that the incident had occurred. But, as legend, it rings true.

Meanwhile, Blake's actual life kept to its own obscure course. A small circle surrounded him: the Swiss painter Henry Fuseli, the sculptor John Flaxman, Captain Thomas Butts, Muster-Master General, who bought his paintings for thirty years. Loyal friends; but one wonders about their resources to appreciate his own. Nor was his art or poetry ever popular. Neglect and poverty often weighed on him. And therefore his productivity is the more striking: his tremendous number of engravings, water colors, and poems steeped in his own cavalcade of mythic men and women— among them Los, Creative Imagination, the originating force of the universe; two of his sons, Rintrah, Prophetic Wrath, whom we know to herald the marriage of Heaven and Hell, and Bromion, Reason, the rapist of love and sexual freedom; and the consort of Los, Enitharmion, or Spiritual Beauty (modeled after Blake's wife Catherine). We easily recognize these today as psychic daemons; they are virtually the names of Jungian archetypes. But Blake invented them on his own, in solitude. He belongs to that band of isolates among great writers, like Emily Brontë of Yorkshire, and Emily Dickinson of Amherst, Massachusetts.[27] In Blake's case, one may wonder about the toll of this isolation on a marriage; and Catherine is known for an incisive criticism. "I have very little of Mr. Blake's company," she remarked once to a friend. "He is so often in Paradise."

So often there, we gather, without Eve.

And yet, at the same time, this exclusive vision never narrowed his grasp of real human conflict as we understand it. Wrath and Pity, for us as in his prophecies, war against the cold mind. Love and Hate are lasting Contraries, as apt in our time for the spiraling of human progress as in his perception of them. I am sure he would find the modern Greek poet Elytis, in his *System of Signs*, aphoristic after his own heart: "Far away, in the deepest depth of the lamb, the war continues."[28] Or to alter the image to Blake's own: "In the depths of the lamb resides the tiger."

And throughout his Contraries, most deeply, his faith in energy persisted. We ourselves can imagine him casting coins with relish, in the manner of the *I Ching*, and producing afresh his own divinatory text for each day. Like:

> If the Sun and Moon should doubt,
> They'd immediately go out.[29]

Once again here the visionary speaks to us. He makes us feel what doubt would do to the sun and the moon, as — on the same debit-line of the spirit — self-doubt does each day to our self-esteem. But the sun and moon are not, as he knows we know, going out. The picture Blake leaves, lastingly, is of faith in impulse, its sewing and reaping; and of what he might have called *the health of Hell,* its pungency, its expanse, its many-sidedness. "The eyes of fire,...the beard of earth." Awake to ourselves, we are aglow and rooted. And free from absolutes: "Everything possible to be believ'd is an image of truth." We hear an ultimate reply to all dogmatic theorists, within psychology and without.

Clearly, too, he would not suggest to us a single correct therapeutic technique. We would call his faith in energy, faith in intuitive understanding. But if empathy, one's readiness to feel the energy of the other person, is in conflict with intuition, Blake asks us to put empathy first. "The most sublime act is to set another before you." And interestingly, it is science-minded Freud himself who echoes this view: that the psychotherapist "surrender himself to his own unconscious mental activity, in a state of *easy and impartial attention,* avoid so far as possible reflection and the construction of conscious expectations, not try to fix anything that he heard particularly in his memory, and by these means to catch the drift of the patient's unconscious with his own unconscious."[30] This is moment-to-moment contact, whether in psychoanalysis or in Gestalt therapy. It is the one therapeutic process, Blake has foretold us, to be trusted. And it begins in a boundless trust in oneself.

The breadth of Blake's inner life stayed with him through his dying; in this case the stuff of legend is plain fact. Long ill from gallstones, he was in his 70th year. He was working on engravings that had been commissioned for Dante's *Divine Comedy.* Catherine was with him. A friend at his deathbed reported: "Just before he died, His Countenance became fair — his eyes Brighten'd and He burst out in Singing of the things he Saw in heaven." The eyes of fire kept open, and the eye of the mind. Joy, to the last, stayed coequal with woe, and he left his life with the grace of his living it.

Heinrich von Kleist, a German writer contemporary with Blake whom he knew nothing of, makes use of a biblical image he would have enjoyed; it combines two of Blake's grand directives, "Excess" and "persist in...folly." Kleist and a friend have been talking about marionette theater.[31] Their ideas have ranged from the perfection of mindless puppets to that of godlike knowledge; the latter, after all, we are somewhat nearer. Then Kleist recalls Adam and Eve's first folly, the disobedience which banished all of us to toil and stress. He muses: "And so we'll have to eat again of the Tree of the Knowledge of Good and Evil to return to a state of innocence." This excess of knowledge, this persistence — aren't they requisite? His friend replies: "To be sure. That is the last chapter in the history of the world."

Chapter 3

RAINER MARIA RILKE: WHEN WHAT IS NEAR YOU IS FAR

"You are so young, so before all beginning," Rilke writes in the fourth of his *Letters to a Young Poet*,

> and I want to beg you, as much as I can, to be patient toward all that is unsolved in your heart and to try to love the *questions themselves* like locked rooms and like books that are written in a very foreign tongue. Do not seek answers, which cannot be given you because you would not be able to live them. And the point is, to live everything. *Live* the questions now. Perhaps you will then gradually, without noticing it, live along some distant day into the answer.

Rilke was writing in the summer of 1903, from Worpswede, the artist colony near Bremen in north Germany where he was staying with his wife, the sculptress Clara Westhoff. He was himself widely esteemed as a poet, the author of a dozen volumes of verse and lyrical prose. We hear in his letter his own confident tone. There are nine others in the series (I leave to one side, for a while, whom he addresses); they give a detailed, subtly rendered charting of mental process and mental health, of the slowness of maturation, of tolerance toward others and toward one's own complexity, and of a faith in life more vital than the solutions and the comforts we usually seek from it. More than 80 years after the letters were written, we find that we can take our bearings afresh from them, as we shall soon see on a fuller look. And we could hardly guess — one must just know the fact — that the letter writer is himself a young man. All but the last brief one were written within a two-year period, when Rilke was 27 and 28.

First of all, then, a question about this man who asks us to love questions (we may get no final answer, but may see a pattern): what has gone into the making of this voice, young and ardently warm and yet so lofty-wise; this air, at once confiding and self-contained, of unobtrusive leadership; this large, decisive perspective on how to live?

Rilke was born in December 1875, into a middle-class family in Prague, and named René, in memory of a sister who had died as an infant the year before. A middle name, Maria, honored the Virgin Mary. He was dressed as a girl and given dolls for toys until he was five. His Alsacian mother always wore black, was devoted to the *Almanach de Gotha*, the official listing of European nobility, and, Rilke noted bitterly to a friend years later, "used to pray as often as other people drink a cup of coffee." She insisted that he never learn Czech, it was beneath him; as a small child, he spoke German and some French. His father, an aspiring career man in the Austrian army, had to leave the service because of poor health and never received the rank or pay of officer that he wanted. He worked as a railway employee. "I am almost convinced," Rilke wrote as an adult, "that [my father] was incapable of loving; right to the end he had a kind of indescribable fear of the heart." Mindful of his thwarted ambitions, the father sent his son, at age 11, to military school at Sankt-Pölten, near Vienna. The shy cadet was miserable with the tough boys, wept through sleepless nights, prayed for death, and began to write poetry. Once, struck by school fellows, he said to his assailants: "I endure it because Christ endured it, silently and without reproach, and while you were hitting me, I prayed my good God to forgive you." This remarkable reply, of use on the grounds of a military school only for derision, tells some salient things about Rilke's development. He speaks from within. He has found a noble — the noblest — historical example for his sense of personal misfortune. And the real audience he addresses is inward too: the spiritual host who could hear such words.

In *Out of Africa,* Karen Blixen comments: "Obscurity is the privilege of young things." The boy René somehow managed, under the glare and pressure of his parents and his schooling, to shelter his own obscurity. The hardness that was supposed to shape the cadet invited him, instead, to nourish his emotional life, in spite of the difficulties, or perhaps because of them; and Rilke was to become the great apostle of "the difficult." His early identification with Christ suggests, too, a recurrent note: a certain self-conscious striking of an attitude. He recruited his strength in this way, but isolated himself the more. And continued isolation, among a multitude of relationships, marks his life.

Pleading persistent ill health, Rilke finally left military school at age 16 with his father's permission. He began stretching himself in his own way. Briefly he tried a school of commerce, then the University of Prague, declared college "Pfuscherei" (bungling) and at 21 went to Munich to write. There he met Lou Andeas-Salomé, the energetic and stimulating woman 13 years older than he, whom Nietzsche had once sought in marriage and who was now herself married to an Oriental scholar. She was the first of many brilliant, sympathetic women with whom Rilke had, as far as is clear, love affairs of the spirit, and who acted like so many vibrant caryatids to support the structure of his soul.[1] Now, too, "René" was gone for good. Lou renamed him with the German, strongly masculine equivalent: "Rainer."

He began his lifetime of travel: to Venice and Florence, where he made friends with the artist Heinrich Vogeler, then with Lou and her husband to "holy Russia." They met the aged Tolstoy (later in life, but not at the time it happened, he could joke about this ill-starred visit to the great literary and spiritual master at his estate, Yasnaya Polyana. He found a 72-year-old man in a screaming match with his wife, preoccupied for the rest of the day, and quite unconcerned with the reverential young German). In 1900, Vogeler invited Rilke to Worpswede. The romantic meeting with the sage of Russian letters had misfired; not so the scene now with a young daughter of the Muses. From a diary note of a party, September 10, 1900:

> Clara Westhoff came. She was wearing a gown of white batiste without corsets in the empire style, girded high under the breasts and falling in long, smooth pleats. Her fine dark face was framed by cloudy black hair which flowed over her cheeks in open ringlets, her coiffure according with the style of her dress....I noticed that she looked quite beautiful more than once during the evening — when she was listening, and the too-decided character of her features was softened by her awareness of something unknown....

Their courtship flowered during the next year, in delightful countryside scenes that included Clara's friend, the painter Paula Becker. By the next April, Clara and Rilke were married, and they lived in Worpswede during the following year, through the birth of their daughter. Rilke also wrote a monograph on the Worpswede artists. But he wasn't settled in any regular, wage-earning profession, nor did he wish to be. He was in fact ready to leave. He appealed to a wealthy married woman interested in his work to help him finance studies in Paris: Russian literature and, especially, the sculpture of Rodin, Clara's teacher, the great, calm genius 35 years Rilke's senior, a prototypical good father, about whom he would also write. As to himself and Clara, he told a friend: "[T]he purpose of our marriage was that each of us should help the other to realize our own individuality and our artistic task more fully. I hope we will be able to settle down not too far from each other." Beneath this gentle and well-reasoned talk lay an iron conviction that life with another wasn't right for him; closeness seems to have worn only the oppressive face of military school, or the claustrophobic quality of his early years at home. Clara and he remained on good terms for life; her own independence and spirit made this possible. But deeper in him was the need to face solitude; that is how he would best "live the questions...unsolved in [the] heart...."

The time of the *Letters to the Young Poet* is almost at hand. But their presiding daemon is the same as that of all Rilke's poetry, and we must take this in a little, if only in the silhouette of it one gets from translation, to sense the pulse of the *Letters* more fully.

From his earliest published writings, his concern was the movement of inner life:

> This is my strife:
> dedicate to desire
> through all days to roam.
> ...
> and through pain far beyond life to ripen,
> far beyond time.[2]

As his outward scope broadened, he saw this movement subtly revealed in the actual life around him. In the behavior of a woman at a tea party who is going blind:

> She was moving after the others,
> withheld,...
> ...taking a long time,
> as though something had not yet been surmounted;
> and yet as though, after a crossing over,
> she would no longer walk, but fly.[3]

For a caged panther, at the zoo, where the movement of life is at ebb:

> Supple, strong, elastic in his pacing
> ...his circles much too narrow for a leap,
> like a dance of strength around a middle
> where a mighty will was put to sleep.[4]

Or movement celebrated in its tumult:

> ...Life, Life, strange time
> reaching from contradiction to contradiction,
> going often so badly, so heavily, crawling,
> and then at once, with unspeakably wide-
> spread wings like an angel,
> oh inexplicable....[5]

His generalizing bent is always present, but also the fine detail, the fresh word for the fresh perception, revealing "that shade of a shade," as Henry James said, "by which, and by which alone, one really knows art."[6]

Over the years, Rilke's view of the pathways of desire deepened. It transforms life, bringing about existence first of all in the *mere possibility* of existence, as in his late poem on the unicorn:

> ...Love supplied
> its need of being....
> ...they did not give it corn,
> but fed it with their feeling that it *might*,
> somewhere, exist. Were able to confer
> such strength, its forehead grew a horn.[7]

Within the senses themselves lies our own alchemical power to change, ourselves to "turn to wine,"[8] — most of all, to turn in quite the opposite direction from the unicorn: that is, to grow invisible. So Rilke wrote to Witold Hulewicz, the Polish translator of his *Duino Elegies* about "that transformation of the visible into the invisible [which] we are performing..." — as though the hidden freedom of his boyhood had become for him the thrust of all human life. And Clara's bronze bust of her husband shows him moving in this fashion into himself, the eyes half-closed, mouth and moustaches drawn down, the whole broad face sweeping inward, where the grail of his quest lay.

All this speaks of Contradiction (*Widerspruch*); it is his crucial generality; we have already heard him hail it as life's recurring nodal point. Rilke uses Contradiction where Blake had used Contraries, the rebellious opposites in man's nature — love and hate, reason and emotion — by which he lives and advances. But hospitable Blake's word evokes something that is already allowed for: Contraries can coexist, guests under the same roof. Rilke, more self-centered, feels the full thrust of a No to his life. As a visionary poet, he sings of Contradiction — from depths to heights, from the unicorn's nonexistence to its existence; but the man feels something else, that undercuts him, akin to death pangs, that must be struggled with, like Jacob wrestling with his angel. "Terror seized me," he wrote about Paris, a few months after arriving there, "before all that which, as in an indescribable confusion, is called life." Again, in a letter from this time to the Swedish writer Ellen Key, "On bad days, I have only dead words, and they are so corpse-heavy that I cannot write with them, not even a letter. Is that bad, weak? And yet God wills it so with me." He feels "awkward in life." Like the woman in his poem who is going blind, he would "cross over" to freedom, but brambles from the restrictive world, long viny roots from it, cling to him. The crossing-over is imperiled. In a letter to Lou, the next year, from Rome: "My progress is somehow rather like the steps of a convalescent, uncommonly weightless, tottering, and beyond all measure needing help. And the help is lacking." And then came the good days, when he wrote with power, conviction, assurance; for *Widerspruch* works both ways. The angel blesses Jacob too. One's resources are precisely to reach out — as Rilke advises us in a late poem:

> Take your practiced powers and stretch them out
> until they span the chasm between two
> contradictions.[9]

The contradictions, no less, of life and death. And the epitaph he wrote for his own death, at 52, begins:

> Rose, oh pure contradiction (*Rose oh reiner Widerspruch*).[10]

The first word is his recurrent symbol for beauty; the penultimate word, a homonym on his own first name; the last word, his virtual synonymy for life. The line of the verse is a cryptograph that puns: "Beauty — oh Rilke alive!"

And now for the origin of the *Letters*:

At 27, Rilke, the nascent author of his epitaph, was in Paris, for the first time alone, when a special thing happened. He got a request from a troubled young cadet, 19-year-old Franz Kappus, at the Military Academy in Wiener-Neustadt, southwest of Vienna. Kappus had been reading a little volume of Rilke's early poetry, *A Festival for Me*. The pastor at the Academy stopped by the student, recognized the author's name, and remembered that Rilke had been his own student over 15 years before at Sankt-Pölten. Franz Kappus, as a young poet himself, felt that the Army was wrong for him; he wanted understanding and advice; and he promptly sent his poems to

Rilke with a covering letter in which he asked for his opinions of them — and for more. "I unreservedly laid bare my heart as never before and never since to any second human being."[11]

Here, with a vengeance, is *déjà vu*! Another poet at a military school — as good a contradiction as life offers! Rilke began writing to the young man. At first he criticized his verses. They "have no individual style, although" — he softens his words — "they do show quiet and hidden beginnings of something personal." He gives advice. "Say what you see." "Seek the depth of things." "Don't write love poems"; they take "a great, fully matured power." Above all, "Go into yourself"; write only if you *must*, "without ever asking what recompense might come from outside. For the creator must be a world for himself and find everything in himself and in Nature to whom he has attached himself." The first three letters, written over as many months, are full of literary opinions and recommendations, as straightforward as the Earl of Chesterfield advising his son. And then, with the fourth letter, Rilke's tone changes. From now on they are a work of his heart, the disclosure of a life that has found its own center early, and has a special reason now for sharing it. We hear the sage, warm yet challenging, whom I quoted at the start.[12]

Whom, mostly, does he challenge? One can describe the letters to Kappus, as Rilke's biographer E.M. Butler does: "largely self-communings." The two men, in fact, never met; this is a relationship *as it were*, on paper. And certainly the husband and father who prefers to live alone is writing of himself, when he speaks of love as "high inducement to the individual to ripen," and of solitude as the basic truth of human existence. But Rilke can equally well throw himself into the concerns of the other. In his fifth letter he is distressed that published verses of Kappus which were sent him may have been lost in the mail. In the seventh letter he goes to the trouble to copy in longhand a sonnet of the young poet, saying:

> I give you...this because I know that it is important and full of new experience to come upon a work of one's own again written in a strange hand. Read the lines as though they were someone else's, and you will feel deep within you how much they are your own.[13]

As we read Kappus' lines ourselves, like

My hands gropingly reach out for love

we find a slighter, paler sensibility than Rilke's, and sense in him a faintheartedness that all the more evokes the older man's resilience. Yes, a relationship between two persons is certainly here, and with the special candor and intensity that physical distance sometimes provides. In the youth under duress, Rilke could well have seen his own problems, past and present, concentrated, as in a centrifuge.

In fact Franz Kappus, as a needy youth, grants him an unusual opportunity. Throughout his life, he accepted and liked his dependence on women for their encouragement and support — strong women with strong, multisyllabic names: Katharina Kippenberg, the wife of his publisher, who wrote a memoir of him; Nanny Wunderly-Volkart, who got him invited to Castle Berg, in Switzerland, where he lived and wrote for a season; the painter Mme. Baladine-Klossowska, who settled him to his work at Château de Muzot, in the Alps, during his last years; Princess Marie von Thurn und Taxis-Hohenlohe, who gave him the hospitality of her castle Duino on the Adriatic, and of another castle in Austria. He maintained a voluminous correspondence with these women, as with Clara and Lou and Ellen Key: hundreds of letters with his views about literature and art and his own needs as an artist. Modest Herr Kappus is something else. He is a youth *befriended* by Rilke, someone invited over, from a dark trail, to the older poet's campfire. The talk is direct and intimate, about confusion and love and sex and emotional pain. Rilke's tone, to be sure, is typically exalted; this is a campfire, if there were one, out of El Greco. But the exaltation is kindly, always without airs;[14] rather than upward, it looks and moves, in Rilke's way, *inward.* And this time the sensitive poet is befriending not a mood of his own, nor a unicorn of his imagination, nor a caged animal, but a fellow human being.

He doesn't need Herr Kappus for anything, and his voice conveys a special, warm disinterestedness: "my wishes accompany you"; "my confidence is with you"; "be glad and confident." We hear this fervor again and again; it is a generosity that comes from his own generativity. His letters carry forward the German literary tradition of the education of the soul in its contact with the world, from Goethe's *Wilhelm Meister* through our century in Hesse's *Demian* and *Siddhartha* and Mann's *The Magic Mountain*. But Rilke shares an exclusively interior life; he has little interest in specific outward events. Even when he speaks glowingly of the body, one feels he is at an almost disembodied level, like the courtly, warm Brothers of Henry James' story, "The Great Good Place," or the shade of Virgil as he leads the heaven-seeking Dante.

We do not have Herr Kappus' own letters. He did not consider them important beside Rilke's, nor, indeed, did he later leave the Army or become a significant poet. But we know from the great poet Dante himself his side of the soul's journey, being led by an artist-mentor. Rilke, as guide, tells us what the journey is like for Virgil.

So Kappus had begun writing, in the fall of 1902, full of his soul's confusions. Here, drawn chiefly from three letters, are Rilke's replies.

We are in Purgatory: this Virgil speaks everywhere of a work of purification. "Perhaps you do carry within yourself," he writes to Kappus in his fourth letter,

> the possibility of shaping and forming as a particularly happy and pure way of living; train yourself to it — but take whatever comes with great trust, and if only it comes out of your own will, out of some need of your inmost being, take it upon yourself, and hate nothing.

The tone is at once urgent and cautious: the urgency is that one must trust; the caution is to assess that the matter is important enough to trust. In turn, Rilke identifies what is unquestionably important: "a pure way of living" — the purity, that is, of its being one's own. We have already heard his basic advice about it: "*Live* the questions...unsolved in your heart." He goes on now: "...then you need no longer be afraid of losing yourself...." His own orientation to the inward heaven is certain. "Do not be bewildered by the surfaces," he continues; "in the depths all becomes law." It is clear that, unlike Dante's, the home of this new Virgil is not a Heaven-denied Limbo, nor yet the spirit-world free of all confusion, but Purgatory too.

It is clear, also, that his speech has a simple, tender eloquence, and that the eloquence lies in the subjectivity, the "need of your inmost being." When, for instance, Rilke talks of subtle new experiences which come like shy birds into our lives when we love, his phrase is "The approach and flight of gentle, divining things." This is the subjective detail he sees — just as he had appealed to Herr Kappus, in his first letter, to "say what you see."[15] It is worth noting, too, that Rilke's prose translates with rich fidelity. I've quoted here from Herder-Norton's translation, which comes verbatim from the German ("*das Nahen und Fliehen leiser, ahnungsvoller Dinge*"). The same ring of strangeness and freshness is in the original.

What he sees, what he can offer to Herr Kappus' sense of being a misfit, is that one's misfortune and marginality are one's growing edge, and that there one locates one's proper voice. And so, he exhorts him,

> [D]ear sir, love your solitude and bear with sweet-sounding lamentation the suffering it causes you. For those who are near you are far, you say, and that shows it is beginning to grow wide about you. And when what is near you is far, then your distance is already among the stars and very large; rejoice in your growth, in which you naturally can take no one with you...but believe in a love that is being stored up for you like an inheritance and trust that in this love there is a strength and a blessing beyond which you do not have to step in order to go very far!

So solitude sings its song, offers itself as a fertile infinite space, and yet by no means is easy. Its value, in fact, is just in what contradicts ease. "It is clear," Rilke writes in his seventh letter, the next spring from Rome,

> that we must hold to what is difficult; everything alive holds to it, everything in Nature grows and defends itself

> in this way and is characteristically and spontaneously itself, seeks at all costs to be so and against all opposition...solitude is difficult; that something is difficult must be a reason the more for us to do it.

He evokes a world, like Blake, of experiment and risk, where the very attention to discovery makes one bold. Kappus, now an Army officer, has been telling of outward constraints in his life, and of sadnesses that have passed, yet even the passing annoyed him. But in Rilke's next letter (five months have gone by; he writes from Sweden; this Virgil is almost always in suitcases), he keeps the tone of challenge. "[P]lease, consider whether these great sadnesses have not gone through the center of yourself?" For especially in sadness, something *new* enters into us. If the sadness is suppressed, it is "lost life, of which one may die." But on a clear look: "I believe that almost all our sadnesses are moments of tension that we find paralyzing because we no longer hear our surprised feelings living." The poet of Contradiction becomes here, explicitly, the spokesman for renewal:

> We are alone with the alien thing that has entered into our self....[W]e have changed, as a house changes into which a guest has entered. We cannot say who has come, perhaps we shall never know, but many signs indicate that the future enters into us in this way in order to transform itself in us long before it happens. And that is why it is so important to be lonely and attentive when one is sad: because the apparently uneventful and stark moment at which our future sets foot in us is so much closer to life than that other noisy and fortuitous point of time at which it happens to us as if from outside. The more still, the more patient and more open we are when we are sad, so much the deeper and so much the more unswervingly does the new go into us, so much the better do we make it ours, so much the more will it be *our* destiny, and when on some later day it 'happens' (that is, steps forth out of us to others), we shall feel in our inmost selves akin and near to it.

Thus, inner stasis, the paralysis of depression, as our inattention to life, to its "surprised feelings" in the moment. And the impersonal future as a fiction: for exposed to the subtle new things that happen now, we are like sensitive photographic film. The impression registers clearly; but a print of the film may be made only much later, in our seeming future. Or we can say: the future pierces us early, in painful moments, slowly gestates within us, and finally is delivered to daylight.[16] Hints of this destiny are a challenge to present alertness, which shows, if we look sensitively, how what is inner contains and foresees the outer. We meet here the wisdom of the Buddhist *Dhammapada*'s opening maxim: "The mind is the forerunner of all things." But Rilke delineates this further as a subtle interplay of the present moment, the new things which we *can* notice as they "enter into" us. And so his challenge continues:

> Why do you want to shut out of your life any agitation, any pain, any melancholy, since you really do not know what these states are working upon you? Why do you want to persecute yourself with the question whence all this may be coming and whither it is bound? Since you know that you are in the midst of transitions and wishes for nothing so much as to change. If there is anything morbid in your processes, just remember that sickness is the means by which an organism frees itself of foreign matter; so one must just help it to be sick, to have its whole sickness and break out with it, for that is its progress.

And along with this, challenge, a plea to trust:

> You must think that something is happening with you, that life has not forgotten you, that it holds you in its hand; it will not let you fall.

And a great Perhaps:

> How should we be able to forget those ancient myths that are at the beginning of all peoples, the myths about dragons that at the last minute turn into princesses; perhaps

> all the dragons of our lives are princesses who are only waiting to see us once beautiful and brave. Perhaps everything terrible is in its deepest being something helpless that wants help from us.

This awareness, he keeps repeating, is difficult; but the difficulty is itself a *privilege* of life. So, too, are its joys. And therefore one must unveil these slowly and with care, like delicate new garments which are intricately wrapped. In this way he comes to speak of sex.

Rilke's fervor on behalf of the body, its potency and integrity, recalls the apostolic note struck by D.H. Lawrence also, before the First World War. Our century has moved on to a total debasement of sex in supermarket pornography, films, books, and magazines. But it began with a kind of physical mysticism. "I conceive a man's body as a kind of flame," Lawrence wrote from Lago di Garda to a friend,

> like a candle flame, forever upright and yet flowing: and the intellect is just the light that is shed on the things around. And I am not so much concerned with the things around — which is really mind — but with the mystery of the flame forever flowing, coming God-knows-how from out of practically nowhere, and being *itself*, whatever there is around it, that it lights up.[17]

The same sense of awe is in Rilke, though more connected to the *unity* of the physical and mental. "'The thought of being creator, of procreating, of making,'"[18] he writes in the fourth letter to Kappus,

> is nothing without its continuous great confirmation and realization in the world, nothing without the thousandfold concordance from things and animals — and enjoyment of it is so indescribably beautiful and rich only because it is full of inherited memories of the begetting and bearing of millions. In one creative thought a thousand forgotten nights of love revive, filling it with sublimity and exaltation. And those who come together in the night and are entwined in rocking delight do an earnest work and gather

sweetnesses, gather depth and strength for the song of some coming poet who will arise to speak of ecstasies beyond telling.

So body and spirit are one, and each moves, of its own, to fullness. Sex ripens in love. Spirit ripens in God, "the final fruit of a tree whose leaves we are."[19]

Like everything creative, the sexual is many-sided; as with esthetic creation, the individual needs to "achieve a relation to sex wholly [one's] own (*not* influenced by convention and custom)...." Rilke goes on:

> In the man there is motherhood, it seems to me, physical and spiritual; his procreating is also a kind of giving birth, and giving birth it is when he creates out of inmost fullness.

The man thus awakens to his own femininity. And so, with a new depth, can the woman. Psyche need no longer be Amor's plaything, nor, for that matter, the imitator of Amor who covets the freedom to have sexual playthings. "The girl and the woman," Rilke writes in his seventh letter,

> in their new, their own unfolding, will but in passing be imitators of masculine ways, good and bad, and repeaters of masculine professions. After the uncertainty of such transitions it will become apparent that women are only going through the profusion and the vicissitude of those (often ridiculous) disguises in order to cleanse their own most characteristic nature of the distorting influences of the other sex....This humanity of woman...will come to light when she will have stripped off the conventions of mere femininity in the mutations of her outward status....Some day...there will be girls and women whose name will no longer signify merely an opposite of the masculine, but something in itself, something that makes one think, not of any complement and limit, but only of life and existence: the feminine human being.

So Rilke, in 1904, sums up the whole 19th century Woman Question, and prophesies, too, beyond the late 20th century caricature of the competitive, acquisitive woman, the inverse image of the "female eunuch." All that is social role. Social role means deception. To be real, sexual communion must circle back to the central reality. "It becomes always clearer that [solitude] is at bottom not something that one can take or leave. We *are* solitary." From this base, he parses the normal losses of love.

> Young people (in whose nature it lies to have no patience)...fling themselves at each other, when love takes possession of them...scatter themselves in all their confusion....And then what? What is life to do with this heap of half-battered existence which they call their communion and which they would gladly call their happiness, if it were possible, and their future? Thus each loses himself for the sake of the other and loses the other and many others that wanted still to come. And loses the expanses and the possibilities, exchanges the approach and flight of gentle, divining things for an unfruitful perplexity out of which nothing can come any more....

So, as famous examples, the young Werther, suicide-bound, speaks of being "engulfed" in love "as though engulfed by an abyss";[20] so the tormented Heathcliff and Catharine Earnshaw feel that they *are* each other...and, significantly, have no relationship at all. But where, Rilke goes on, love flowers with the flowering of the individual, then it comes out of "your first deep being-alone...the first inward work you did on your life." Then it flowers as we have not yet seen it in our culture, beyond all social role,

> infinitely considerate and gentle, and kind and clear in binding and releasing...the love that consists in this, that two solitudes protect and border and salute each other.

Thus his concept of love, at once tender and exacting — exacting because the solitude it requires always takes great courage. But so it must be: all the themes of the letters, difficulty, sexuality, transformation, faith in life, are illumined by this solitude, that is, by the love that is its flame. Kappus' only choice is to trust it. "Believe me," his Virgil says: "life is right, in any case."[21] The young man who had first written for advice is finally asked to dare not to seek it, to let himself be (so Rilke takes leave of him in a brief, Christmas letter four years later) "that unique, not repeatable being which at every turning of our life we are." This is the word of the spirit which Rilke, throughout the letters, has been shaping anew, the deepest contradiction in life's changes, the message again of Goethe almost a century before from the *West-Eastern Divan*: "*Stirb und Werde*." "Die and become."

Rilke's summons to young Kappus to explore and to trust his solitude was occurring at just the time that Freud, in Vienna, with four colleagues, began the weekly meetings of the "Psychological Wednesday Society"; these, some five years later, became the Vienna Psycho-analytic Society. Freud, too, had spent years in solitude, had trusted himself, had investigated the powers of the unconscious, and had begun to speak forthrightly about sex. But the thrust of his thinking is quite different from Rilke's. For him, unconscious drives often clash with reality; they harbor infantile dependence, grandiose dreams, antisocial impulses (where the seven deadly sins enjoy free rein).[22] And so the goal of his analytic treatment is to get control of oneself, to learn how to set realistic limits to one's irrational drives while consciously acknowledging their presence and pressures. Within developing psychoanalysis, the great break from this view came with Jung, who, 10 to 15 years after Rilke's *Letters*, turned the picture around. For him, the psyche at its core is self-nurturing. Between its conflicting impulses — regressive and grandiose on the one hand, adventuresome and compassionate on the other — it moves toward a reconciliation of opposites. Freud's view of a continual warfare is limit-setting and cautionary; Jung's, of an advance toward harmony, trusting and optimistic. The contrast between the two marks a differing conception of how to be a good parent to oneself. Or, perhaps, of what to emphasize as a good parent. Rilke's *Letters*, in turn, glow with the Jungian faith in experience, and skirt some of the tensions in living which Freud steadfastly addressed.

We are particularly prepared today to appreciate his faith: the impetus in psychological work, for the past 25 years, has been toward self-unfolding and self-regulation: in humanistic thought, in Gestalt therapy, and in physical modes such as bio-energetics and Charlotte Selver's work with sensory awareness. All these disciplines emphasize, as Rilke does, openness to everything one experiences, the nonautomatic quality of one's life, self-support. And countless testimonials, in popular psychology today, witness to the power and success of self-confidence: so that Rilke's voice now, if anything, may liberate us afresh to *uncertainty*. His "love the questions themselves," includes, after all, even Hamlet's most famous question. He would have us doubt everything, even life itself, for doubt "become[s] a good quality if you *train* it."[23] Knowledge grows as sap rises, without force, with time. "*Patience* is everything."[24] In all directions he is anti-gospel. "Whether my letters can really be a help, I often doubt. Do not say: yes, they are. Just accept them, and without much thanks, and let us await what comes."[25]

And so he gives full weight to what is difficult in life. No other inspirational writer has ever stressed difficulty so much; we note this all the more today, when spiritual teachers would open us to easeful, healing powers, or hypnotists assist us effortlessly to "access" the unconscious in order to live smoothly, or tranquilizing drugs "restore" us to normal function. But perhaps all these helps are basically distractions, which create new difficulties when they fail, needing ingenious new solutions: an expectable *vicious cycle*. Suppose, in Rilke's sense, that we ask: What if inner rough paths and distress are *life's ideas* of the normal? What if problem-solving — to keep my job or leave it, whether I should get married or stay married, or just how to cope with being left by my husband or my wife — what if all this is too rational, too goal-minded, too much a checklist of pros and cons? While something deeper — for instance, my continuous longing for both intimacy and self-expression — only serves up the surface problems which I need to solve; and any of us seeks therapy, or for that matter becomes a therapist, in order to satisfy the deeper longings. What if the answers we seek can only evolve slowly, as we probe and endure the longings? Then the answers may come of their own; as the future may already lie in the recesses of the present; as the image may literally be true (to quote Nabokov's remarkable words in *Bend Sinister*) that "...we live in a stocking which is in the process of being turned inside out...." And if so, to an extent we must be disoriented; for, his image continues, we can't "ever know...for sure to what phase of the process our moment of consciousness corresponds." Our *Gestalt* is never so wide.[26] But accepting the process, we cultivate a *virtuous circle*. We are responsible, as we trust life. As we trust life more, we grow more responsible.

And so Rilke speaks about solitude; for responsibility, like charity, begins at home, with ourselves. And he allies love with solitude: "it is a high inducement for the individual to ripen;"[27] and it is a protection and salute to another's solitude. But isn't this approach to love a strange one; like his stress on the virtue of what's difficult, almost grim in its austerity? For it solves nothing we would like love to solve. Shouldn't love leave solitude behind, and even difficulties with another? That, of course, would be much easier...always assuming one can slip in and out of relationships when they grow painful, like in and out of a seat belt: as the airplane stewardess says, "Just lift the handle." But we cling to our hopes, even when they fail, and we fear to be alone, even when that may succeed, and we do not notice how much we are alone, always, with both hope and fear. Rilke's voice returns to us here. "We *are* solitary...this is at bottom not something that one can take or leave."[28] And he would urge us to feel trust, fidelity, courage in the fact: so the *Letters* exhort us, with their telling warmth and heartening guideposts for what we can find within.

> [A]bout emotions: all emotions are pure which gather you and lift you up; that emotion is impure which seizes only *one* side of your being and so distorts you. Everything that you can think in the face of your childhood, is right. Everything that makes *more* of you than you have heretofore been in your best hours, is right. Every heightening is good if it is in your *whole* blood, if it is not intoxication,

> not turbidity, but joy which one can see clear to the bottom. Do you understand what I mean?[29]

At the same time, for all his acceptances, one senses that something is ignored in this Purgatory. Rilke was, after all, less courageous about intimacy than about solitude; or rather, he didn't dare to mix them. His yearning that leads on to pure invisible being leaves out, in fact, life's unremitting visibility, and the conflicts and shadows that go with the visible.[30] He believes in Contradiction — he said once that psychoanalysis would be wrong for him; if he lost his devils, his angels too might leave[31] — and yet he gives the angels the last word. For him, life is never accidental nor wayward nor really tragic; the darkness of existence, like Sleeping Beauty, only awaits the Prince's kiss. It isn't a darkness that stays.

But what of this, in our own daily affairs, do we know? We are aware, rather, of a tension between spiritual grace and our own shortcomings; of a polarizing, as well as a sharing of concerns, in friendship and love; of hatreds and of griefs in us that seem unending; of unity with others as well as solitude among them, and of the disturbing pulls that unity and solitude make against each other. As to the great improvements that can come about in mental life — having faith in ourselves, accepting our mortality and failings, giving up destructive addictions, loving others who are imperfect and feeling lovable while we know we are imperfect — all that happens in a world of continuing frustration and pain, in which Freud's words on behalf of psychoanalysis ring out nobly: "Much will be gained if we succeed in transforming neurotic symptoms into common unhappiness."[32] In his own way, Freud was much more a spokesman of Contradiction than Rilke understood: near the end of his life he remarked how regressions from mental health to neurosis occur often; they call for further analytic work and represent a perhaps endless opposition.[33] And we can add to his view, putting the matter at its most extreme, that the darkness of life justifies insanity as the dark side of sanity: Sleeping Beauty, at the best, fated to sleep again and to toss in a world of bad dreams. I trace here the road from Rilke to Kafka, and soon we shall be following it; it is the road from an idealizing to a refractory picture of life.[34] But to stay a little longer with

Rilke: we appreciate his breadth, as well as his limits, in giving us a world modeled on its possibilities for beauty, a world, so to speak, without prose.

And yet that is not nearly to say enough. For his idealism was *grounded*, too, cultivated by his patience, trust, and confidence in the constantly renewing, increasingly ripening soul. It is pleasant to note, too, as regards his grounding, that he had his light side. He was known for his charm and sense of humor, and some of his correspondence attests to it: for instance, his dancing attendance on the temperamental aging actress, Eleanora Duse, in 1912, on one of the islands near Venice, when a peacock approached her unnoticed and screamed in her ear. Or recalling the fiasco of his early pilgrimage to visit Tolstoy. But on the whole, the picture he leaves with us is that of the earnest eremite of poetry, whose steady outward journeys through Europe and North Africa were a symbol of continual traveling within;[35] devoted to his muse through its years-long withdrawal from him, then its ecstatic recipient when it brought a flood of inspiration: five of his long *Duino Elegies* and all 55 of the concise, metrically intricate *Sonnets to Orpheus* were completed in a few weeks of winter, 1921. And their message is precisely of secret arrivals, protean existence:

> Silent friend of wide distances, feel
> that your breath still adds to space...
> Become, in overwhelming night,
> the magic power at the crossway of your senses...
> Say to the unmoving earth: I flow.
> And to the rapid water: I exist.

He kept his conviction of the senses' magic throughout the rapidly fatal leukemia of his 52nd year. He refused all pain medication: now, too, he would let "the organism have its whole sickness...the point is, to live everything...life is right, in any case": these were the truths that, twenty-three years before, he had so well stored up toward his own dying. His last letter, to a French poet a week before his death, alone in a sanitarium in Valmont, Switzerland, broken and in agony, still maintained the voice of praise, even the tone of elegance, which he had so remarkably upheld throughout his life: "I think of you, poet, friend, and in so doing I still think of the world — poor shard of a vessel that remembers being of the earth."

When Rilke withdrew from Kappus, in his Christmas message of 1908, he described him as "somewhere in a rough reality being solitary and courageous." He leaves him alone there, as Virgil left Dante at the top of Mount Purgatory. And it is good to recall the last words Dante gave his Latin mentor, almost 700 years ago, for they ring with the faith in facing one's own destiny that Rilke felt for his own young poet, and that imbues the goals of therapists with their clients today, both within psychoanalysis and outside it:

> Expect no more of me in word or deed:
> here your will is upright, free and whole,
> and you would be in error not to heed
>
> whatever your own impulse prompts you to:
> lord of yourself I crown and mitre you.[36]

Chapter 4

FRANZ KAFKA: HOLY FIRE

Prague: March 1913. A gray, drizzly day. A young Jewish man leaves his office at the Workers Accident Insurance Company. Outside on the Josefsplatz, the cobblestones are like the backs of a sea of dormant turtles that just might start to move. He walks straight to his parents' flat. To his relief, neither they nor his sister are at home. He throws open the window in his room to bathe for a full minute in the cold air. It ruffles his dark hair, parted strictly in the middle and slicked back; his angular face and solemn eyes relax. Then he trips against the side of his desk as he sits down at it. He pauses, smiles, picks up a blank sheet of paper and writes: "The True Way goes over a rope which is not stretched at any great height but just above the ground. It seems more designed to make people stumble than to be walked upon."

In fact we don't know just when, or under just what circumstances, Franz Kafka wrote this aphorism, the first of 104, numbered consecutively on separate sheets of paper. But it is a mark of his achievement to invite me to imagine a prosaic scene, at once commonplace and ambiguous, filled with the sense he noted about himself in his diary, of "sea-sickness on dry land." He will explore this sense fully, in terms prosaic as rope, the merchandise from a hardware store; but rope, that is, that trips you up. For he will be, to our age, the great mentor of ambiguities, of shadows and stumbling, and of the soul's truth inseparable from these. After Kafka, mental health, and the theory of mental health, keep a dark side, like the moon. No one else has ever revealed this more cogently, nor made our acceptance of it more irrevocable.

Ordinary living, indeed, was a conundrum to Kafka; and by an irony that exceeded any calculations of his own (for he believed that he lived quite inconsequently), his life has become the most famous case history in modern literature. Like Rilke, he spent his childhood in Prague at the end of the last century. Unlike him, he grew up and remained a Central European, the bachelor son of a Jewish family who stayed home and worked at an office job, with occasional vacations abroad. His father was a shopkeeper selling "fancy goods": gloves, umbrellas, haberdashery. His mother was devoted to the father and worked with him in his business. Three sisters were born before he was 10. The crucial blow for Kafka, simultaneously depth-wound and wellspring of his later vitality as a writer, was his subjugation to the despotic, bullying father. "You asked me recently," he begins the *Letter to His Father* which he wrote at 35, in the last years of his life, already ill with the tuberculosis that killed him and wanting especially to probe his sense of unfitness for marriage,

> You asked me...why I maintain that I am afraid of you. ["Maintain" suggests already that the father considers him wrong.] As usual I was unable to think of any answer to your question, partly for the very reason that I am afraid of you, and partly because an explanation of the grounds for this fear would mean going into far more details than I could even approximately keep in mind while talking.

But now, with the benefit of the written word, he gives details. He recalls, from his early years, "whimpering for water, not, I am certain, because I was thirsty, but probably partly to be annoying, partly to amuse myself." The father, "after several vigorous threats had failed to have any effect," took the boy out of bed and locked him alone outside on the balcony in his nightshirt. The description shows Kafka's usual regard for fairness; he is provocateur as well as victim. And so he is in other images of horror; here is one from a note to the *Letter*:

> I was defenceless confronted with [a] figure, calmly it sat there at the table, gazing at the table-top. I walked round it in circles, feeling throttled by it. And around me there walked a third, feeling throttled by me. Around that third there walked a fourth, feeling throttled by him. And so it went on, right out to the circling of the constellations, and further still. Everything felt the grip at the throat.

He continues his letter for 41½ grim pages, intimidated and accusing, about the father's disparagements of his work, of his Judaism, of his choice of women friends. Then — for always, with Kafka, the incisive scalpel exposes the warm beating heart — he concludes:

> Naturally things cannot in reality fit together the way the evidence does in my letter; life is more than a Chinese puzzle. But...in my opinion something has been achieved which so closely approximates the truth that it might reassure us both a little and make our living and dying easier. Franz.

And then?

Then he gave the letter to his mother, to give to his father. She read it and returned it to him, believing it could do no good. Was he afraid to give the letter himself? Or didn't he quite want to, and know for sure that she wouldn't? Or had he assigned her a special role? The one to intervene on his behalf? The one whose approval was first of all necessary? The one to whom, between the lines, the letter was most of all addressed, in reproach for her not having intervened in the past? She may have felt some, or all, of this tangle, or simply have seen no point in intervening now; the purpose of the document may have looked hopeless.

But its intent was not hopeless. And with her return of his letter, the chance for "reassurance" that Kafka had spoken of was gone.

Certainly, his giving *her* the letter was typical of the indirection in which his life abounded, and which, Hamlet-like, forestalled his acting. About a year later, he wrote to his friend Max Brod: "It seems to me that I'm wandering around like a child in the forests of maturity." And this was, indeed, the circuitous path he had long since taken: studying law at the Deutsche Universität, to please his father, not himself; stifling his rage at home when one of his sisters sat down in his room with a book when he was preparing to write, then took a card from a tray and fiddled with it between her teeth. Finally she left. "With departing rage," he notes in his diary, "of which only a stinging vapor remains behind in my head, and with dawning relief and confidence, I begin to write."

But *this* had really happened in his life: he had begun to write. Earlier, at the University, he had discovered Marcus Aurelius, Meister Eckhart. "Books," he wrote in those days to a friend, "often work like a key to unknown rooms in one's own castle"; he had found indeed the sense of his own royalness. Also he had made friends, most specially with small, humpbacked Max Brod, one year younger than he, and a charismatic figure equally devoted to literature. Brod was to be a lifelong support to Kafka's inner life, much as Theo van Gogh was to Vincent. And during the next decade, in stories, sketches, and fragments, Kafka found himself — found himself, that is to say, *unthrottled*. "The special nature of my inspiration," he noted in his diary, in February 1911, his twenty-eighth year,

> in which I, the most fortunate and unfortunate of men, now go to sleep at 2 a.m....is such that I can do everything, and not only what is directed to a definite piece of work. When I arbitrarily write a single sentence, for instance, 'He looked out of the window,' it already has perfection.

It is as if the savage man Friday, or even a preverbal animal, had suddenly discovered he could speak. And, indeed, animals do speak in Kafka's work: one recalls his ape who "broke into the human community" with his pealing "Hallo!"[1] But it is also true that the human community is a brainwashing prison, barring the ape forever from his former free life in the forest. And Kafka, too, stays barred. Language is a master key; he achieves with it an unbounded sense of connection and of wholeness, but all within the prison complex, where only a few skylights open a crack onto the sky. This, in fact, becomes his great lucid theme, the theme of human inextrication.

I've spoken of Contraries, in Blake's view, as a root force in human nature, and of Contradiction, in Rilke's. With Kafka, one touches the same depth in the idea, Paradox. (Though he does not use the word, like they use theirs. It is too close to him for that, it is the air he breathes.) Just how does paradox unfold? A thing is a thing as we know it — and its opposite. "If it had been possible to build the tower of Babel without ascending it, the work would have been permitted." ("Yes," we note. "If men were free of self-interest. But on the other hand, how can you build it *without* ascending it?") Or the image is given in reverse: "We are digging the pit of Babel." ("I see," we think. "We must dig down, into humility. Our pride is already too high. But how do we do that, without destroying ourselves?") In either direction, the action is self-canceling; or else, somehow, the opposites must be attuned. Kafka himself, we have already heard, is "the most fortunate and unfortunate of men." What good fortune is this? And when an innocent event occurs, is it innocent? "It was summer, a hot day," begins the anecdote "The Knock at the Manor Gate":

> With my sister I was passing the gate of a great house on our way home. I cannot tell now whether she knocked on the gate out of mischief or out of absence of mind, or merely threatened it with her fist and did not knock at all.

Exact facts — and the dream-vague opposite: "I cannot tell." And the consequence — after this safe, innocuous beginning — is total danger, loss, punishment. Horsemen ride in with spears through the now wide-open gate, then out, following the man and his sister. He sends her away; she obeys reluctantly. He is taken to a farmhouse and judged and sentenced. For what? The bright summer's day is now the darkest mystery. And yet, has he expected anything else? For he concludes: "Could I still endure any other air than prison air? That is the great question, or rather it would be if I still had any prospect of release." What has he done to lead him to this resignation, he who had not even touched the gate — or is it actual acceptance of guilt? Is he *both* things at once, innocent and guilty? But then paradox turns a corner, into nightmare.

Literature, much less psychological understanding, has no precedent for an approach like this. The nearest thing to it was the farcical nightmare of Gogol, three generations before in Russia: his story, for instance, of a runaway nose with a life of its own, or his picture of surreal depravity in small town politics in the play *The Government Inspector* have the flash and conciseness of Kafka. We feel, in Gogol, our fragmentation and our deceptiveness laid bare. But he allows us *some* explanations, no matter how implausible. A drunken barber has cut off the nose before we chance to see it, on the street, in "a gold-braided brightly colored uniform, buckskin breeches, a three-cornered hat, and a saber." We hear that the Judge's clerk, from his play, smells continually of vodka "because his wet nurse dropped him when he was a baby." (This is an explanation?) But in Kafka, daytime nightmare happens *sui generis*, quite unexplained.

> When Gregor Samsa woke up one morning from unsettling dreams [so begins his story "Metamorphosis"], he found himself changed in his bed into a monstrous vermin. He was lying on his back, as hard as armor plate, and when he lifted his head a little, he saw his vaulted brown belly, sectioned by arch-shaped ribs, to whose dome the cover, about to slide off completely, could barely cling. His many legs, pitifully thin compared with the size of the rest of him, were waving helplessly before his eyes.
>
> "What's happened to me?" he thought. It was no dream.

Normal questions of how to cope — the matter of feeding Gregor, of confining him, and so on — preoccupy him and his family until his eventual death in the same room, the body "now completely flat and dry." Kafka's tone throughout is matter-of-fact, offhand, comically macabre à la *Gogol*. (He was known, when he read his tales to his friends, to laugh so hard that the tears streamed down his face and the reading had to stop.)

Or a still more sustained nightmare: Joseph K., the hero of the novel *The Trial*, is "arrested one fine morning without having done anything wrong." He spends much time hunting for an explanation, without avail, and is finally slain one evening at the edge of town, near a stone quarry, by two polite men sent by the authorities. (It is as though the whole action of the book, from opening morning to closing night, is all in a day's work.) And until the end, his guilt or his innocence unresolved, nightmare or waking unclarified, defeated K. keeps his paradoxical hope. About to be killed (now we hear Kafka, still simple but at his most lyrically intense):

> His glance fell on the top story of the house adjoining the quarry. With a flicker as of a light going up, the casement of a window there suddenly flew open; a human figure, faint and insubstantial at that distance and that height, leaned abruptly far forward and stretched both arms still farther. Who was it? A friend? A good man? Someone who sympathized? Someone who wanted to help? Was it one person? Or was it mankind? Was help at hand? Were there arguments in his favor that had been overlooked? Of course there must be. Logic is doubtless unshakable, but it cannot withstand a man who wants to go on living. Where was the Judge whom he had never seen? Where was the High Court, to which he had never penetrated? He raised his hands and spread out all his fingers.
>
> But the hands of one of the partners were already at K.'s throat, while the other thrust the knife deep into his heart and turned it there twice. With failing eyes K. could still see the two of them immediately before him, cheek leaning against cheek, watching the final act. "Like a dog!" he said; it was as if the shame of it must outlive him.

In all this darkness, what is illuminating? Two generations, since his death in 1924, have gone to school with Kafka's work as a Bible of alienation, in which the creator said, "Let there be enigma," and they have given out variant meanings: fascism, with its ruthless, inaccessible authorities; religion, with an unheeding God; psychological exposé, with unconscious forces beyond reach that govern our lives and make us feel insect-like, obscurely wrong, obscurely condemned. But while all these interpretations are decipherable in Kafka's writings, a larger conundrum seems to wrap them round. How much, here, oddity is commonplace! And what of the drive to destruction, so explicit, for instance, in his story "The Hunger Artist," where a man proudly starves himself to death; or in another story, "The Judgment," where a son kills himself on command from his father? Just what is illumined? Then Kafka himself, in his own life, gave a similar command. In his last will, he asked that his unpublished writings — the novels, *The Trial, The Castle,* and many short pieces including his aphorisms — be destroyed. He trusted nothing in them; he was clear about this. Or was he? For it is as with the *Letter to His Father*; he put the responsibility for his most private wishes in the hands of another, in this case his executor Max Brod, who then (to the eternal gratitude of Kafka's readers) disobeyed the request and published everything.[2] What posthumous paradox is this? Pascal, in his *Pensées,* noted: "Perfect clarity would profit the intellect but damage the will." Kafka's lack of clarity seems to have stimulated both.

We might, after all, do best to say that a misunderstanding of him is unavoidable. It is built into the texture of his vision, as it is into a Zen koan that asks, "What is the sound of one hand clapping?" But the appeal of Kafka, like that of the koan, is the sense that behind the riddle there lies a logic. It is as though Kafka showed us the back side of a tapestry, where all the knots of his conflicts, tensions, and anguish were tied off. But there *is* a tapestry with a front side to it, and there the fabric is harmonious and whole.

The aphorisms, which are our chief concern, show this other side. From where in his life, from what less troubled corner of his heart, did they come? We don't know. But having imagined the origin of the first one, my guess for the others is: from a time of great objective trouble...perhaps when he was facing extreme illness in the summer of 1917. He had spat blood. A specialist told him he was "liable to become tubercular." Leaving his job, his friends, and a troubled courtship in Prague, he moved to Zürau, in northwest Bohemia, the home of his sister

Ottla, with whom he got on very well. It was a good time for spiritual reconnoitering.[3]

And the aphorisms are very much, in the religious sense, "devotions on emergent occasions"; they recall John Donne's great 17th century set of Devotions, written also during a serious illness, as I am imputing these to be. Kafka, of course, doesn't have Donne's sustained groundswell of language. Aphorisms are terse. But his thought is as complete, as much concerned with basic standards, problems, and transformations in life. And may it not be that, just because his situation in serious illness is not commonplace, is more delicate and grave than usual, his own approach is more simple and lucid? Real threat to life may take the wind out of self-destructive thoughts, may turn one fully to what one has.

And so, with all his subtlety and alacrity, he faces himself, alone. Rilke, early in the decade before, had addressed so fulsomely (as we've heard him) his grateful, responsive young poet. Now Kafka, incisive and laconic, addresses the unanswering cosmos. His voice is like one in the wilderness, but not one that cries. Rather, like a spider making its web, methodically, patiently, he comments and notates, uses forethought and care. Watch how he reckons.

First of all, the title is striking: "Reflections on Sin, Pain, Hope, and the True Way." It isn't Kafka's; he gave none. It merely sums up the contents. But we note at once a kind of double entry. Half of the four categories are on the positive side of the ledger. I've already marked the first aphorism as having his pessimistic wit. But may he, through the whole series of reflections, be using in a different way his gift for paradox, his usual making much of little? May he, now, be making much — of much? Suppose we shine a flashlight quickly over these pages, as through a dark cave. The 71st aphorism: "Test yourself on humanity. It makes the doubter doubt, the believer believe." Can this really be our famous pessimist speaking — this Montaigne-like, enlightened skepticism? Or perhaps the incongruity he points to — doubt, belief, both ratified — perhaps this is leading to his familiar ground, a dark place. The flashlight moves. Number 32: "There is no having, only being, only a being panting for its last breath, panting to be choked out." Yes, here is Kafka's life of pain. But wait! Number 39: "The disharmony of the world seems, comfortingly enough, to be merely an arithmetical one." What? Isn't this full of promise, his "comfortingly enough" and "merely"? Hasn't he now a higher mathematics in view? For there is that title, with its Hope. And also (as both negative and positive) Sin, the True Way. These concerns clearly are religious. But just how? The flashlight moves again. Number 44: "The word 'sein' signifies in German both things: to be and to belong to Him." Yes, a good German double meaning all right. So what matters to him here about God is nothing inaccessible and perplexing; on the contrary, it's almost like being held. Is he inviting himself, inviting us — he, the disenfranchised Kafka — to view life from within the sense of *belonging to it*?

Yes. One after another, as we look at them, so the aphorisms affirm. Life is fathomable. Or not quite: with the edge of comfort he is giving us, still we mustn't be bland. Kafka never is. Life coheres, but only with all its paradoxes. Like this one: "Theoretically there exists a perfect possibility of happiness: to believe in the indestructible element in oneself and not strive after it." (66)[4] The paradox, in fact, is immense enough to require his first, ironic adverb; beyond theory, *practice* isn't impossible, but it isn't at all obvious either. We have already heard him in this ironic vein: "If it had been possible to build the tower of Babel without ascending it, the work should have been permitted."[5] And he would be the first to salute the great difficulty in the bare bones of Zen wisdom: "Eat when hungry, sleep when tired" — perhaps notating it with the same adverb: "theoretically." For what about one's anxious eating, one's escapist sleeping, one's insomnia, and so on?

By what route, then, does theory become practice? "Two tasks," he tells us, "on the threshold of life: to narrow your circle more and more, and constantly to make certain that you have not hidden yourself somewhere outside it." (90) Our usual pleasure in sprawling and hiding: isn't this the domain of Freud's Pleasure Principle, into which we seek to withdraw from the demands of real life? This pleasurable detachment is even subtly present in Newtonian science, where we observe from "outside" the system, and don't include ourselves within it, as the viewpoint of modern physics requires. Kafka double-entries the point in a longer, more ardent and sonorous aphorism:

> You can hold back from the suffering of the world, you have free permission to do so and it is in accordance with your nature, but perhaps this very holding back is the one suffering that you could have avoided. (99)

For the ironies don't relent. What is most "in accordance with our nature" is the one suffering we "could avoid...perhaps." Is his "perhaps" *grim* (with the unlikeliness of our not suffering) or *tender* (with hope for it)?

Certainly he is concerned with what it takes to enjoy the world. "How can one be glad of the world unless one is flying to it for refuge?" (22) Flight to it; nothing at all that's grudging or stressful in one's embrace of it, in fact the very opposite of "holding back," like birds on the wing home, or a quiet conversion. So Kierkegaard once noted that a spiritual revolution may go on inside a man on Tuesday, and on Wednesday nothing is discernibly different about him.[6] Kafka, who admired Kierkegaard, imagines a fragment from just such a man's inner life:

> 'But then he returned to us as if nothing had happened.' This is a saying which sounds familiar to us from an indefinite number of old tales, though in fact it perhaps occurs in none. (103)

At the best, we live in a steady motion: "From a certain point onward there is no longer any turning back. That is the point to be reached." (5) Then, so to say, life is *in orbit*. It has achieved its nonstriving. We are back also to Zen simplicity, which is a kind of smallness. "Two possibilities," notes Kafka: "to make oneself, or to be infinitely small . The second is fulfillment, therefore inaction, the first a beginning, therefore action." (86) Another entry — his double entry on the same subject — emphasizes nonaction even more. "What is laid upon us is to accomplish the negative; the positive is already given." (24) For how else but as a negative can we think of our personal, perishing tasks, as we face within us "the indestructible element," the positive?

Whereas the pride we take in achievement and mastery, just herein lies our spiritual debit. Pain and Sin enter precisely with the old heroic cry "Excelsior!" ("Always upward"); it is Satan in our ears at his most beguiling. For such is his nature: to be sly and subtle; to tempt us to good things (what could be better than that first Biblical promise, the knowledge of good and evil?); and for him not even to mind our own arguments against him. Thus, Kafka: "Once we have granted accommodation to the Evil One, he no longer demands that we should believe him." (25) The guest takes over; having entered by one door, he is everywhere on stage. Or, restated: our ego, our vanity foam like a cataract, and drown us. Therefore, "The afterthoughts with which you justify your accommodation of the Evil One are not yours but those of the Evil One." (26) Such, clearly, is the rapidity of our self-delusion. But Kafka makes it still clearer in an extraordinary image added as a pendant to the same aphorism:

> The animal snatches the whip from its master and whips itself so as to become master, and does not know that all this is only a fantasy caused by a new knot in the master's whiplash.

So the Evil One bends and twists us, with elegance. He is the principle of limitation, limitlessly refined. Evil itself — that is, limitation — simply exists, unaccountable, at loose in the world, and Kafka salutes it in an eight-word, eight-syllable ode: "A cage went in search of a bird." (13)[7] Just what does he show us here? Suddenly there passes a procession of his own reduced, fettered, death-condemned characters...and us among them, making death camps and nuclear weapons. We watch, stunned. And then comes his double entry, a new image with the cadence of a Greek chorus. "The hunting dogs are still playing in the courtyard, but the hare will not escape them, no matter how fast it may already be flying through the woods." (41)

But these horrors remain on only the debit side of the ledger. On the column of credits: "The mediation of the serpent was necessary: Evil can seduce men, but it cannot become man."

(48) Yes, the cage is not the bird, it cannot become the bird. And, as a double entry: "Evil is often like a tool in one's hand; knowingly or unknowingly, it will allow itself to be laid aside without protest, if one only has the will." (91)

The last phrase presents our knottiest problem. For how do we mobilize the will, given our laziness and our impatience? "Because of impatience we were driven out of Paradise, because of laziness we cannot return." (3) (The idea has an echo of Rilke, but here its sound is mordant.) Laziness, impatience have a certain proficiency of their own, are so wonderfully convenient and accessible. In the face of them, what can we do?

And now Kafka moves most fully beyond the theoretical. We hear injunctions. "In the fight between you and the world, back the world." (50) Astonishing! To feel this empathy for the other, not in order to deny oneself, but to be free of fruitless self-involvement. Again: "From a real antagonist boundless courage flows into you." (20) The other's energy as a generator for my own; the other's limits helping me define my shape. Even some concentration camp victims, most famously Viktor Frankl, found new resources of spirit in the midst of their brutalized life. As to the patience which can "accomplish the negative": "One must not cheat anybody, not even the world of its triumph." (51)

Which implies no indifference to the world's suffering, only the attentiveness which is the life of the spirit, the True Way. Or still better, more Kafka-like, the Wayless Way: for we are never on it with a technique or a design. Instead of "the way," a technique is a kind of inhibition, is only "wavering." (23)[8] We know the True Way, rather, when we are aware that nothing else exists, or that everything else, the Evil One too, is serving it. Of course, caught in our anguish, our guilt, our sense of estrangement, this realization is not possible, but it can come to us, quite simply, when we free ourselves of comparisons:

> Only here is suffering suffering. Not in the sense that those who suffer here are ennobled somewhere else because of their suffering, but in the sense that what is called suffering in this world is, without any alteration, except that it is freed from its opposite, bliss in another. (93)

"Without any alteration": this is Kafka's constant standard for the single, spiritual world. And so, finally, it is without anything speculative at all, it is as conviction, whether in sickness or in health, that he enters a strong credit for life as we all live it now. "The indestructible is one; it is every human being individually and at the same time all human beings collectively; hence the marvelous indissoluble alliance of mankind." (67)

Thus his vision in its full allowance, and with the warmth of "holy fire" which for him is central. But I have taken the phrase from a poem of William Butler Yeats, where it is a chief image[9], not from Kafka, who in his estrangement could hardly have uttered it, for whom the fire flared as from a distant hearth, like a hint, like a promise, like a memory, across a windy plain. But there are two more aphorisms that speak, without question, of the heat of the fire. The first, about human relations: "Let the face that is filled with loathing and hate sink on your breast." (40) Here, unqualified, the release of tension, the warmth of tenderness, prevail.[10] The second, full of quiet joy, redemptive patience, power beyond words, is his final aphorism:

> You do not need to leave the room. Remain sitting at your table and listen. Do not even listen, simply wait. Do not even wait, be quite still and solitary. The world will freely offer itself to you to be unmasked, it has no choice, it will roll in ecstasy at your feet.

Though Kafka stood at a distance, his hands were always stretched toward the fire, and when the winds didn't blow it away, it warmed them.

In his essay on Kafka, Camus recounts the story of a crazy man fishing in his bathtub. "A doctor with ideas as to a psychiatric treatment asked him, 'if the fish were biting,' to which he received the sharp reply: 'Of course not, you fool, since this is a bathtub.'"

Camus' story is steeped in Kafka: an insane situation is logically dealt with, whereupon its insanity compounds. For why is this clear-headed man fishing? And yet we feel that he knows something, something important, something about absurdity in life, leading to no cynical conclusion that nothing is valid, but to its opposite, that everything is. One can, one might as well, lucidly fish in the bathtub. A doctor with this same lucid standard might have observed: "That's heroic! Since you can't catch anything." And when life, of its own, is equally outrageous, just so much an affront to reason, we can still fish and persevere in it. That is the constant, positive note in Kafka, at one with the "even-hovering attention" which Freud recommends for the psychoanalyst.

The point deserves our widest regard because, on the other hand, nothing is easier to observe than Kafka's pathology, as he is always himself doing. His journals and his fiction are full of his self-doubt, his feelings of confusion and inadequacy. But from one disorder he is remarkably free. He is nonphobic. He avoids, he disqualifies nothing. He has, instead, the vigor and assurance of a hunter (I get the word from him). "I am on the hunt for constructions," reads a diary entry of November 1913. "I come into the room and find them whitely merging in a corner." This is the spirit of the man who loved the Yiddish theater in Prague, who relished fresh air and swimming, and whose Quixotic spirit comes out, now and then, in his writing. Here is a piece called "My Destination":

> I gave orders for my horse to be brought round from the stable. The servant did not understand me. I myself went to the stable, saddled my horse and mounted. In the distance I heard a bugle call, I asked him what this meant. He knew nothing and had heard nothing. At the gate he stopped me, asking: "Where are you riding to, master?" "I don't know," I said, "only away from here, away from here. Always away from here, only by doing so can I reach my destination." "And so you know your destination?" he asked. "Yes," I answered, "didn't I say so? Away-from-here, that is my destination." "You have no provisions with you," he said. "I need none," I said, "the journey is so long that I must die of hunger if I don't get

anything on the way. No provisions can save me. For it is, fortunately, a truly immense journey."

The servant who does not understand or hear — that fellow is stuck "here," in old habits. But the other, who hears and acts and is headed "away-from-here," he is in the Heraclitean flux where the present is always changing; and for all the risks of change, he finds the exultant adverb, "fortunately." This is Kafka à la Whitman, with the freedom from fixity, the readiness to accept what comes, which is the great boon of the nonphobic. And we've followed ourselves, in the aphorisms, how much he accepts; how much, with the clarity of whiteness, comes to "merge" for him, forces of loss, forces of succor; and with what steadiness he could bend them all, like Ulysses his strong bow, to shoot straight at the bull's-eye, the turbulent, needy, abiding human heart.

And yet Kafka's dark side is usually more in view, on the whole not denying, but crowding his powers; often, in fact, it gives a special angle to his perception, a special élan to his strength. This side of him is so important that I want to give it careful attention for its own debits and credits. I quote here a vivid passage from the English psychoanalyst Harry Guntrip:

> [There are] people who have deep-seated doubts about the reality and viability of their very 'self,' who are ultimately found to be suffering from varying degrees of depersonalization, unreality, the dread feeling of 'not belonging,' and of being fundamentally isolated and out of touch with their world. This is broadly 'the schizoid problem,' the problem of those who feel cut off, apart, different, unable to become involved in any real relationships....The problem here is not relations to other people, but whether one is or has a self.[11]

To me Guntrip's excellent description is in error only once: there *are* no other people — though for many, the sense of mere shadowy existence is confined to dreams or to extreme stress. But its general reality surely is the basis of our general interest in Kafka. His images are not intriguing strangers, but images we know. And for some of us, like himself, the schizoid problem looms very large. Then a peculiar liquidity imbues the most certain experience, refracts it into an irregular or broken form. We recall, by contrast, Blake's firmness: "The truth can never be told so as to be understood, and not be believ'd." Kafka, in *The Trial*, makes his own refracted comment: "The right perception of any matter and a misunderstanding of the same matter do not wholly exclude each other."[12] Blake's truth is still here, but offset by an addendum, its broken image. So goes schizoid alienation. But the refracting has its positive side too: the way it makes me question how clear my clarity ever is. When I know, for instance, that my life is mortal, doesn't my pride seek, in this certainly, a kind of immortal refuge? Wanting to be good and in the right, don't I require someone to be bad and in the wrong? Aware of my love for another, don't I at once grow unaware of my self-love that obliterates the other? Do I nourish any life without forgetting that I have also destroyed others, whose blood provides some of the nourishment I now provide? All these refractions evoke, above all, my longing for something else, a sense that is whole and unforgetful, an image that is intact. And yet, alienated from it, I am the more sensitive to closeness — to "flying to [the world] for refuge} — to knowing how grace, in the religious sense, *is* closeness. Thus Kafka, in one aphorism, has yet "a vestige of faith," that God contemplates him, as he passes from a lifetime in a prison cell to the eternal prison of death, and says, "You must not lock this one up again. He is to come to me." (10)

This "vestige," then, seems to refine awareness; it appears to be ironically true that the more solid one's sense of life is, the less one is delicately alert to its ambiguities. In the field of mental health, one can, on the whole, distinguish along these lines the finest therapists from the best theorists. The most effective therapists are relatively unhampered by their personal problems. In fact their help to their clients is just their own *increment of personal freedom*, joined to their technical skill in support, interpretation, and silence. Their freedom invites their clients to risk more freedom. Often they are hardly theorists at all: for instance, Milton Erickson, the virtuosic hypnotherapist, gives us a few generalizations about the wisdom of the unconscious. The freewheeling family therapist Carl Whitaker says some words about how we are all crazy in our sleep. But far more luxuriant theories have blossomed from those entangled in problems and able, with their own *increment of personal understanding*, to give the psyche's subtleties their due. So, for example, overdisciplined Freud formulates "childhood sexuality," 'repression," "the pleasure principle," and "the reality principle"; schizoid Sullivan, the "uncanny dread" and terrifying "not-me" experience of schizophrenia; obsessively logical Bateson, the logic of the "double bind" that underlies schizophrenic nonsense.[13]

And returning to Kafka's aphorisms, we note again their widespread concern with theory. At the remove of his solitary cell, he gives us formal rules of commitment ("From a certain point onward there is no longer any turning back"; "[P]erfect...happiness...theoretically: to believe in the indestructible in oneself, and not strive after it.") He gives precepts ("You are the problem. No scholar to be found far and wide." [19]) — And what can we say about his "You," the chief addressee of his Aphorisms? Kafka's German is "Du," English "Thou."[14] Who is that? Is it Kafka himself, gaining more substance in his isolation by talking to himself? Or mankind, pictured as an anonymous brother? In the last aphorism that I quoted, Kafka's thought has a familiar ring; we recall Rilke writing to his young poet, "Do not seek...answers, which cannot be given you....Live the questions now."[15] But courteous Rilke had used the German pronoun of polite address, "Sie." Kafka's tone, like Rilke's, is ardent. What does his "Du" add? Something *devotional*. And yet, not to a concrete other. The ardor is abstract, the devotion is turned toward theory. Even his specific advice is preceptive, not personal. And so his "Du" is both focused and blurred, abrupt as well as warm, spoken to no one man and spoken to Everyman.

And just this ambiguity informs the whole range of his understanding: how we are at once estranged from each other and indissolubly together; at once self-encaged and belonging to Him. The distancing of theory, combined with the breadth of the nonphobic, permits Kafka all the more to see the other side of things, the riddling nature of experience, what E.M. Forster called "not...the knowledge of good and evil, but the knowledge of good-and-evil."[16] For the opposition is a unity. Our lives are steeped in the absurd. We have no fullness without confinement. Circumstances and inner capacity always restrict us, and death comes soon. We are challenged to find the fullness in our confinement. Therefore paradox itself is a crown, and the faultless paradoxicalist never coasts nor arbitrates, nor seeks to untie a knot.

So the themes of the aphorisms run, and sharpen us, in turn, to the paradoxes in mental health which any good theory must honor: paradoxes that join the sense of restriction to that of freedom; the readiness to doubt, to assurance; perhaps, also, insanity to sanity. In the mid-1950s, Gregory Bateson reported the words of a chronic schizophrenic, an ex-Air Force machinist, now hospitalized for 12 years, whose forms of communication he was trying to understand. The man spoke an obscure, garbled speech. But once he said something as dryly factual as Camus' man in the bathtub. "Bateson," he complained, "you want me to come and live in your world. I lived in it from 1920 to 1943, and I don't like it." Bateson felt silenced. For when mental illness so sanely explains itself, sanity seems only an imposition.

And most of us, as we try to be more sane, do we do anything but impose on ourselves?

In a piece called "On Parables," Kafka developed this idea more fully, with all his wit and finesse. I quote it in full, for it is itself an extended aphorism and cannot be subdivided.

> Many complain that the words of the wise are always merely parables and of no use in the daily life, which is the only life we have. When the sage says: "Go over," he does not mean that we should cross to some actual place, which we could do anyhow if the labor were worth it; he means some fabulous yonder, something unknown to us, something too that he cannot designate more precisely, and therefore cannot help us here in the least. All these parables really set out to say merely that the incomprehensible is incomprehensible, and we know that already. But the cares we have to struggle with every day: that is a different matter.
>
> Concerning this a man once said: Why such reluctance? If you only followed the parables you yourself would become parables and with that rid of all your daily cares.

Another said: I bet that is also a parable.
The first said: You have won.
The second said: But unfortunately only in parable.
The first said: No, in reality: in parable you have lost.

Here is the enigma of mental health, which is the same enigma as Kafka's. In parable, everything is as it should be: that is, it is just as it is, "freed from its opposite," from all comparison. Then, rephrasing St. Paul, one sees through a glass *clearly*. A parable may speak of change in how one lives, like the story of the Prodigal Son. But nothing needs to be repaired for the change to come about. Whereas, in everyday reality, we live with a sense of defect, of something that requires correction. And then we want to be unanxious, undepressed, undriven, cured of worldly cares, ready indeed to become a parable. But just in that wish, we lose the other awareness, to which the virtue of patience belongs, that no basic correction is needed. Or is it possible (for this question hangs in the balance) to keep the awareness of parable, or aspire to it, or gain it back — awareness of everything intact as it is, of good-and-evil together — so we can sense that there's no Paradise without the snake, but that Paradise is our home?

Kafka's own life continued sorrowful. During his stay at Zürau, he broke off an engagement for which he felt emotionally unfit. Longing for intimacy brought him, on two later occasions, close to marriage. But the old self-doubts triumphed. He was not up to it; it was his father's "domain." Perhaps, at bottom, a paradox held which he could never quite embrace: that marriage can protect solitude as well as closeness.

Meanwhile, his health remained broken: bouts of influenza and pneumonia, and finally tuberculosis of the larynx from which, in his 41st year, he died, in great pain. At the end, he said to a young friend at his bedside: "Don't go away." "I'm not going away," the friend answered. "But I'm going away," said Kafka. It was, for the last time, grace sought, and lost.

In a famous aphorism from English literature, Keats observed: "Shakespeare led a life of allegory. His works are the comments on it."[20] One can think of Kafka's works, and certainly his own extraordinary aphorisms, as comments on the allegory he didn't know how to live. The fitful, irresolute adult remained, his yearning never slaked for the father who would choose him as his specially loved son, his delight. And yet the releasing vision was there too, the eye of parable, which recreates the life of the spirit from life that felt like a desert, and posits, in all its aridity, the brooks and meadows of Eden. The paradox that Kafka most personally leaves with us becomes our own grounds for therapeutic humility: I mean, the blending within him of mighty opposites that remain unreconciled. It is as though, in him, we see a man who couldn't swim, but had the gift of walking on the waves.

Chapter 5

MARTIN BUBER: WE TOGETHER

With Martin Buber, we cross a great divide. Blake's Poetic Genius, which defines True Man, Rilke's individual who dares to be alone and is faithful to his aloneness, Kafka's Everyman, lost within himself and taking, as it were, instrumental readings on the True Way — they are each, according to Buber, the fruit of relationship; they are only to be understood and recognized as participants in relationship. The concept of individualism as such unrolls like a magic carpet which then vanishes. One is, in reality, always in connection with another. Even self-estrangement shows a sort of bond, the Ariadne thread twisted in the labyrinth of a relationship, but never broken. Blake had announced, two hundred years ago:

> Great things are done when men and mountains meet;
> This is not done by jostling in the street.[1]

Buber's words, in our century, reaffirm Blake's in a still more sweeping Annunciation: "All real living is meeting." And in his small, packed book, *I and Thou*, he draws a cardinal distinction, fateful in its meaning for philosophy, education, religion, and psychotherapy, between meeting an object, and meeting a presence; between relating to a world of measurable things, our customary, objective world, the world, as he says, of *It*; and relating boundlessly to that which is other than oneself, the realm of wholeheartedness, of love, of *Thou*. From this vision of man's "twofold attitude," he draws a wealth of subtle clarifications. Above all, in his own living he takes the world as *Thou* in heroic and testamentary fashion.

Buber was born in Vienna, in 1878, and his infancy seemed to move in the warmth of Eden. Then, when he was three, the loved child was banished from Paradise. His mother disappeared without a trace. Not comprehending at first, he went to live with his paternal grandparents, in Galicia, as Austrian Poland was called. Later in the same year, a playmate, an older girl, said to him, as they were standing on his grandparents' balcony: "She will never come back." Suddenly he knew. As an adult, he made up a word for what the child had understood. He took the German word for meeting, *Begegnung*, and coined the neologism: *Vergegnung*: a "mismeeting." For the poignance of the loss did homage just to this: the centrality of meeting. When he saw his mother again — it was one time only; she traveled back from Russia, where she had gone and remarried, to visit Buber as a young man, now himself married and with children — "I could not," he then wrote, "gaze into her still astonishingly beautiful eyes without hearing from somewhere the word '*Vergegnung*' as a word spoken to me." Tolling for him, it brought back the pain of his loss, and its importance.

His childhood itself, however, had moved along in an atmosphere of unusual blessedness. His devoted, self-educated grandmother and companionable, scholarly grandfather saw to his education with private tutors until he was ten. A photograph of him, age seven, shows a handsome and thoughtful boy, eyes looking down, hands in his pockets, as if contemplating a task to be addressed, and ready for action. There is an air of sadness, but also of resolve and inner direction; one sees the first stage of a life which is to be, in effect, the education of a teacher.

In his grandparents' home, he spoke not only German, but Hebrew, Yiddish, Polish, English, French, and Italian. After his years of schooling at the Polish Gymnasium, he also read Latin, Greek, Spanish, and Dutch. Love of language, indeed, lay at the core of the young man who heard the word "Vergegnung" in his mother's presence; who came to retranslate the Hebrew Bible into German with a unique fidelity to the original, and special regard to its quality as speech; and who found and described so fully, as we shall soon hear, the "primary words," *I-It* and *I-Thou*. When he was ten, he also resumed close relations with his father, who had remarried. The boy responded to his father's warmth and his gifts as a storyteller; they were a great precedent for Buber's own later recording, in German, the Yiddish Hasidic tales of 18th century Poland.

At 19, he went to the University of Vienna, and soon after to Leipzig and Zürich, studying the history of art, classical German literature, and the German Renaissance mystics Nicholas of Cusa and Jakob Boehme. Now the Renaissance range of the student's own nature was full grown; his vast appetite for learning and his zeal for current Jewish affairs mingled with a tireless love of life. After one sleepless night on a train returning from Berlin, where he had gone with a friend to "rescue" a Zionist meeting from a narrow political to a broad cultural base, he went directly to another meeting in Leipzig, then dressed for a banquet, danced all night at a ball, and proceeded to classes the following morning. One feels the throb of energy packed into this short, lithe man who later wrote, in a lyrical piece playing on the language of St. Francis, "I look at you and call to you, Brother Body, and praise you more than sun and wind."

Amid his youthful "plenitude of possibilities"[2] at the University of Zürich, he met Paula Winkler. She had been raised in Munich as a Catholic. She was 21, a year older than Buber, beautiful — wide-set pensive eyes under a high forehead — strong-willed, with great intellectual and literary gifts, and with a tenderness that both evoked and sheltered his individuality. The hurt child was now the grateful beloved. Instead of *Vergegnung*, full *Begegnung*; and then *Heilung aus der Begegnung: Healing through Meeting*. The phrase is the title of the psychotherapist Hans Trüb's book, for which Buber, in his seventies, wrote the introduction. Twenty years after his marriage, he quotes from Goethe's *West-Eastern Divan*:

> So, waiting, I have finally won through thee
> God's presence in each element.[3]

It is generally understood to be his private dedication to Paula. And while she was still his fiancée (she converted to Judaism for their marriage), he wrote to her in a letter: "I regard you...as my freedom. One must take the whole world-riddle into one's relationship to one person." So the central theme of his life — healing through meeting — became clear early and grew richer, with new clarifications, as he developed.

In his "Maxims for Revolutionists," Shaw wrote, "He who can, does. He who cannot, teaches." (Thus, strangely enough, Ireland's most active teacher!) Buber's own sense of renewal in living held to the maxim: "He who consumes life, destroys it. He who hallows life, lives and teaches." To hallow life is itself an action, it brings forth one's will; but this will is, as he says in *I and Thou*, "without arbitrary self-will." It is Taoist willing without willfulness, of which Kafka speaks too in his aphorism: "What is laid upon us is to accomplish the negative." At the same time, Taoist spontaneity evokes the mystic's understanding: that life is fulfilled in presence, ineffableness, inward harmony. How is this to be reconciled with an activist social conscience and a commitment to intellectual formulation and discrimination? After his marriage, Buber edited Jewish periodicals, but this work was not enough for his mystical side. He sought his own special teachers in the rabbis of Hasidic Jewish life, those men of four to seven generations before who taught by example in Polish villages.

He had seen them as a child, when his grandfather took him to the still-remaining Hasidic community of Sadagora, in Galicia, and he watched the Hasidim exult and dance with the Torah. This was sacrament: "the outward and visible sign of inward and spiritual grace."[4] And beyond all pious observances, the Hasidic rabbis saw the same sacrament in daily life. Many stories about them — their good humor, their wise, earthy friendliness — had been handed down in Polish folk tradition, and beginning in his late twenties, Buber spent five years collecting and translating these tales from East European Yiddish into German. Here is one of them:

> Rabbi Shemuel told this about Rabbi Rafael of Bershad: "When he was going on his summer trip, he called me and asked me to share his carriage with him. I said: 'I am

afraid I should crowd you.' Then he said to me in the manner he always used to express special affection: 'Let us love each other more and we shall have a feeling of spaciousness.' And after we had prayed, he said to me: 'God is a great-hearted friend.'"

Friendliness like this showed in Buber himself. The Dutch humanitarian Frederik Van Eden noted about him at a meeting of educators in Potsdam, in 1914, when the First World War was threatening: "The slender, fragile, subtle, but strong Buber, with his straight look and soft eyes...yet deep and sharp, the Rabbi, but without the narrow mind, the philosopher, but without the aridity, the scholar, but without the self-conceit."

In fact, his own tendency to mystical exaltation troubled him. In 1913, he had published a little book called *Daniel*, in which the problems of living with others serve as vectors for inner realization, and show the inward unity of one's own life — even more, "the unity of life and death." This self-realizing is the glory of life; and, as perpetual adventure, it is also a constant risk. Buber named it "the kingdom of holy insecurity." But whatever truth this phrase contains, he later found it to be couched "extravagantly,"[5] and he came to call the whole Song of Myself which *Daniel* expressed, "an exalted form of being untrue.[6] In an essay of 1929, "Dialogue," he recalls a crucial experience soon after writing *Daniel*. A soldier of the First World War, a young man named Mehé, came to see him to talk about life. Buber had, just that morning, felt "lifted out" of himself in religious rapture. He listened to the man, he was friendly and attentive. But he was still inwardly absorbed. He did not guess the other's despair. Two months later, a friend of Mehé visited Buber and told him that Mehé had died at the Front: not exactly a suicide, but at the same time, in the despair "of no longer opposing one's own death." Mehé had needed from him a presence, Buber understood, beyond the best that conversation could provide. All this had for him the force of conversion; the earthy Hasid in him came back, and he renounced mystical rapture like a man who has hit bottom on an addictive drug. "Since then," he writes in "Dialogue,"

> I have given up the 'religious' which is nothing but the exception, extraction, exaltation, ecstasy; or it has given me up. I possess nothing but the everyday out of which I am never taken. The mystery is no longer disclosed, it has escaped or it has made its dwelling here where everything happens as it happens. I know no fullness but each mortal hour's fullness of claim and responsibility.

He joins himself to the motto Karen Blixen came to live by: "Je responderay"[7] — "I will respond." He joins himself to Goethe's call: "What is your duty? The challenge of every day."[8]

As public servant, during the war he founded and edited *Der Jude,* which became the leading journal of German-speaking Jewry. Zionist and anti-Zionist, socialist and literary pieces were published. Kafka submitted a section of *The Trial.* Buber rejected it, but, as Kafka wrote to his fiancée, "with a letter that was more respectful than any ordinary acceptance could have been." Now Buber's own constant practice with others was: *to be present.* To the Czech poet, Franz Werfel, who had written him in distress that he could no longer produce poetry, Buber replied:

> You should for the time being set aside the work and live without it. It is nothing more than waiting and accepting God's tempo. Consider only that the things are there for you and the more you have trust, the more you originate and give of yourself....[T]he only thing you have to fear is just this anxiety....I know this anxiety from a period of my own life, and I feel more than fond of you: joined with you.

We recognize the tone; it is that of Rilke's response to young Kappus. At the same time, the dialectical Buber knew his own differences from Rilke: for the poet, to live in spirit is to be assimilated to the invisible; for Buber, it is to be fully concrete in relationship; as music is not "within" the virtuoso performer, but "out there" in his performance. One must indeed, so the dialectic proceeds, *be* inwardly a unity, in order to enter fully into relationship. Buber's old question of how to synthesize inner and outer commitments, soul-yearning and world-loyalty, has turned round. How could they *not* be synthesized? What the classical Greeks called *paideia* — the integrated education of the inner life, leading to literary cultivation and wisdom — is, for him, a still wider *Gestalt*. It is the sacredness of the everyday, and the interwoveness, indeed the deep identity, of education, psychotherapy, and religion. He felt called on to describe how we ever manage to ignore all this and to live otherwise; how the world of interhuman fakery, which is so much of our culture, comes about. But it is more than fakery: we all, even the most honorable, live in two different kinds of relationships: the one unbounded, the other measured. It is our lack of clarity about this, or our ignorance of it, or our lumping the two together, or treating one as if it were the other, which generates and maintains so much of the pain of life.

For all these things, the subject of *I and Thou*, the scholarly Buber of 1916 had in mind a five-volume work, "systematic and comprehensive."

But once again, and to our own good fortune, the Hasid in him triumphed. After the war, the philosopher Franz Rosenzweig founded a new humanistic free Jewish House of Learning in Frankfurt, and he invited Buber to work with him. So it is as a teacher talking to his students, in a course called "Religion as Presence," that the actual *I and Thou* arose. Buber used transcriptions of his spoken word to base the text on, and many passages are essentially verbatim from the class. Now, with this little book of some 100 pages, published in 1923, his own education as a teacher was ripe.

I and Thou is in three parts, with a postscript of 14 pages that Buber wrote 34 years later. I shall be discussing the first part,[9] though I bring in the others, which make up most of the book and, much more heavily pedagogic than the beginning, elaborate matters of history, philosophy, and theology. But all of this is drawn out of the first part, as from the reserve supplies in a storeroom.

Part 1, 30 pages long, is divided into 28 sections, like so many chapters of a book in the Bible. And there is a definitely biblical quality to the writing. This Book is part genesis, part psalm, part gospel; it is at once unfolding and rhapsody, exposition and illumination, doctrine and song. In the Bible to which it belongs, it could be called "The Book of Epiphanies."

I and Thou is a difficult book. It is a Principia of human phenomenology, in which each sentence contains a subtext for epistemology, education, ethics, religion, and psychotherapy. Buber's mind is dialectical, richly qualifying, and full of images. His style has much grace and power, but also an imperviousness, like tough bark. It will not yield or melt. But to abstract or condense him is to undo his meaning; as he once wrote to the Zionist Viktor Jacobson: "You can only be rid of my style together with me." Some people might wish his little book more "systematic and comprehensive." I am glad it isn't. As an old man, he commented to his American biographer, Maurice Friedman, that his thought was "wildgrown"; and in this central text of his life, he wisely let it stay wild. Themes and images are developed more or less, here and there, like flower beds in an English garden. But sometimes images, or a whole passage return; notes are struck again, like artfully recurring *leitmotifs.*

And yet, too, the book is simple. Its one concern is to identify what is involved when one says *Thou.* And the German word is still plainer, not at all, like the English, alien to the ear. It is the *Du* of common speech, the singular "You" which one speaks to a child, to a family intimate or close friend, to a lover, or to the God of one's faith. And what is more evident than the theme (central to *I and Thou*): "To be is to be related"? Or: To be accepted by being cherished as one is, allows one to blossom. All this is simple as the wheel is simple, which seems altogether obvious once it is discovered, and has untold uses for the fulfillment of our lives.

But wait! To speak of "usefulness" is already to approach one of the book's complexities. Buber will have much to say on the cunning traps of being useful. And in a sense, just as a blessing isn't an acquisition, so his book can't be used. Had he thought of it, he would have been pleased that in *I and Thou,* a year before Kafka's death, he fulfilled Kafka's prophecy. He sought no gain. He "built the Tower of Babel without ascending it." And therefore his own achievement is blessed.

The title itself is annunciatory. It gives the characters of the drama — only two, and known only as pronouns. But just these two, with just these pronouns, comprise the basic human situation. Or rather, they comprise a specific *way* in which they are related to one another. What is this way? It is direct relation. It is mutual relation. It is meeting. It is *between* I and Thou. It is exclusive: not that "nothing exists except [*Thou*]. But all else lives in *his* light."[10] It is not "to be experienced and described," for one experiences and describes that which is set apart from oneself, and with *Thou*, I am always included. And in all these ways, it is "the cradle of the Real Life."

What, clearly, is it *not*? It is not what most of life is: what we observe, measure, categorize, integrate. It is not set in space, time, order, and causal sequence. It is not the product of the past and the useful present. And yet, for all these myriad phenomena, we don't need any other characters in the drama. Rather, we change our relation to the other, who becomes, now, a kind of thing, a sum of qualities, something "for the record," something which can be computed. The other is no longer *Thou*, but *It*. (Or He and She, which can replace It: all the third person pronouns are equally thing-like.) And the *I* with *It*, the measuring and appraising *I*, is different from the *I* with *Thou*.

Take, as Buber likes to, an example from literature. Here is Whitman's poem:

> When I heard the learn'd astronomer,
> When the proofs, the figures, were ranged in columns
> before me,
> When I was shown the charts and diagrams, to add,
> divide, and measure them,
> When I sitting heard the astronomer where he lectured
> with much applause in the lecture-room,
> How soon unaccountable I became tired and sick,
> Till rising and gliding out I wander'd off by myself,
> In the mystical moist night-air, and from time to time,
> Look'd up in perfect silence at the stars.[11]

The astronomer's learning, the world of *It*, deserves its applause. But like a biblical prophet, the poet says what counts to him for more — it is just the "unaccountable" in him. From that arises, "from time to time," like the wind that bloweth where it listeth, his look "in perfect silence"; the stars as *Thou*. Their physical distance, the fact that the light now seen from them was emitted eons ago, all this means nothing; billions of miles, to *Thou*, are as close as the mother to the child she nurses. So Goethe once said of the stars, as a mother might say of her children, "They are my conscience." Or, the mother's baby, her *Thou*, "fills the heavens." *Thou* itself is a cosmos. In another phrase of Buber's, it is "the heaven of *Thou*."

We are hearing him as poet. But his mind is also dialectical; he tells us of *Thou* and *It*, first of all, through the dialectician's method of sorting general ideas. The book opens with the pronouncement: "To man the world is twofold, in accordance with his twofold attitude." And over and over as he proceeds, he describes this twofoldness through the opposing or complementary principles that inhere in man's social world, in his religious life, and in his grasp of his own potentialities. On the one side, "the community that is built up out of relation" — like the Hasids Buber had seen as a child; on the other, "the collection of human units that do not know relation — modern man's palpable condition of lack of relation." As to religious experience: "solitude is the place of purification, necessary even to the man who is bound in relation" (we hear echoed Rilke's paean to solitude); and, in contrast, there is solitude, "the stronghold of isolation, where a man [only] conducts a dialogue with himself — the real fall of the spirit" (a distinction Rilke does not spell out). Again: to man's freedom in development belongs the idea of *destiny*, which "is not his boundary, but his fulfillment." Destiny appeals to "his grand will," free of "arbitrary self-will." On the other hand, *fate* is a closed idea, as both causality and conditioning are closed. These three notions only snatch at a reality which eludes them: causality belongs in space and time; conditioning, as defining our nature, is only partial; fate is a false credo. A man "must sacrifice his puny, unfree will, that is controlled by things and instincts, to his grand will, which quits defined for destined being."

But in the thick tapestry of these distinctions, and basic to all of them, is figured the much simpler dialectic, the two relationships, *I-Thou* and *I-It*: the one of combination, the other of separation; the one of presence, the other of objects. "I" plus "He" (or "She" or "It") does *not* add to *Thou*; "I" and "He" make

It. And *It* is always "we" divided. Though the same two entities, I and another, are involved, the addition is quite different. Buber's German prose neatly brings out a connection and a difference, for the first two syllables of each salient word are the same. *Gegenwart* is English "presence," *Gegenstand,* English "object."[12] But in both languages we have from him, the master dialectician, the four elementary monosyllables that tell the tale: *Ich, Du; Ich, Es. I, Thou; I, It.* They could be words in a nursery rhyme.

In fact it's fitting to talk here of the human infant: Buber himself spends much time, in Part I of his book, speculating on infancy, and its special absorption in "the flash and counterflash of meeting." He begins anthropologically with the childhood of mankind, then turns for evidence to primitive cultures today. Theirs is a "lived relation" with Nature, inseparable from it, direct, bodily, powerful. And as Picasso, two decades earlier, had found in almond-shaped masks of the French Congo a new vitality for European art, so Buber gives us, for vitality in language, "the ever fresh Kaffir greeting, with its direct bodily relation, 'I see you!' or its ridiculous and sublime American [Indian] variant, 'Smell me!'" In our own "worn-out formulas...in 'Hail!'" he asks rhetorically, "do we discern even dimly...the original conferring of power?"

And this grand relational unity, the person bound to his body and to Nature in a "blood-stirring *Thou,*" is still more apparent to us in every child. It has known, in its mother's womb, just that "perfect silence" Whitman's poem spoke of (Buber, as though adding an image to Whitman's poem, talks of the "cosmic quality" of the prenatal bond). After birth, the infant lives for some time only in relation. "It is simply not the case," Buber stresses,

> that the child first perceives an object, then, as it were, puts himself in relation to it. But the effort to establish relation comes first — the hand of the child arched out so that what is over against him may nestle under it; second is the actual relation, a saying of *Thou* without words, in the state preceding the word-form....I become through my relation to the *Thou;* as I become *I,* I say *Thou*....In the

beginning is relation — as category of being, readiness, grasping form, mould for the soul.

And among these proclamations, Buber gives us another term which acknowledges the separate organism: for just as, biologically the infant has germ cells for later sexual function, designed by nature for union in relationship, so he also has, in his individual being from the start, what is required at once to establish relationship; he has "the *a priori* of relation, *the inborn Thou.*" By virtue of this *a priori*, he can make contact; he learns "mutual relation, 'tenderness.'" Later he comes to personify and to converse with what is "over against him." So the child's soul develops; it is always, Buber continues lyrically (for *Thou* indeed is the lyrical mode of our being, and in his very striving to be exact, Buber's voice is lyrical) — the child's soul is always "bound up with longing for the *Thou*, with the satisfaction and the disappointment of this longing, with the game of his experiments and the tragic seriousness of his perplexity." What is tragic? Not only *meeting* happens. As we know, so does *mismeeting.*

But we have not yet said enough about the importance of *Thou*. As the origin, acknowledgment, and confirmation of our existence, it makes us human. It defines what is apt for our existence. It lives only in the present and can only be spoken "with the whole being": as Socrates spoke to other men and they to him; as Goethe gave himself to nature, and nature gave itself in return; as Jesus "calls his *Thou* Father in such a way that he himself is simply Son and nothing else but Son." And just as moral good "can only be spoken with the whole soul," so *Thou* always is good, is healing, whenever I say it and whenever it is said to me.

Then, for the child comes the next great developmental step: "Through the *Thou* [he] becomes *I*." Buber fills out the picture. "That which confronts [the child] comes and disappears, relational events condense, then are scattered, and in the change consciousness of the unchanging partner, or the *I*, grows clear, and each time stronger....The separated *I* emerges, transformed." And so *the world of things* is produced.

> Shrunk from substance and fullness to a functional point, to a subject which experiences and uses, *I* approaches and takes possession of all *It* [now] existing "in and for itself"....With the magnifying glass of peering observation [the person] bends over particulars and objectifies them, or with the field-glass of remote inspection he objectifies them and arranges them as scenery, he isolates them in observation without any feeling for their exclusiveness, or he knits them into a scheme of observation without any feeling of universality.

Thus, the world of *It*, of whatever can and does *accumulate*: things, experience, good intentions — and bad. *It* is solid life, with "object constancy" (to use a phrase of the psychoanalyst Margaret Mahler[13]). Or, in Buber's words again: "the world...set in the context of space and time." And, of course, it is a world indispensable to us. "Every *Thou* in our world must become an *It*." The person I love is also "he" or "she," with a history and a daily life; as am I to him or to her; as am I to myself. "This is the exalted melancholy of our fate," Buber sings; melancholy because *It* is always less than *Thou*; exalted because of all the recognizable good that may come of *It*: scientific knowledge, the body of the law, civilized culture with its traditions and customs.

But the real trouble, our ultimate "melancholy," is that *It* may fail to become *Thou* again. *Thou* must become *It*, but for *It* an option exists. *Thou* may be forgot. And the good of *It* persists only when *Thou* is remembered; when I reconfirm *It* as *Thou*. When I do not, then *It* becomes the Pandora's box out of which all the moral ills of mankind fly. For with *It*, divorced from *Thou*, we have not "whole being," but life carved up and classified; and we know overtyrannical man, overmethodical man, the conventionalized and hypocritical world of rules in which I keep up appearances and do what is expected. Already in infancy, the child's world is blackened by the mother who forsakes him as *Thou*, and represents, with her culturally derived prescriptions and regulations, a too-unyielding *It*. She becomes his Bad Mother, from whom, in turn, the child learns the identity of Bad Me. All enmity with oneself and with the environment arises out of the loss of *Thou*. As to the environment: whether it be the air I pollute with toxic chemicals, the workers in a factory whom I, as their management staff, oppose and sue, the customer or the lover whom I sell or conquer, or the political enemy whom I, as a loyal American, build bombs against, they are each *only* my adversary as I fail to say *Thou* to them.

For myself, loss of *Thou* leads, in Buber's phrase, to "self-contradiction:...the *a priori* of relation, the inborn *Thou*...strikes inward,...develops where there is no place at all for it to develop." What, clinically today, we call *autism* may result, the individual shut up in his or her private world. Or a man may learn, through his parents and his culture, to take himself as *It*: the individual, forlorn of *Thou*, closed in his self-aggrandizement. So Buber speaks of imperial-minded Napoleon:

> He sees the beings around him...as machines, capable of various achievements, which must be taken into account and utilized for the Cause. In this way, too, he sees himself — except that he must continually ascertain anew by experiment his power of achievement (whose limits he does not experience): he treats himself, too, as an *It*.

Yet Buber also, with his own many-sidedness, admires Napoleon. For though the emperor understood himself as *It*, he did so without illusion; he did not seek personal power but, no matter how mistakenly, an experience of "consummation." His passion had grandeur; and — here is Buber's Blakean tones — all passion imports good. "The man who straightforwardly hates," he asserts, "is much nearer to relation than the man without hate and love." Moral evil comes when passionless *It* is master. In *It*, always, there is fundamental indecisiveness. The fishing line of one's being trails slack. Only with whole being is it taut again; only whole being, which says *Thou*, can be decisive. "If there were a devil," Buber goes on, "it would not be one who decided against God, but one who, in eternity, came to no decision." We hear Blake's proverb echoed: "Expect poison from the standing water."

In the last long paragraph of Part I, Buber, the psalmist, sings the interplay of his two realms, the "bare present" of *Thou*, the assembled formulations of *It*, with full deference to the intrinsic values of each. The world if *It* is where one

> has to live, [where] it is comfortable to live, [it is] the world indeed which offers [men and women] all manner of incitements and excitements, activity and knowledge. In this chronicle of solid benefits, the moments of the *Thou* appear as strange lyric and dramatic episodes, seductive and magical, but tearing us away to dangerous extremes, loosening the well-tried context, leaving more questions than satisfactions behind them, shattering security....

And yet this elfin *Thou*, fluid and glimmering, provides the source-relation, the rich, unified loam from which both *I* and *It* have come; *Thou* is the larger and sturdier reality. Buber is emphatic about its many larger relations, wider categories, though he makes these emphases soft; some of them are almost conversational asides. "Prayer is not in time but time in prayer, sacrifice not in space but space in sacrifice, and to reverse the relation is to abolish the reality." Again: "Feelings dwell in man; but man dwells in his love. This is no metaphor, but the actual truth." And again: "Spirit appears in time as a product, even as a by-product of nature, yet it is in spirit that nature is timelessly enveloped." In each instance, he means a literally greater reality, not an abstraction, for *Thou* is always concrete, a person *in toto*, from whom no element of *It* — color of hair, tone of voice, posture, intention — can be detached. For the abstract, Buber has a scorn like Kierkegaard's toward Hegel; and he can sound the same note. "Many a man," he tells us dryly in the first pages of his book,

> has raised over and above himself a structure of ideas, in which he finds refuge and repose from the oncome of nothingness. On the threshold he lays aside his inauspicious everyday dress, wraps himself in pure linen, and regales himself with the spectacle of primal being, or of necessary being; but his life has no part in it. To proclaim his ways may even fill him with well-being.

What counts is everyday dress, real life. It is that to which, more inclusively than all the usefulness of the world of *It*, love and prayer and sacrifice refer. "Love" — Buber gives us a brief and sweeping definition —

> is responsibility of an *I* for a *Thou*. In this lies the likeness...of all who love,...from the blessedly protected man, whose life is rounded out in that of a loved being, to him who is all his life nailed to the cross of the world, and who ventures to bring himself to the dreadful point — to love *all men*.

The example of Jesus leads us directly on to prayer and spirit, that is, the religious domain of *Thou*. But to feel this in its full force, first we must return to the concrete person, *I* in the world.

This *I*, formed from the original *I-Thou* of early life, has its own stability, its own locus and limits. But strictly speaking, it exists always as *I*-with-*It*, or as transformed again into a further *I*-with-*Thou*. It is never isolated; it never wanders like a hermit; it has no other fullness than that of its connections. And here Buber, the student and polemicist of religion, takes pains to be explicit. There can be no single soul's mystical "absorption [in] universal being"; no oneness of the mind with Nature, as Andrew Marvell sang:

> Annihilating all that's made
> To a green though in a green shade.[14]

Neither is there a Nirvana emptiness, uprooting even oneness, in which mystical unity too is revealed as illusion, and all hard-and-fast reality ceases. There *is*, indeed, as the Buddha knew, a goal of "undivided mystery." There is, as many mystics have said, "The soul's becoming a unity." But with this power of becoming that a man has, he *does* something. He may carouse with his power in the realm of *It*, and thereby dissipate his being. But to cultivate inner unity is also to grow decisive; and decisiveness, as we have heard, is preparation: it prepares a man for *Thou*. Then, "concentrated in unity, he can go out to [this] meeting." He meets the other, human or nonhuman. In either case, with *It* or with *Thou* he is himself indissolubly in relation. And relationship in its own right always speaks of otherness, of a reality which remains *other than* oneself.

Buber talks in two special ways of the nonhuman other. In the otherness of artistic form, "man is concerned with an act of his being." Thus he draws forth from sound, as his *Thou*, the form of music; from stone, the form of sculpture. Buber's own phrases, "To produce is to draw forth; to invent is to find," are, in the German text, untranslatable wordplays: "Schaffen ist Schöpfen, Erfinden ist Finden." Once drawn forth, or found, the finished artistic work then enters the world of *It*: it is for experiencing, for communication, for sale. And sometimes, of course, it meets the receiver as his *Thou*.

But in God — here is the great, the incomparable distinction — in God we address Otherness that can have no form; we address "the eternal *Thou*." For this *Thou* "cannot become *It*....[it] remains present. By its nature, the eternal *Thou* is eternally Thou."[15]

And it is the eternal *Thou*, God's Otherness which will not yield to any formulation, that is the Temple in which each meeting of "real life" occurs. Only in relation with Him, is the inborn *Thou* consummated. By virtue of Him, the "holy insecurity" of each mortal *Thou* is imperishable and blessed forever.

Early in Part I, foreshadowing his much later talk of God, Buber announces, "In each [*Thou*], we are aware of a breath from the eternal *Thou*; in each Thou we address the eternal *Thou*." He speaks, as he must, in generalities, for God is the most inclusive reality: as each mortal *Thou* is more than *It*, so God is more than each mortal *Thou*.

And of course, therefore, we cannot prove that He exists. His unprovableness, rather, is only proof that we are fragmentary and mortal. "Hast thou an arm like God?" the Lord says to Job, "or canst thou thunder with a voice like him?" Appeal to unproof, indeed, is the burden of those who do not witness Him. But those who are his witnesses witness, here as elsewhere, the *mutuality* of all *I-Thou* relations. Buber insists always on this mutuality, although sometimes he has to tug at it to keep it in shape. How, for instance, does mutuality exist between a man and physical nature, when he says *Thou* to it? Poets may simply "feel nature's response." But in the Postscript to his book Buber reasons (his own poetic soul flying to the dialectician for refuge) that, with stars and tree, we are at the "pre-threshold" stage of mutuality. In the case of man and God, the eternal *Thou*, Buber quotes Nietzsche's words on inspiration: "taking but not asking who gives." And yet again, as dialectician, he cannot resist a further note: God is unconditional, absolute, beyond measurement, beyond concept and image; but — here comes a word that sounds, amid these pealing carillons, positively droll — in addition, God is a *Person*. Buber is aware of the trombone slide downward with the word; he acknowledges it elegantly: "it is...necessary to add that God is *also* a Person." Mutuality, once again, requires this; how else can we, as persons ourselves, meet Him? But for Buber, the paradox here is only to be embraced; not paradox, as in Kafka, with nightmare reversals, a bewildering Yes and No together, but paradox which is contrast, as within a rich stained glass. So, in language as occult as that of the *Upanishads*, he proclaims: "Our relation to [God] is as above contradiction as it is, because he is as above contradiction as he is." Or — in a passage that could be out of the medieval Catholic mystic, Meister Eckhart — "You need God in order to be — and...in the fullness of His eternity [God] needs you....'Thy will be done,' [you say]; but truth adds...'through me whom Thou needest.'" Or again — the polemicist gone, the psalmist singing and abjuring no images of immediate power: "Of course God is the 'wholly Other'; but He is also the wholly Same, the wholly Present. Of course he is the Mysterium Tremendum that appears and overthrows; but He is also the mystery of the self-evident, nearer to me than my I."

So, rhapsodically, man *addresses* God; so, in more prosaic language, a relationship *speaks of* otherness. These verbs evoke a final concern of Buber's thought which, in *I and Thou*, is also a first and fundamental one: the primacy of *words*. Relationship, of course, has its own clear primacy. And when it is expressed as Meeting, its sensory mode is usually *visual*: we *see* how relationship happens. Meeting, too, can be *tactile* — and Buber in fact never disparages any of the senses. Cultured European that he is, we've heard him extol the Indian greeting: "Smell me." But for him, still more deeply than Meeting, perhaps out of the depth of the imageless *Thou* that God is, it is not the visual nor the tactile, but the *aural,* God who speaks, man who is addressed, man who addresses the world, man who addresses man, which brings out the essential nature of *Thou.*

And here, in the midst of his unshakable worldliness, his Platonizing sense of language, of a language behind language, comes into view. There is, for him, a kind of speech that precedes language, speech that is a wider reality, speech already resident in the wider reality of spirit. Thus, from an unpublished Forword to *I and Thou*: "Speech is the primal act of the Spirit whose human execution the spoken languages...serve." We have already heard the first sentence of his book, announcing his dialectic of man's "twofold attitude." In his second sentence, the dialectic is enfolded in his Platonic sense of words; and we hear an echo of St. John's "In the beginning was the Word" as Buber follows his own thought: "The attitude of man is twofold, in accordance with the twofold nature of the primary words which he speaks."

We already know this "twofold nature" as relationship: *I-Thou* and *I-It*; the "whole being" of the one, the "shrunk substance" of the other. Now we are hearing it also as the primal words *I-Thou* and *I-It,* words "spoken from the being," *I-Thou,* of the whole being, *I-It,* of less. In actual speech, of course, the primary words may employ any verbal expression. "Hello" can signify the plenitude of *I-Thou,* or the dryness of *I-It.* "The form of the words," Buber insists many times, "proves nothing." But basically, the primary words, with their own differing *I*'s, are always inseparable pairs, as the primal relationships, with their differing *I*-s, are inseparable. Indeed, the primal words and relationships are themselves inseparable, though, by virtue of their Platonic character, the words have a certain precedence. And so Buber says: "The world *belongs to*[16] the primary word, *I-It*....The *primary word*[17] *I-Thou* establishes the world of relation."

In turn, each primary relationship and primary word maintains, within itself, a kind of unity. Not a mystical one, which would imply that *I* and *Thou* are fused. This never happens, except as delusion. But "the relation itself [keeps] its [own] vital unity," its "enrapturing dynamic." Mysticism, if one dare speak of it at all with Buber's developed thought, is transposed by him into the field of relationship; it is the flash of being that ignites between two persons, as words flash in the realm of spirit. But in neither case is he referring to a separate metaphysical world; rather, he speaks of phenomena in their full presence, imbued with the depth and the resonance of *Thou*. So, "when a primary word is spoken [and] the speaker enters the word," he speaks the words of daily life. So the "vital unity" of relations is expressed always as the relations of ordinary life. And so too, with the widest, most inclusive reality, "God's speech to man." It "penetrates what happens in the life of each one of us and all that happens in the world around us, biological and historical, and makes it for you and me into instruction, message, demand." This spirit-imbued sentence, from the last page of Buber's Postscript, written in 1957, circles back over 35 years to his opening pages, where he has spoken of a man's taking his stand "in the sanctity of the primary word."

Thus his book begins, like the several instruments of chamber music, with all the levels of his thought in play: dialectical, Platonic, secular, sacred. And therefore I have saved for last, after each of these levels has been discussed in its own right, a fuller look at the first page. We can hear all the instruments now.

> There is no *I* taken in itself, but only the *I* of the primary word *I-Thou* and the *I* of the primary word *I-It*.
>
> When a man says *I*, he refers to one or the other of these.
>
> . . . .
>
> The primary word *I-Thou* can only be spoken with the whole being.
>
> The primary *I-It* can never be spoken with the whole being.

The many levels, it is now clear, make one strong harmony of the life we live.

But I believe we get as vivid and clear an impression, too, beginning with Buber's beginning, if, from the first, we *listen* to his words, listen as if they were said aloud. We recall that his book, with all its biblical overtones, was in its own origin, like the Bible, largely spoken. The teacher was speaking to his students in Frankfurt. And as we ourselves listen, we hear in his words, commingled, the voice of a poet, of a prophet, of a refined Talmudic dialectician, and always, too, the voice of a man to whom language, from his childhood days, was dear. Most of all, we hear a simple, speaking voice. Indeed we read his book best hearing as its first, introductory words, as in the many Hasidic tales Buber has given us: "The Rabbi said."

Yes, in essence *I and Thou* is simple. *Thou* is the other, met openly and without design. Love is caring for *Thou*, and it tempers self-assertion. Without love, the other becomes an *It*, any use of whom is, in a sense, a misuse.

Has Buber just spun the obvious into an involved dialectic?

Certainly his basic ideas have passed into the stream of our progressive thought. The *I-Thou* bond is now a commonplace of humanistic psychology: "personal regard," "warm contact," "human equality" — we know these synonyms for it. And his vision of presence, dialogue, community — our current words are "immediacy," "responsiveness," "mutuality"; isn't that all clear? Or is it? Have these for us slipped down too easily, like smooth-coated capsules? But there is a fiber in them, and a range and intransigence of meaning, nonclinical, not even secular, which a therapist and client must assimilate slowly.

In a letter to a friend, the Southern writer Flannery O'Connor tells of a brilliant, intimidatingly brilliant, dinner party in 1950 at Mary McCarthy's. After several hours,

> the conversation turned on the Eucharist, which I, being the Catholic, was obviously supposed to define....[Mary McCarthy] thought of it as a symbol and implied that it was a pretty good one. I then said, in a very shaky voice, "Well, if it's a symbol, to hell with it!"[18]

This is a story after Buber's heart: a Western, urban, non-Jewish Hasidic tale. For its concern is direct relationship to God. A symbol, by contrast, *stands for* something, is a special kind of *It*, a link to the thing. But it's a screen too, partitioning the thing off. Where then is direct relation? Is the Eucharist

Thou, or isn't it? We have heard Flannery O'Conner's response. And in psychotherapy: is the therapist *Thou*, or a symbolic *It* bearing the client's pattern of relations from his parents in childhood? Is the client *Thou*, or *It* with an objective pathology? And if both relationships apply, what is their relevance to the goal of the therapy? So Buber's concepts move us to a new depth, invite us to swim in unformulable waters.

Some things, of course, we can formulate with all the precision of *It*. A client is entangled in unconscious complexes — feelings of inadequacy, self-demands for perfection, and so on — and needs help with freer, fuller self-assertion. The therapist officiates as an impersonal expert. Symbolical reenactments of the past occur: the therapist as tyrannical father, unresponsive mother, and the like.

But in Buber's view, the contours of the therapy are recast. And its essence is nothing symbolic. It is direct relation in the consulting room. It is the saying of *Thou*.

The therapist teaches the saying. His support of the client, his evocation of past thought and feeling, his confrontations in the moment, his interpretive responses, all make way for *Umkehr*, or the *turning back* of his client to being *Thou*.[19] Most of all, the therapist's presence says the primary word. And so the client begins to sense himself as an intact other, not the *It* belonging to his parents that he was, growing up. He begins to feel confirmed in all his aspects, adult and infantile. In his essay, "Distance and Relating," Buber speaks of "the wish of every man to be confirmed as what he is, even as what he can become, by men; and the innate capacity in man to confirm his fellow men in this way."[20] *Confirming* is the seal of the presence of *Thou*. As the therapist grants it, the client moves toward self-recognition, and therefore new clarity. For instance, a husband and wife can learn to ask of each other, as their quarrels and accusations had failed to ask, "Take good care of me." If they cannot offer this care, then at least they can part after really meeting, rather than in the dark. They can come to confer on each other an intact otherness, which, in either a successful or a failed relationship, itself confirms the other, says *Thou*. So, too, the client comes to say *Thou* to the therapist: a man long aloof and critical of the therapeutic work may reach out to shake the other's hand.

In a lecture at the Washington School of Psychiatry in 1957, Buber described, through a dialectical pairing of opposites, just *how* the therapist teaches.[21] He is concerned with Being, as distinct from Seeming; he wishes to have Being central between himself and his client. He speaks, as the Buddhists say, Right Speech, truthful without abuse. His concern is to unfold his client's being, rather than impose anything on it; to develop, so to speak, *the consenting adult* by first of all appealing to and restoring to awareness *the consenting child and infant.* He accepts the client, like the good parent does the small child, as unique and whole, literally not able to be objectified and taken apart. He feels his way into the client's being by imagining his reality, "imagining the real."[22]

These concerns sound, as I've said, familiar today; they evoke the warm, empathic psychotherapist of film and television. But Buber is full of unfamiliar distinctions. At a seminar with psychiatrists of the Washington School, he spoke further about "imagining the real."

> The therapist must feel the [patient's] side as a bodily touch, to know how the patient feels it. [He experiences from his side and from the [patient's], but there is no reciprocity there.] If the patient could do this, there would be no need of therapy.[23]

What is this? Is he saying that *I-Thou* equality isn't possible between therapist-teacher and client-pupil? He is. A few weeks after the Washington seminar, Buber met in Michigan with the noted client-centered psychotherapist Carl Rogers, who remarked about therapy, rather assuming he would harmonize with Buber: "[It] is a meeting of two persons on an equal basis." "Dr. Rogers," replied Buber dryly, "we must say to one another, 'We disagree.'"[24] For how can client and therapist be equal when the equality is just what is to be taught by the one, learned by the other?

And now let me, Buber-like, apply his "imagining the real" to Freud and himself. Freud stands beside him, saying: "Of course! Patient and client, as you say, aren't equal. The client's mental and emotional distortions from childhood experience inhibit this equality. In fact the therapist is only a stand-in for parental figures with whom the client has unresolved problems. That is the analytic work. It may, in a fortunate course, conclude with an equality of understanding." But Buber differs again. He replies: "Yes, the therapist is draped in old associations, ghosts from the client's childhood. And these ghosts have a strange solidity. They are a kind of *It*, twining complexly around the therapist as *Thou*. But from the start, the client sees beyond the drapery. He sees a man whom he wishes would meet him and all his ghosts, who would light him up and reveal their ghostliness, as a lighted torch can rekindle a second torch. And the torch of both is lit from the *Thou* of the heavens. If the relighting fails, the therapist must ask himself: 'Did I meet the other? Or did I merely see his ghosts, or my own?' Every hour in the consulting room is a piece of Hasidism, faithfully or faithlessly observed."[25]

And now, one further imagining of the real. Jung stands beside Buber and says: "Of course! No secular psychology is enough. The analyst is the friend of the client's soul, whose goal is to find God. This inward truth is the one spiritual truth we know: God and God's Otherness are of the soul." But Buber differs yet again.[26] "The client's becoming unified within is a good goal," he says, "but only a partial one. Merely personal truth keeps the truth relativized. It's a loose shutter banging in the wind. It's the Eucharist as symbol. With what warrant do you say that God's Otherness is less 'out there' than are the stars? Why should God's Otherness be any more 'within my soul' than the therapist himself is? As pure *Thou*, in fact, He is less 'mine' than any thing I can possess. And therein lies my salvation. For we know that isolate being is being that is bereft, shut up as in a cocoon, while actual existence lives in confirmations: child and parents with one another, a worker with his colleagues, client with therapist, lover with lover. Just so, man with God. And therefore the Hasidic Rabbi Nahman of Bratzlav celebrated a cosmos divided, so that its members can have the joy of meeting. He sang *The Torah of the Void*:

> Without the void
> All would be One.
> But then
> there would not have been any creature — any world.

> So the void is a kind of
> Divine Wisdom of not being
> so that there can be division
> between one kind of being
> and another."[27]

So Buber, to return now to his own words from *I and Thou*, "takes his stand in relation." So his stand redefines and reilluminates therapy, makes it, for both members, one more piece of what he called "each mortal hour's fullness of claim and responsibility."

In his own life, the claim was indistinguishable from action, and often was expressed as a special way of behaving. We might call it the *Thou* of action: for these are things done by a man which themselves speak deeply to other men. And this German-Jewish teacher could act heroically. Here are three vignettes.

Buber in his late fifties, under the Nazis: in November 1933, he reopened the House of Learning in Frankfurt, where much of *I and Thou* had been presented some twelve years before. Non-Jews as well as Jews were invited to attend courses. A few months later he became the leader of the "Central Office for Adult Jewish Education" in Germany. For the next four years (he finally left for Palestine with Paula in the winter of 1938) he taught Jewish religion, learning, and culture with an eye to understanding and mastering present-day Jewish problems, and he maintained, under constant Nazi scrutiny, complete intellectual freedom. A respectful Gestapo official, after listening to one of his talks and making notes, shook his hand and said, "Stay well." Alone with Paula, Buber translated the words to mean, "God grant that we do not have to kill you." During these days a stranger accosted him on the street: "You Jew!" Buber replied at once: "You oaf!" Regarding incidents like these, he remarked to a friend, "I do not understand how one can live at all without courage."

Buber in his mid-seventies, returning from Jerusalem to receive the Peace Prize of the German Book Trade in Frankfurt: this gift from a country which (he pointed out in his acceptance speech) "about a decade ago...killed millions of my people in a systematically prepared...procedure,...organized cruelty [that] cannot be compared with any previous historical event," caused outrage in the Israeli press, and in Europe and America. It is easy to imagine Buber, esteemed worldwide as a Jewish teacher and philosopher, rejecting the gift. So much closer to the Holocaust than we, so much more its symbolic victim, he could have raised far more passionate objections than were expressed in 1985 toward President Reagan's visiting the cemetery at Bitburg. But this was a peace prize; for him the symbol went the other way. His speech continued: "The becoming of one humanity is, in the present hour, the highest duty on earth. To obey this duty is laid on the Jew — a surviving arch-Jew — chosen as a symbol, even there, just there, where the never-to-be-effaced memory of what has happened stands in opposition to it."

Buber in his eightieth year, meeting with psychiatrists in Washington, D.C.: Long known for his "great, comfortable warmth," he was asked if his seminars could be filmed, or at least taped. He declined; "modern technical contrivances" injure the spontaneity of dialogue. And anyway — a charmingly debonair aside from a man devoted to immortal truth: "In twenty-five years no one will even know what I am talking about." During the seminars, the noted psychiatrist David Rioch asked him: "What can you say about God in healing?" Buber, the most theocentric of men, who during his life has talked of little else, declined again. "In the moment when the name of God is mentioned," he answered,

> most human circles break asunder without knowing it. In that moment the consciousness of thinking — the fact of thinking together — is disrupted....People say God without meaning reality, merely as a sublime convention of the cultured person.

This was, at once, reproof — God isn't to be a smooth capsule — and a toast to the unutterable. Dr. Rioch commented later that, of all Buber said and did in Washington, his refusal to speak about God impressed him the most.

Buber's austerity in speaking about God had increased with the years. One can imagine the look askance that he would take at spiritual cults today: gods in Cadillacs; gurus commanding their devotees how to live; success named a measure of enlightenment. Had he not, already in *I and Thou,* said that you do not profit from God? Our world is his world of Seeming and Imposing; Thou is in the catacombs; the imageless God — "'The God of the gods,'" as he once quoted Hölderlin — is in eclipse; or if with us anywhere, He is in Mother Teresa's vision of the Calcutta beggar: "Christ in his distressing disguise."[28]

Nor would Buber accept our interests in a scientifically minded religion.[29] Has he not said that God's existence cannot be proved? Has he not, in effect, condemned the "transpersonal"? For in its depths, reality is *interpersonal*: God, the limitless *Thou,* we remember, is "also a Person," with whom we, as persons, consummate our own reality as we address Him.

Buber's perceptions are a constant critique of the secular world that is not sacred, of the sacred that is not ineffable, of the ineffable that is not everyday. He has put himself, as he said, on a "narrow ridge," neither subjective nor objective, neither materialistic nor idealist; the realm of life "where there is no sureness of expressible knowledge but the certainty of meeting what remains undisclosed."[30] This ridge is high on the mountain where, Blake proclaimed, men do great things. On it, simplicity, an encompassing simplicity, can come, but openness, an unpartisan openness, also stays. For it is there that one heeds best Whitehead's great injunction: "Seek simplicity and distrust it."[31]

Perhaps Buber didn't distrust it enough. All that life gives us of loss, of pain, of irony, he takes into his grand view, accommodating them, greatly illuminating them. And yet, in part, they stay in shadow; the grandeur suffers from a certain lack of pathos. That may come from an arrogance in the man. For instance, after the conversation with Carl Rogers, he remarked to Maurice Friedman, "I was very kind to him. I could have been much sharper." When Buber is right, he is totally, unshakably right. This grants him majesty. But it crimps his sense of humor and, perhaps too, his awareness of God's humor, the wryness of the life given to us, with which our own wry candor can reckon. Buber tells us, for example, that art is a great potency; it stands "against the world becoming alien."[32] Perhaps so. But one misses Flaubert's ironic bow to art: "Of all lies, art is the least untrue."[33] Or again, in Buber's sovereign terms, I belong in the world, addressing *Thou,* utilizing It. But also I stand amid mischief and foul play, others' and my own, where the heart is blinded and the mind cruel, and the tragedies of Desdemona and Madame Butterfly occur. And there is indifference, others' and my own. And far within, disconsolate, rooted in *Vergegnung,* am

> I, a stranger, and afraid
> In a world I never made.[34]

To feel the truth in all this takes a certain lack of confidence, bred of a poignant sense of life's pain. But Buber's *I-Thou* moves always, "seductive and magical," in a world of felicity. His God is always able to be found. His Jesus, "nothing but Son to Father," seems to have no moment on the cross when the son feels forsaken by the father.

And yet, too, Buber's grandeur lights up this pathos. From all estrangement and moral evil, there is always the possibility of *Umkehr,* turning back. He doesn't deny pain and loss and difficulties, but he is himself, like the great Hasids he has brought to light for us, a fundamentally *cheerful* man. He doesn't dwell on the ironic and the tragic. And yet his vision denies them no dignity. It invites, above all, fullness of response, and gives us, in all aspects of life, a new way to ask after this fullness. For psychotherapists in particular, it provides a clear goal: the reclaiming of the client's freedom to feel himself, or herself, a *Thou,* and be able to say *Thou* to another.

Buber's death at 87, in a biblical old age, gives a sense of fullness completed. *Begegnung* had by now happened on the widest scale of world recognition. One feels Goethe's maxim fulfilled: "The happiest man is he who can join the end of his life with the beginning.[34] And *Begegnung,* always, is the renewal of one's living. "Tell me something about life," Buber exclaimed to a woman friend who visited him during his last illness, from uremia. (This is a final Hasidic tale; now the teacher is teaching from his deathbed, in Jerusalem.) She tells him that a course is soon to be taught on *I and Thou.* "That is not life," he says. Another book of his, she goes on, is being translated into Hebrew. "That is still not life," he insists. Finally she says, "My husband passed the Israeli bar exam."

"*That* is life!" says Buber. Renewal in action: that is life. In his own time he had become half mythic; and it is as though, through his living, he shows how the sense of renewal that myth itself provides begins always with *action*. "In the beginning God created the heaven and the earth."

Certainly he located his own myth of the "primary words" in life's action. And we, too, feel the power of his word *I-Thou* in life as we know it and as it renews itself in us. From cellular division to sexual difference, from nursing mother to human community to man or woman addressing God, the basic unit in life is *two*. "I" plus "Thou" make "We." And "We" are always "We Together."

Chapter 6

LAO-TZU: THINGS AS THEY ARE

"There are two types of life. The one is mere thoughtless living, using life up until its extinction; the other is the eternal change and its unity in spirit. He who does not allow himself to be consumed in his life, but incessantly renews himself and just through that affirms his self in change — he attains the eternal change and self-affirmation." So Buber, in rather heavily abstractive Germanic prose, introduces the concrete and pithy teaching of the Tao, the ancient Chinese source of all phenomena and the unified ground of life. Buber's particular concern in his essay, written in 1910, is the fulfillment of Tao in the unified man, the one who "attains the eternal change and self-affirmation"; and twelve years later he formulated this unity another way and in the manner of song. It became, as we know, the *I-Thou* of relationship. His developed concern is the connection between things: how the beads are threaded on the string. But in the *Tao Te Ching*, translated *The Way and Its Power* and ascribed to Lao-tzu,[1] the vision is of the nonseparation of things: it is of the string which threads the beads. At the same time we enter the human sphere of permissiveness, of receptivity, of graceful and total letting be. Though rare, this note has been struck now and then by the wisdom of the Occident. We have already heard it in Blake:

> He who kisses the Joy as it flies
> Lives in Eternity's sunrise.

In Rilke:

> Let life happen to you. Believe me, life is right,
> in any case.

In Kafka:

> What is laid upon us is to accomplish the negative; the positive is already given.

And, of course, in Buber's *Thou*: a man attuned "to the course of being...intervenes no more;...he meets" the world. All these assertions are Taoist.

With Lao-tzu, we shift to a chiefly legendary figure; indeed we know him only in the idealized recollection which is myth. He is said to have been immaculately conceived by a shooting star, carried for sixty-two years in his mother's womb, and born white-haired, in 604 B.C.; thus the very name "Lao-tzu," which may mean "Master Lao," but also "the Old Boy." So much for the extravagant origins and ripening of his wisdom. Ssu Ma Ch'ien, a historian who lived in the second century B.C., tells us that, as an adult, Lao-tzu was curator of the royal library at the Court of Chou in Loyang, the northwestern province known today as Honan. In person, "he was a superior man, who liked to keep himself unknown." Later, disheartened by the cruelties of the Chou dynasty, he mounted a water buffalo and rode westward to the barrier gate at the Hankao pass, leading toward what is now Tibet. Ssu Ma Ch'ien continues:

> Yin Hsi, the warden of the gate, said to him, "You are about to withdraw yourself out of sight. let me insist on your (first) composing for me a book." On this Lao-tzu [withdrew for three days and] wrote a book in two parts, setting forth his view on the Tao and its attributes in more

than 5000 characters. He then went away, and it is not known where he died.

So he recedes from our view, absorbed into the landscape like innumerable figures in Chinese paintings, and we sense that we know as little of him as he wished. He is like the Native American, too, who walks silently through the forest, leaving no trace. And this picture is so consonant with the way of the Tao itself, of life lived altogether unobtrusively, that one is persuaded the myth is of a man who *should have lived.* In accord with tradition that is controversial but has not been disproved, I shall take Lao-tzu as, in essence, historical, and the author of the *Tao Te Ching.*

His times are better known, and give us a familiar historical scene for the rise of a religious reformer. By the 8th century B.C., the Chou dynasty had established and presided over a multitude of baronies which were almost always at war. During the early centuries of the Chou, a code of chivalry controlled much of this warfare; the enemies, Homeric-like, would exchange compliments and even weapons before battle. Later, the code broke down completely, with sudden raids, surprise attacks, and mass slaughters of over 100,000 people that included women, children, and the aged — a boundless destructiveness reminding us of the 20th century Anno Domini.

It took just this chaos for an opposing boundless force to assert itself.

> When men lack a sense of awe, there will
> be disaster (72)[2]

says the *Tao Te Ching.* We are struck at once by the nature of this counterforce: the sense of awe. Not "the law of God," the religious force we customarily think of as opposing the lawlessness of man. Lao-tzu even gives special credit to the horrors of moral evil.

> All can know good as good only because there is evil. (2)

For the moral sense to exist at all, and for it then to be able to come into balance, we must allow for its opposite. Though religious zeal in the West, too, has arisen in times of political warfare and upheaval, we sense that its temper is quite different; that it stands for an extremity and a partisanship we are not hearing in these words of the Tao. To take the full measure of Lao-tzu, as Westerners, let us look first at this difference.

Christianity celebrates *passion.* It opposes its passion of martyrdom to the ubiquitous human passion for cruelty. And the Passion of Our Martyred Lord, immortalized in Western visual art and in Bach's music, is the special emblem of Christian devotion. Whether feeling is controlled, as in Giotto, or exalted, as in El Greco, we deal with the play of emotion, with suffering, and with rapture "that passes understanding"; in which "all things will be added unto you."

> The anguish
> of man in God,
> and in man, God's joy.
> Two things so much alike, so
> interchangeable, so
> strange to all existence.

So St. John of the Cross, in his poem on the birth of Christ, sings, from 16th century Spain, of Christian martyrdom and happiness. And Kierkegaard, a century ago in Denmark, in his *Concluding Unscientific Postscript,* writes with all possible force of feeling: "Christianity wishes to intensify passion to its highest pitch."[3]

But in the East, in the figures of Lao-tzu and the Buddha, it is *compassion,* a far gentler tenderness, aglow rather than afire, which radiates. One can even speak of their *dispassion,* of the freedom from the heat of emotions in the bliss of the Buddha. An Indian Bach would compose "The Dispassion of Our Lord." For as Christianity gave an unparalleled dramatic form to religion, the pure suffering servant nailed to the cross on the hill of Golgotha in the consummation of his passion, Buddhism gave it an unparalleled psychological form, the Buddha at peace under the Bo tree, aware of the fatal sorrows of attachment, consummating his enlightenment in dispassion. Jesus, a young man, dies violently, as a storm drowns the land. Then he is resurrected to light. Buddha dies in old age peacefully, as the seasons change. No resurrection is needed.

We feel this difference, too, in a differing sense of personhood. Jesus is the special messiah; and in Christianity the Godhead is embodied indeed in *three* persons. Jesus himself "stands in" for all mankind. According to the Creed of St. Athanasius, he "suffered for our salvation"; because of him is the remission of human sin. And Jesus himself dramatizes a conflict of the persons within the godhead. The Gospels say: "Not my will but thine." But Buddhism, in its original form, gives no god at all, and no importance, much less conflict, to person. "Buddha" names only a state of being, "the awakened one." No one else can add his grace to you, though the Buddha, it is true, is an example, and all other human beings can be, like him, awake. Lao-tzu, too, who is perhaps known to us only by a nickname, wished to be a concealed and unknown person. His one exemplar, in the *Tao Te Ching*, is the sage who "makes no show" (72). If Tao be taken to be the same as God, it is an entirely impersonal God which *allows*, not the personal God of Western tradition who *decrees*. The Tao itself is not meant to be uplifting. It is, as Suzuki Roshi says of Japanese Buddhism: "nothing special." A natural accent lies in everything. Accent is wrongly displaced by efforts of accentuation.

One must in turn distinguish between the tone of Buddhist and Taoism. The Buddha gives us methodical analysis of the Dharma, of the way things are: that we live in suffering, in birth, in illness, in our many griefs, in aging, in death; that we suffer because of our attachments, our resistance, that is, to inevitable flux; that attachments can fade in our detached mindfulness of them, neither holding onto things nor avoiding them nor pushing them away. Then a person, according to one of the Sutras, "abides in onlooking equanimity." In Lao-tzu, the same message is terse and unsystematic, but quite clear in image, precept, vision. Do we know the value of what is empty?

> Cut doors and windows for a room;
> It is the holes which make it useful. (11)

Do we know the pain of attachment?

> There is no greater sin than desire....
> Therefore he who knows that enough is enough
> will always have enough. (46)

Do we know that a simple life is fuller?

> In the pursuit of learning, every day something
> is acquired.
> In the pursuit of Tao, every day something
> is dropped. (48)

Buber's own words on Taoist wisdom with which I began, to be thoughtlessly consumed in life or to affirm oneself in change, have themselves the intellectual ring of Buddhism. But the *Tao Te Ching,* in its eighty-one verse sayings, is full of allusions and pictures. We see artisans and emperors, thorn bushes, muddy pools, and the river flowing home to the sea. And yet, beyond image — "the ten thousand things" of the phenomenal world — something else is before us too; something elusive and as real as it is elusive, not to be seen, not to be heard, and also not to be exhausted, the source and the endless unity of what we see, hear, exhaust.

We shall be turning to the Tao in detail. But Lao-tzu's sense of permissiveness and flow is so unusual that I want to suggest the feel of it at first in a few more preliminaries: to take a serpentine course, so to speak, through the outskirts of the Tao, referring us further to what it is not, and to what it may seem to be like, and to what it begins to be like, and so, by slow windings, to move into its own landscape.

Haven't we, in the West, heard Lao-tzu's song of unity before? If not in traditional religion, perhaps in philosophic thought? I think of Professor Arthur Lovejoy's identification of a Chain of Being in Western cosmology, with underlying principles of plenitude, continuity, and gradation. It is as though, across a universe of many separable panels, a single, fully drawn portrait was painted. The vision endured from classical Greece into the 18th century A.D.; already, in the 4th century, St. Augustine describes it elegantly in a retrospective tribute:

> Plotinus the Platonist proves by means of the blossoms and leaves that from the Supreme Lord, whose beauty is invisible and ineffable, Providence reaches down to the things of earth here below. He points out that these frail and mortal objects could not be endowed with a beauty so immaculate and so exquisitely wrought, did they not issue from the Divinity which endlessly pervades with its invisible and unchanging beauty all things.[4]

The Tao, "intangible and elusive, and yet within [it] is image" (21): aren't we listening here to a Western celebration of the same power?

But something is different. There is a static perfection in Plotinus: too much a finished portrait rather than moving life, *all too full* of clarity and light. Already we have heard Lao-tzu require a sense of awe and vindicate evil. His wholeness is not so rationalistic.

We Westerners, meanwhile, have ourselves learned to know a far less simple cosmos. The 19th century brought evolutionary theory, with its gaps and jumps between species, as though there were something capricious in the organic world. Continuity and gradation were gone, as well as an encompassing creator. And physical science today is full of breaks, quick changes, unpredictable energy transformations, as though the cosmos itself showed something of the disorder and disruption that we also see around us today in the social world. Fragmentation everywhere. Or can all this be an evolving tumult, a move toward a new sense of order, close to Lao-tzu's wide-flung sense of the One?

So, intrigued by resemblances, Fritjof Capra wrote *The Tao of Physics*, bringing the Eastern view to bear on quantum mechanics and relativity theory. In quantum thought, static particles have disappeared. There is only energy, which manifests itself in one form in the mass of a particle. And the subatomic particles cannot be clearly differentiated from the forces binding them, so the particles and forces must be taken together as an inseparable whole. In relativity theory, also, events in time are ordered differently depending on the velocity of the observer: one is always inseparable from what one observes. Here, too, reality exists and transforms as an inseparable whole, and evokes the unity of which Lao-tzu speaks.

But the Chinese sage isn't, after all, concerned with concepts of physical structure. He does write of the governing order of the cosmos, but he doesn't hold a special view of it, neither static nor relativistic nor quantum-like. There is no "Physics of the Tao."

Instead, his world vision of an unceasing flow — rather like our sense of the "stream of consciousness"[5] — seems to be steeped in psychology; and that is a special flowering of our time. Do any of our ideas about the inward life meet his?

There are claimants. Jung, for one, understood the Tao as expressing his own view of the primordial formless self, combining inner and outer reality. Our ego, in contrast, establishes personal identity. It is a fragment of self and subordinate to it, as all form is less than the Tao. But a psychic development is possible: the integration of ego with self, which is "the bringing about of Tao [as] conscious life."[6] Jung, however, treats this goal more as a Chinese psychological ideal than a Western therapeutic reality. At least it is not one that we have yet assimilated.

Gestalt therapists, in the second half of our century, have been perhaps more presumptuous. They have often seen their work as "The Tao of Psychotherapy": the concern, that is, with the receptive openness of clients to the ground of their experiencing. Then each successive moment is, so to speak, drawn up from the inward creative void. I don't myself know anyone who would say that his life, or hers, reflects this pattern, except in rare moments. But it beckons as a real possibility. Meanwhile, the Gestalt focus on process, not content, suggests a further unity which is part of Taoism: the "pure process view which links...man to the macrocosm."[7]

But, as with physical theories, something in all these schema of inner growth is different from Lao-tzu, is more structured than he. The "creative void," as we speak of it, is hard *not* to conceive of but as our own limited creation, "a concept or symbol too human in spite of everything."[8] Let's pause a moment over a famous legend.

It is said that Lao-tzu met once with his great contemporary, the reformer Confucius. For the troubled dynasty of their time, Confucius sought to formulate a new social order based on courtesy, unselfishness, benevolence, and respect in family and in political life. But Lao-tzu swept this vision aside. "Put away," he said admonishingly, "your proud air and many desires. Life is too incalculable for any set code of conduct. It changes, like the snake losing its skin. It's clever, like the rich man who looks poor among thieves. Let it be. Let it find its own level: which means not new schemes and new actions, but the ending of all willful action."

Not that peaceful Lao-tzu, for his part, seemed at all quiescent during this speech. On the contrary. Returning to his disciples, Confucius said:

> Of birds I know they have wings to fly with, of fish that they have fins to swim with, of wild beasts that they have feet to run with...But who knows how dragons surmount wind and cloud into heaven? This day I have seen Lao-tzu and he is a dragon.[9]

The beneficent dragon of Chinese mythology, bringer of rain, and the man for whom right action springs from vital nonaction, from an alert repose — all this suggests how Lao-tzu would receive our Western allusions to him. For the Tao,

> Born before heaven and earth (25)

does indeed give an answer to our science, philosophy, and psychology, as these abide among "the ten thousand things." It permits, that is to say, all our borrowings. As their infinite source, it can illuminate them. But it does not covet them; it does not ask for them; it resides in an obscurity which, like that of Lao-tzu himself, is its central and prevailing power.

And so we have arrived at the Tao, but with what sense of enigma? For if it is a sort of cosmology, it is not precisely delineated. It is primordial, what the Germans call an *Ur-Kosmologie*, which can give rise to many others. And yet, better delineation is not possible, since in essence it is not translatable from itself. And yet, untranslatable as it is, it allows for everything.

What is it?

The Tao that can be told is not the eternal Tao.
The name that can be named is not the eternal name. (1)

Thus *The Way and Its Power* begins its affirmations: with negatives. We are in the mystical tradition of the *Via Negativa*, of a reality which extends beyond anything that can positively be asserted: as the Indian *Upanishad* sings of the primal light, "neither existence nor nonexistence";[10] as the Chinese Chuang-tzu, 300 years after Lao-tzu, sings also of the Tao, "author of causes and effects, but not the causes and effects."[11] For Lao-tzu, it is clear that "the eternal name" is "no name," just as it has "no beginning...no end" (14). Or he chants, with another negative:

I do not know its name. (25)

The best single words for it are "darkness," "mystery" (1). But at once, with the rapid extension of thought typical of him, he shifts us in his first verse to a balance of the unnameable and the named, negative and positive. They are joined together:

These two spring from the same source.... (1)

From the formless essence of Tao arise all the forms of the phenomenal world. And we ourselves can appreciate this order of precedence, the generative nature, that is, of the mystery and its stillness. It is indeed precisely in our own stillness that we do this appreciating.

Ever desireless, one can see the mystery.
Every desiring, one can see the manifestations. (1)

So, at times, we have the sense of being stopped in our tracks by experience which is too much, by wonder, by awe, wordless, not this, not that. "What is incomprehensible," Einstein said, "is that the universe is comprehensible." The scientist takes in the logic of subatomic structure, or of our own biology marvelously differentiated from a few primitive tissues, and senses the inexplicable, the not-to-be known, in the known. Within cosmic stillness and the world of phenomena, the microcosm of our own existence is a legatee of Tao, a renewed source of the Way and its power.

And just as the positive springs from the negative, so our human capacity to fathom this connection arises from opposites: we know beauty because of ugliness, long because of short, good because of evil. So the Buddha, first with a sick man, then with a dying man, discovered mortality as an adult, from which his earlier, fairy-tale existence had been shielded; and after that he came to embrace life as it is. The Tao itself is known as great through the ridicule of fools who laugh at it:

> If there were no laughter, the Tao would
> not be what it is. (41)

These polarities fill out Lao-tzu's second verse. And now begin the great swinging leaps of his Therefores.

> Therefore the sage goes about doing nothing,
> teaching no-talking.
> Working, yet not taking credit.
> Work is done, then forgotten.
> Therefore it lasts forever. (2)

From what does his first Therefore follow? From the natural balance of the polar opposites, which require "nothing," no extra force, to come into play. And more than that: from the mystery, the generative source, in which all the balance rests. The sage knows this source in himself, keeps in view the order of precedence, and doing so, he takes in the world at its inseparable depths; in Buber's word, he takes the world as his *Thou.*[12] Therefore his work is beyond time, and so forgotten. But also, with the logic of the timeless, Lao-tzu's final Therefore: "It lasts forever."

His first two verses in fact are the core of his book. And by another of its grand leaps, this text which begins by celebrating the inexpressible Tao becomes, in its completed shape, a manual for success in worldly life just as specifically as Machiavelli's *The Prince.* Lao-tzu's, indeed, is the first "How-to-be" book, full of counsel and admonition; in this case the success in view is "How to be wise." And the path he shows is no less arduous than that of Machiavelli's tyrant. The Tao, like the Prince who lies and cheats for his people, sweeps everything before it:

> Heaven and earth are ruthless;
> They see the ten thousand things as dummies. (5)

And so we know geological convulsions like earthquakes, and physical pain and illness, and fear and grief and loneliness. Yet, too,

> The Tao is an empty vessel; it is used,
> but never filled. (4)

Therefore the sage who exemplifies *Tao* stands protected by his basic selflessness.

> Observers of the Tao do not seek fulfillment. (15)

But Lao-tzu plays nicely on the word "fulfillment," so agreeable to our ears. Again:

> Through selfless action, [the sage] attains
> fulfillment. (7)

For this selflessness is *also* a fulfillment; it is the freedom not to cast one's own shadow over one's actions, to make no claim on "the ten thousand things." In his nothingness is the sage's balance. His one concern is:

> He helps the ten thousand things find
> their own nature. (64)

And his guiding method is *to yield* to the thing before him. Therefore the Tao, which we have heard sung as *immeasurably greater* than all things, from the point of view of the things themselves is something *far less* than they. For it gives way to them; to all effects, at first it loses to them. But Lao-tzu also points out:

> Under heaven nothing is more soft and yielding
> than water.
> Yet for attaching the solid and strong,
> nothing is better.
> The weak can overcome the strong;
> The supple can overcome the stiff. (78)

The full principle is:

> Yield and overcome. (22)

In this fashion the Tao shows its own power in things, the power of *Te* (the middle word of the book's title): that is, of a thing's inner drive to fruition and its adaptability in getting there. So flowers find paths in which to grow through cracks in the cement. And for human beings, *Te* means inward openness: letting ourselves be ruled by the same regulations that govern breathing and heartbeat. Then we have the resilience of the unconscious, and its lasting power:

> The mother principle of [this] ruling holds good
> for a long time.
> This is called having deep roots and a firm foundation.
> (59)

Lao-tzu names the principle after "the mother," the female *yin* of the *yin-yang* polarity. The imagery of the *Tao Te Ching* brings in the yang too, connecting it very early in the text with the political and social order; Lao-tzu hails the Tao as "the forefather of the emperors" (4). But the *yin*, like the basic mystery of the cosmos, receives special emphasis:

> The valley spirit never dies;
> It is the woman, primal mother. (6)

Again:

> The beginning of the universe
> Is the mother of all things. (52)

Of himself Lao-tzu says:

> I am nourished by the great mother. (20)

And yet again, as special precept:

> Know the strength of man,
> But keep a woman's care. (28)

Maternal care is the *Te* of Tao, its power to let things be, let them run their course as they are, setting up no opposition, either of correction or of reform, fostering rather the changes which are in the nature of the thing, as the tree grows from the sapling. It is in Lao-tzu's own feminine side to attach no strings to his own life, not "to pluck...honor from the pale-faced moon,"[13] nor covet success or remembrance. For *Te* is life accepted in As-Is condition and so brought to its fullness. There is skill and art in this, too, as in building a fine house, or shaping a good community, or nourishing crafts and the arts. But it is art which follows the dictum of *The Winter's Tale*: to

> mend nature — change it rather —
> But the art itself is nature.

So his book itself, true to nature and the feminine, develops from the embryo of its opening verses to show us the life we know: its impersonal depths of Tao, its personal abuses and coercions. We recall that he has said evil is necessary to know good. But he doesn't justify it.

> Some things are not favored by heaven. Who knows why?

he asks, and boldly leaves the question unanswered:

Even the sage is unsure of this. (73)[14]

And yet: so we are made. We want things to go our way, though we develop hypertension and peptic ulcers in the process. We block ourselves with neurotic and psychotic defenses. We deny what we don't like, even the most basic facts, like our own death. So, too, with the ills of public life. Tyrants neglect and mangle the people. They "eat up money in taxes." They "interfere too much." (75) Deceit, exploitation, and murder become second nature. And are we so sure that it is second?

Lao-tzu is sure. For him, constraint in living betrays it; and this can happen indeed with the greatest subtlety. For even good laws, a code of social virtue itself, appear only when a basic acceptance of life has been lost:

When the great Tao is forgotten,
Kindness and morality arise.
When wisdom and intelligence are born,
The great pretense begins.

When there is no peace within the family.
Filial piety and devotion arise.
When the country is confused and in chaos,
Loyal ministers appear. (18)

And now negatives enter Lao-tzu's vision in a new way. Now they signify neither something more, nor something less. They mean, literally, the ridding of external controls:

Give up sainthood, renounce wisdom,
And it will be a hundred times better for everyone.

Give up kindness, renounce morality,
And men will rediscover filial piety and love.

Give up ingenuity, renounce profit,
And bandits and thieves will disappear. (19)

The words sound abrupt, almost nihilistic. But certainly the tone is not. It appeals to the lithe unadorned reality, in which he has unbounded confidence:

The universe is sacred.
You cannot improve it. (29)

For to him, the "still point of the turning world" exists in all that turns; it is the basal pulse of the universe, beating in every chasm and in every bloom. It is present action, or rather, the yielding non-action of the Tao itself: what is called *wu-wei*. For just as we have heard the Tao described by what it is not, so right action too is made clearest by negations:

Practice non-action.
Work without doing. (63)

The whole range of Lao-tzu's understanding comes into this acting-without-action: his freedom, vigor, ease, astuteness. For nothing in *wu-wei* is resigned or passive. It is acting to bring out an inherent power, the fundamental nonaggression of organic growth that he has saluted in *Te*. We know it ourselves as a special esthetic form: the Japanese martial arts of judo and aikido. And it is the great societal message in our century of Gandhi and Martin Luther King, the power of what does not resist, that registers the impact of assault without provoking new assault, that, bending under blows, like a tree in the wind, maintains its integrity. In nature, of course, there is much violence. Interspecies survival involves predators. But only mankind preys on its own species and this is the travail, at odds with the Tao, that *wu-wei* addresses and sees through:

A good soldier is not violent.
A good fighter is not angry.
A good winner is not vengeful.
A good employer is humble.
This is known as the Virtue of not striving.
This is known as ability to deal with people.
This since ancient times has been known as the ultimate
unity with heaven. (68)

The sage, accomplished in *wu-wei,* knows that life of itself takes sudden turns; sometimes we get up with a hangover, and there had been no wine the night before. Then it may seem as if a gratuitous malevolence held sway. But it isn't malevolence. It is the many-sidedess of life and the world, with nothing out of tune. We may wake to a jingle-jangle morning, but we can't jangle the *Tao.*

And therefore, personally, Lao-tzu permits himself a very wide field. At times he sings:

> Oh, I drift like the waves of the sea,
> Without direction, like the restless wind. (20)

To keep in touch with his own drift, he travels light.

> In the pursuit of learning, every day something is
> acquired.
> In the pursuit of Tao, every day something is
> dropped. (48)

And in this simplicity he is "supple...as a newborn babe." (10) He meets whatever comes directly and without fear:

> He who knows how to live can walk abroad
> Without fear of rhinoceros or tiger.
> He will not be wounded in battle.
> For in him the rhinoceros can find
> no place to thrust their horns,
> Tigers no place to use their claws,
> And weapons no place to pierce.
> Why is this so?
> Because he has no place for death to enter. (50)

So the path of *wu-wei* brings its own power, free of the frailty death overcomes, or free to die in the moment and be reborn; for accepting himself beyond any set *Gestalt,* at one with loss as he is with gain, willing for both, Lao-tzu allows his life to work out its own harmony. And

Knowing harmony is constancy.
Knowing constancy is enlightenment. (55)

Finally, too, for the political ruler, the same principle. As the sage stands for noninterference in life, the worldly sage king stands for restraint:

Whenever you advise a ruler in the way of the Tao,
Counsel him not to use force to conquer the universe.
For this would only cause resistance.
Thorn bushes spring up wherever the army has passed.
Lean years follow in the wake of a great war.
Just do what needs to be done.
Never take advantage of power. (30)

On the contrary, to rule well is to rule gently, lightly:

Ruling the country is like cooking a small fish. (60)

The great chef's *savoir-faire,* leading but not dominating, applies also to the relations between countries:

Therefore if a great country gives way to a smaller country,
It will conquer the smaller country. (61)

Thus the Hellenistic world after Alexander where, as Rostovtzeff tells us "the Greeks did not force their civilization upon any one," and so triumphed throughout the Mediterranean, except in Judaea, where the ruler used force, and provoking a Jewish revolt, failed totally.[15] And in our time the instances of countries — Czechoslovakia, Poland, Vietnam — forced by outside aggressor and fighting back, are clear.

Why are the people rebellious?
Because the rulers interfere too much. (75)

But, worldly-wise, Lao-tzu is clear that rule by restraint is much more difficult in large countries, with their many currents of counter-interests. He flatly recommends "a small country" (80).

And in the West we must look to a very small government for such restraint from a ruler. In the words of the governor of Saxe-Weimar at the end of the 18th century, himself busy with refurbishing the state exchequer, running the schools, building roads and bridges, and planning foreign policy in a time of upheaval — in the manner, indeed, of a Taoist king, the prime minister Goethe notes: "Love does not dominate. It cultivates."[16] We have returned to the generative nature of the Tao, with which Lao-tzu's book began.

Through all its interplay of cosmic nature and civic need, of ideals and practical advice, the tone of the *Tao Te Ching* keeps a unifying lyricism. The passages I've quoted are filled with it. Now, as a coda, a few more lines. On transience:

> To talk little is natural.
> High winds do not last all morning....
> If heaven and earth cannot make things eternal,
> How is it possible for man? (23)

Of the timeless source of things:

> Tao in the world is like a river flowing home to the sea. (32)

Of fullness in life:

> Green plants are tender and filled with sap.
> At their death they were withered and dry.
>
> Therefore the stiff and unbending is the disciple of death.
> The gentle and yielding is the disciple of life. (76)

It is Lao-tzu's steady flow of imagery which encourages me to think that one man said it all, said so much, so briefly, from so many angles, with such lightning comprehensiveness.[17] And it is a wonderful reversal that his sense of the wordless truth has become, in his writing, vivid expression: the formless Tao, "born before heaven and earth," but present here in the form of his verses, as he sings its force and grace, renewing our life in each moment with its unceasing power.

And so the Tao extends infinitely, nourishing everything. It is of change and nature, of wind and water, and of mankind as wind and water, when it lets itself be.

All this is pleasing to the ear. One can be lulled by it, as by the refrain we have heard in recent years: Go with the flow.

But isn't it also a paradox, as deep as any in Kafka?

For it's clear that Lao-tzu does not mean, by "Let be," an amoral free-for-all: that whatever is, is right. On the contrary, the Tao has its own specific morality against constraint, denial, and intrusion. And yet we live with these things, protecting, defending, empowering ourselves as on a natural battlefield of life, and we must, in honesty, be perplexed by his claim, "The universe is perfect." Are we mistakenly not seeing the paradise he speaks of? Or, yearning to believe him, do we mistakenly seek a paradise where there is only a battlefield?

Mystic though he is, it is his own practicality that helps us with this dilemma. For the eternal Tao, after all, is not to be told:

> It fulfills its purpose silently and makes no claims. (34)

But the battlefield also is real; on it, we interrupt others and ourselves, and the human condition is in its poignant enmity with Tao. We "carry sharp swords [and] love to be sidetracked." (53)

But just here, too, the principle of the Tao, *wu-wei*, can really affect us, crucially change life, reverse our interruptions at the very point that they occur.

Some examples from psychotherapy:

1) A story is told of the Buddha curing a woman who could not accept the death of her infant child. She kept the baby in her arms, chanting wildly, "He *must not* be dead." She heard of the Buddha as a great healer, perhaps a wizard, and she rushed to him. "Please!" she begged. "You have special powers.

Bring my baby back to life." "I will help you," he said, capturing her attention like a good therapist. "But first," he went on, "you must do something." "Anything. What is it?" "You must bring me some grains of mustard seed from a house in the village where no one has died."

His action is *wu-wei;* it is, in a sense, nonaction. He has left the woman to busy herself with her own plan. But we perceive the altered course of her story. At the first house where she knocks, a child died last year; at the second, a grandparent a month ago; at the third, a friend just yesterday, and so on. She goes back to the Buddha, still holding her baby, but calm now, and she says, "I knew after the tenth house, but I went to ten more to be sure I knew. He must be buried."[18]

It is in fact her own return to life that the Buddha made possible. Now, through her grief at the loss, the sap can run again in her.

2) Milton Erickson reported the cure of a woman with a severe washing compulsion, up to twenty hours a day.[19] She had been in psychoanalysis for several years, with no success. Erickson said: "I didn't go into the cause or the etiology; the only searching question I asked was 'When you get in the shower to scrub yourself for hours, tell me, do you start at the top of your head, or the soles of your feet, or in the middle? Do you wash from the neck down, or do you start with your feet and wash up? Or do you start with your head and wash down?'"

Once again, the minimal impact of *wu-wei*, but with the fateful effect of releasing the woman from her isolation. The therapist was really interested in her; that was enough. Her self-interruptive actions could stop.

3) A young man said to me: "My wife and I just found out that we're going to have a baby. Isn't that fantastic? I know you've been telling me, 'Why not have a baby, since your wife is concerned about her age?' And I've always said, 'I just can't afford to.' Well, this happened. All I could feel at first was that it was wrong, unthinkable, that I was cornered. And then suddenly: it was still unthinkable. But it was right. I felt that something I couldn't control had happened and I'd trust it *just because* I couldn't control it. I'm already indebted to the baby for that. I'll make it work, somehow."

Here is the yielding of *wu-wei*, to which I could add only my assent. And it brings in the Taoist paradox: the control you feel when you dare to trust the uncontrollable.

From these instances it is clear that *wu-wei* also has radical consequence for therapists. They can't follow any formula of technique, not with the openness that they need. Their model is no less than the sage of Lao-tzu:

> He brings men back to what they have lost.
> He helps [them] find their own nature. (64)

Are they then, like him, pure exemplars of Tao? But how could that be? Leaving the Buddha of my tale aside, we all remain human beings on a battlefield. Lao-tzu's sage casts no shadow and has no persona. Whereas we, in mortal frailty, fall back on the "selfless persona" of the therapist, in order to cover the ego-claims we don't wish visible in the consulting room. Or, in a more subtle expression of the persona, we admit to weaknesses and ego-claims, but as though to say that our basic selflessness is untouched by them. I don't mean these thoughts cynically, nor to discount our seriously taking the sage as a guide. We fall short of him. But he gives us direction.

This direction is simplicity. And here another practical matter, the therapist's language, his chief tool, comes into view for critique.

Years ago, I heard Harry Stack Sullivan speak of a psychiatric trainee who described the "narcissistic cravings" and "power maneuvers" of his patient. Sullivan suggested something — a form of Behavior Modification therapy for the therapist. "You've been working very hard, Doctor," he said. "And I think you've been confined to your professional circles. Take a breather. Get out in the community with what you know. Give a talk at a Rotary Club or a PTA meeting. And be sure to ask for questions." The trainee did so, and his language changed. Now his patient, he told Sullivan, was "blind with desire," "drunk with power."

Theoretical writing in psychology perhaps can't be content with common speech or metaphor, but its phrasing can be as direct. And yet contortion is sometimes the rule of the day. Here is Heinz Kohut, explaining narcissistic disorder. It arises when the child's "cohesive grandiose-exhibitionistic self (via his relation to the empathically responding merging-mirroring-approving self-object" is too frustrated.[20] Does he mean: "A child's pride is deeply wounded when his self-love isn't nourished by another's love." Or James Masterson depicts borderline personality. It results from split "rewarding and withholding part-units...[in] the intrapsychic structure," derived from the mother's rewarding the child when he clings, and pulling back when he wishes to separate.[21] Does he mean: "To feel that he is good, the child lives as his mother wishes, submissive to her will; for she withdraws from him whenever he is independent, and then he feels abandoned and bad." These writers are influential teachers with valuable ideas.[22] But the words I quote clog the mind's pores, estrange rather than connect us to the persons they describe. How can we be fair to complex variants within people, and yet evoke a common human bond? That is the challenge of Lao-tzu's simplicity, which at once unites mankind and embraces a paradox: the twofoldness of our natures as limitless Tao and limited form. It is surely as true of the narcissist and the borderline person as of the rest of us: "I am God in nature. I am a weed by the wall."[23]

Lao-tzu's simplicity is perhaps hardest for us to apply as political advice. In psychological work, we deal with people one-to-one, or in families or small groups, where the nuances of the inner life can be honored. But politics means mass man, and not even, today, the small country he would like. We cope, instead, with interwoven world problems and international bargaining, in which his wise ruler seems still more implausible than his psychologist sage. What becomes, in fact, of benevolent leaders and issues, as we know them? Gandhi and Martin Luther King are assassinated. Ecological conscience and activism for the common good are entangled in partisan self-interest. Does a politician care about racial equality or sexual equality as a human right, or in order to get votes? Will industrial greed pollute us to extinction — smog, nicotine, oil spills, and the rest? Do we help Russia with a crisis of famine, or is our concern national security, so that we add in some economic aid when basically we finance the dismantling of their bombs?

But Lao-tzu's voice, on matters like these, is not naive. Rather, he predicts our problem. For anything uncompromised, he says, must begin with the individual:

> A man of Virtue performs his part,
> But a man without Virtue requires others
> to fulfill their obligations. (79)

This is politics from within. Perhaps, today, only a man of soul, like the former Czechoslovakian president Václav Havel, embodies it, a man who indeed governed a small country after having been a political prisoner in it, and who knows an abyss of uncertainty in his own existence. He has said:

> If I am a better president than many others would be in my place, then it is precisely because somewhere in the deepest substratum of my work lies [a] constant doubt about myself and my right to hold office. I...would not be in the least surprised if, in the very middle of being president, I were to be summoned and led off to stand trial..., or taken straight to the quarries to break rocks.[24]

Here, from the heights of public life, is the basic self-questioning, and acceptance of an absurdity in existence, that can lead as Lao-tzu wants, to politics beyond reasons, even good ones:

> Just do what needs to be done. (30)

And the questioning springs from what is most vulnerable, unformulable, within us. It accepts inherent contradictions: failure with success, weakness with strength, death with life. And so it returns us to the Tao, but not comfortably. We go with this flow only at a cost, for it asks of us a yielding in which nothing is fixed, in which we become, like it, a mystery.

But in the end there is no other way to see things plain or, without any pressure or constraint, to know ourselves. When we let things be as they are, we shall have become as we are.

Chapter 7

GREGORY BATESON: METADISCOURSE

> [T]o people like us, work, meaning the devotion to some purpose, the nobility and worth of which we cannot question, is the one and only thing that helps in time of trouble....To set oneself to find out something, even a little bit, of the structure and order of the natural world is, and will be for you I dare foresee, a splendid and purifying purpose....

These words, written in 1922 by the leading geneticist of his day, William Bateson, to his youngest son, Gregory, ring with the exhortation, the assurance, and the high-minded faith in science of the Victorian age. The young man, not yet 18, was to become the behavioral scientist of the 20th century with the most searching range of theory: the creator of the double bind for understanding schizophrenia, and of a new science of mind coterminous will all life. He was to contrast himself repeatedly with clinicians who shoot first and ask questions afterward. For him, only the questions — questions of "structure and order" — illuminate action. And to see clearly into the questions, to let oneself expand into them, is to begin also to see the world differently. This was his doing-through-not-doing, his *wu-wei;* among experimentors and manipulators in psychology, he was a Taoist. In him, too, we shall be hearing again the voice of the Victorian father, the confident teacher clear about what he knows and what he doesn't know; so he will speak to us in the fictionalized conversations with his daughter which he called Metalogues.

Science permeated Gregory's boyhood. "I grew up in the midst of natural history and beetle collecting," he recalled in his late sixties. William had named him after Johan Gregor Mendel, whose work on hereditary "differential characters" — dominant and recessive — Bateson evangelized in England; he had also coined the word *genetics* from that work. But in spite of strong family ties, Gregory at home sensed that he didn't belong. In his mid-teens he shot up to his six feet five inches, typically quiet, feeling unnoticed in spite of his height: family photos show a reflective, good-looking face over a gangling body. He soon became a sole survivor. His oldest brother had died in the First World War, his middle brother by suicide after a failed love affair.

At first obeying family tradition, he went to the University of Cambridge to study zoology. Then, at 18, he got engaged to the daughter of one of his father's Swiss colleagues. His parents found that the girl wasn't good enough. Her father, observed his mother, "was a sturdy peasant." "They were just ordinary people — in addition to being foreigners," said his father. Gregory broke the engagement. "What right have [my parents]," he thought, "to be hurt?" His emotional reticence was akin to that of Lewis Carroll and A.E. Housman, other great, timid University men. But something else, long dormant, stirred in him; it was the independent cat of Kipling, "the wildest of all the wild animals...[who] walked by himself...waving his wild tail and walking by his wild lone — and all places were alike to him."[1] By the time he was 21, Gregory would no longer be just "son of," the visible namesake of Mendel. He switched his field to anthropology. "I'm afraid you will be terribly disappointed in me in this," he wrote with care to his father. In a lifetime of many Grants applications, this personal one may well have been his hardest to write:

> I'm afraid you will be disappointed...but...I do not feel able to throw myself unreservedly into [zoology]....I am much

> more likely to get into trouble through going on as I am...than by changing into a branch of science which is personal where I should be able to take root a bit....I do not think there is any reason to worry over our relationship....I am taking up a much more honest position, instead of quietly worrying.

The letter stood as his diplomatic reply, over three years later, to his father's wishes of him in 1922, and William took it in good grace. Three months later, in the midst of his still busy career, he died of a heart attack. The next year, Gregory set sail for his first field work, in New Guinea.

What began, in fact, was a life work in which he made zoology personal too, and came to understand the world of animals as alike to that of the human. His own life, if we give it his sense of relevance, is important only for the illustration and the development of his ideas. He held to Bertrand Russell's motto: "A fact, in science, is not a mere fact, but an instance";[2] and the statement holds equally when the fact is one's own existence. His particular phrase for the thing "instanced" is "the pattern that connects"[3] — connects his own or any other single life to the clearest, most discriminating, and most comprehensive ideas about it; that absorbs an individual life's pattern into their pattern. Keeping with this credo myself, I shall follow how his ideas began, and how they grew, clustered, and elaborated their own network.

"The pattern that connects" can be described another way: it shows how the world of experience fits together. Gregory's concern here is akin to Buber's, whose work he later admired. But in the late 1920s, observing the headhunting tribe of the Iatmul along the Sepik River in New Guinea, his own framework began with the concepts of the leading British anthropologists of his day. Malinowski, a brilliant field worker, had proposed a functional theory of culture. Gregory summed it up dryly in later life: "Natives plant X to eat them."[4] He objected. Too simple. Of course food is needed to keep people alive. But also "food can be provided to give...social status, to ornament festivals, any number of things." Radcliffe-Brown, the other main theorist of the day, took a more organismic view of societal life. Social structure as a whole, he said, determined the individual's behavior: thus marriage legitimized offspring into a society. But to Radcliffe-Brown, "culture was a vacuous...concept."

Gregory liked the sense of *system* in Radcliffe-Brown, and he sought himself a finer discrimination of system-behavior, its color, feel, and logic. He proposed concepts of his own. 1) *Eidos* (from the Greek for "form"): a culture's standardized *style of thinking*. Iatmul eidos, for instance, led to a male infant's inhaling smoke from a bespelled fire, so that he would grow up erudite in the totemic names of his clan. A learned adult would know 20,000 such names of four to five syllables. On the other hand, 2) *Ethos* (from the Greek for "character") is a culture's standard of *emotional tone*: for example, the value male Iatmuls set on pride, harshness, and spectacular display. And centering specifically on interaction, 3) *Schismogenesis* (from "schism"): separation, within a system, into balanced polarities. For example, in *complementary schismogenesis*, Iatmul women, as audience, admire their men's spectacular display in ritual performances; this enhances the men's exhibitionism, which intensifies the women's spectatorship. *Symmetrical schismogenesis* occurs in rival male groups that bully the young men before their initiatory rites into adulthood — an escalating rivalry. This escalation is then countered by complementary behavior in a ceremony called *naven*, which accompanies the initiation: the youth's mother's brother, dressed as a woman, approaches him and caricatures a passive homosexual act, for instance, rubbing his buttocks against the length of the boy's leg. Within the masculine values of the culture, this action is not seriously tolerable. It is a piece of theater, after which the newly designated adult-son begins a symmetrical assertiveness with his father.[5]

Examples of schismogenic balancing in Western life: a dependent wife establishes equality with her husband on the tennis court. A rivalrous couple find new intimacy when one is ill and taken care of by the other.[6]

All these concepts evoke the complexity of a human system. But in themselves they are disjointed, swatches of a pattern in want of development. More than a decade after first describing them, at the Macy Foundation Conference in 1946, Gregory heard the mathematician Norbert Wiener speak about *servo-*

mechanisms, and about Bertrand Russell's *Theory of Logical Types.* And his ideas wove together, and expanded.

A *servomechanism* is a circular mechanism, like a steam engine with a governor. The more power delivered to the piston, the faster it moves, the faster then the governor spins, the more the weighted arms of the governor diverge, and the *less,* then, the power supply. The machine, in short, is self-correcting, and oscillates around a steady state. Such mechanisms are well-known in physiology: for instance, the reciprocal inhibition of anterior pituitary hormone and sex hormones, or of blood sugar and insulin; or the sequential connection, at high altitudes, between lessened oxygen supply and increased speed of breathing and heartbeat, leading then to enriched hemoglobin in the blood, and *slower* breathing and heart rates. Just such a circulatory effect, or *negative feedback,* as Wiener's language of cybernetics has it, marks the alternation of symmetrical and complementary schismogenesis. Might not a larger description of personal and societal adjustment also be understood cybernetically?

In turn, schismogenesis, eidos, and ethos are all involved in processes of *learning*; and over the years Gregory had concerned himself with various modes of experimental learning; for instance, Pavlovian and rote learning. It became evident to him that a dog's Pavlovian learning, buzzer followed by meat powder in a fixed period of time, sets up *another* learning, a learning of *fatality* about how events proceed. Fatality is the eidos that arises from Pavlovian contexts. (We can conceive the accompanying ethos to be fortitude, or patience. Negatively felt, it could be depression.) Rote learning, on the other hand — learning to say syllable B after one has said syllable A — conduces to another kind of learning: to see sequences as self-contained and complete. Gregory noted correspondences in human societal life. A Balinese child learns to dance by a sort of "muscular rote." The teacher guides by example, or literally holds and moves the child's limp limbs. The adult Balinese, in turn, shows a passive, stylized sense of flowing with life — with a sense, too, of the ever-present risk of *faux pas.* In contrast, the Western industrial factory worker, whose life is regulated by a timeclock and fifty workweeks a year, lives in a Pavlovian schema; pay and a little leisure follow set signals. He can easily feel an immovable, pessimistic fatality governing all human things. If an exception to such a fate exists, it too is beyond control, a sort of caprice, like winning the State lottery.

In each case, one learns *from how one learns;* and the second-order learning is on another, more generalized level. And just this structure of hierarchical levels is presented by the *Theory of Logical Types.*[7] Bertrand Russell distinguishes rigorously between members of a set (say: 2, 4, 6, 8) and the set itself (even numbers), which is of "higher logical type" than its members; these two are like nesting Chinese boxes.[8] For all its abstractness, the theory bears a striking correspondence to concrete organic life: how, for instance, the whole brain and spinal cord "nest within" primitive ectodermal tissue, itself therefore the ground plan of the nervous system, and so of "higher logical type" than it. We are speaking here of physical *context.* And isn't there a series of nesting contexts, I in my body, in my family, in my culture, in the world environment I know, in the cosmos I do not know but imagine, a series comparable to Russell's logical levels? The greater the generality, the more "abstracted from" small contexts, the more inclusively real. And may not these levels serve also for a more inclusive theory of learning, as well as for understanding confusions in learning?

By the 1950s, Gregory's anthropology centered on Western communicational patterns; he became, in effect, a research psychologist studying schizophrenics and their families at the Veterans Hospital, Menlo Park, California. And he noticed a curious correlation with Russell's types. The schizophrenic behaved as though he felt punished *but wasn't supposed to realize it;* as though, Gregory wrote to Wiener in 1954, the patient understood he would be "punished for cringing," since he is supposed to believe himself loved. Couldn't this knowledge which has to be denied, be described as a prohibition against the learning one has learned? As being put in the wrong for what one knows? The larger framework — the higher logical type of being unloved — is confounded by the smaller one, with its semblance of familial harmony. Wouldn't a child or a very dependent adult child, neither feeling affection nor able to deny feeling it, be compelled, by the logic of the case, to disordered behavior? So, for example, the schizophrenic giggles foolishly when his mother speaks to him, or appears emotionally paralyzed, or says something bizarre but meaningful, like "The woman is a submarine no one can see."

The description is appealing. But there is a jump from fact to thought which troubled his co-workers of the time, Jay Haley and John Weakland. Jay Haley reminisced later:

> We were trying to find out what on earth Gregory was talking about. And he couldn't tell us....We were asking, "How do you know that a schizophrenic is so because he is punished for feeling punished?" It took about six or eight hours, and finally he said, "Well, that's *the sort of thing* that must be happening." Then we knew what he was talking about....It was a hypothesis really, that Gregory pulled out of the sky, on the basis of looking at the way people communicated.

Later they had the data, and the double bind theory, as this structure of denial came to be called, attracted much attention in psychiatry. But it was always rooted in something intuitive, subjective, and created:[9] like Einstein, as a youth, asking "What would the world look like if I rode on a beam of light?" and proceeding, by degrees, toward the Special Theory of Relativity. Such an approach is more akin to Blake than to data-collecting and measurement. It brings out the personal factor in science: how, in observing behavior, it is I who detect and combine the clues; in the pattern that connects, it is I who connect it. Gregory called his theoretical stance "a sort of pincers maneuver": matching observation to fundamental theory. But he emphasized that his sense of relevant data, the interactive field — and of basic theory, the logical types — came from his own discriminations.

So his thoughts were turning when I met him, in 1955. The context of our meeting deserves a little digression.

I was in serious trouble at the time. I was a first-year resident in psychiatry, with quixotic ideals, working at the Langley Porter Institute in San Francisco, on a locked ward. One of my patients was a 22-year-old Irishman called Wayne, himself a San Franciscan, who had been transferred from a maximum security hospital in another place to be evaluated now for a prefrontal lobotomy. Wayne had a long history of school truancy, car theft, assault with a deadly weapon, and episodes of rage and confusion in which he had threatened people's lives. These had resulted in several hospital commitments; the present one was his fourth. Prefrontal lobotomy, in those days, was still common coin in institutional psychiatry, and the University of California Medical Center had on its staff a neurosurgeon very skillful in the procedure. During the several weeks I had known him, Wayne was definitely not psychotic. He was, in fact, a charmer — bright, friendly, observant about the ward of schizophrenics around him and only a little apprehensive about the surgery that lay in his path. *One Flew Over the Cuckoo's Nest* had not yet popularized the destructive nature of the operation. Its personal appeal to him was that, afterwards, he could stay out of hospitals.

One evening, when I was on call, he caused a sudden commotion on the ward. He came to the nursing office, furious and belligerent, and demanded the hospital keys. I was summoned at once. When I appeared, he calmed down a little. He said he just wanted to visit friends in the neighborhood for an hour. He would come back after that. I believed him. Could my belief, I wondered, affect his fixed conviction of being distrusted? I asked for an extra set of keys. The head nurse, facing this outrageous request, although it was from the doctor in charge, refused. I gave Wayne my keys. Then there began a kind of dance between us. He walked to the door of the ward, stopped, turned around, and threw the keys on the floor in my direction, yelling, "Don't *give* them to me!" I said, "Why not?" "I don't know." I picked up the keys and threw them back to him. "*Don't*!" he yelled again, and threw them back to me. We exchanged the keys a half-dozen times; it began to have the character of a game, a game of "catch." Finally he unlocked the ward door. Then we performed the same dance, or game, on the stairs down to the main lobby, and then at the door to the street. At last he let himself out, throwing the keys back and, in effect, returning them to me now that he was done with them. The nurse meanwhile had alerted the police. They didn't find him. An hour and a half later, he rang the front doorbell, and returned calmly to the ward.

I am glad to say that, in the end, Wayne was not considered to meet the criteria for prefrontal lobotomy. But I had blackened my own name. In flagrant disregard of the situation, I had given keys and liberty to a committed patient with a history of serious social menace, who had been brought to the city in confinement, solely for the purpose of having the menace controlled. No one wanted to discuss with me our "dance"; his extraordinary repeated *refusal* to be given the liberty. His return was considered lucky. My poor conduct in letting him go swallowed up anything creditable about my judgment in his coming back, or any recognition of a therapeutic good to him in my respecting his promise to return. He was transferred at once to another doctor. I was put on probation.

In my confusion, I sought out Dr. Jurgen Ruesch, who held a research post at Langley Porter and was a well-known psychiatrist. Dr. Ruesch heard my story, leaned back in his swivel chair, cupped his hands behind his head, and lectured me briefly. Throughout history, societies have expressed a need for standards of professional competence. One accredits oneself by meeting these standards. He inquired about past episodes in my life of troublemaking behavior (I could think of a few), and he recommended that I seek psychotherapy. I began to look as sociopathic to myself as Wayne looked. But, even more, I was puzzled. I felt more like a shortsighted explorer, more an ignorant than a purposeful fool.

During this time, I was reading the book *Communication*, co-written by Dr. Ruesch and Gregory Bateson, and had warmed to Bateson's ideas. He had criticized *energy* theory in psychoanalysis, a concept that Freud, searching for a basic principle of science, had got from physics. But in physics, Bateson pointed out, energy is indestructible, whereas in life "patterns are destroyed in order that other patterns may be created." Constant energy is needed, of course, for *physical* metabolism; but the coming and going of psychological pattern ally better with another basic principle in science, the concern with *order* in the Second Law of Thermodynamics.

Bateson's sense of relevance felt to me bold and penetrating. And wasn't I myself, perhaps, trying now to create a new pattern in my work life? I phoned him in nearby Menlo Park. He told me that he kept Tuesday evenings at his home for Stanford psychiatric residents whom he taught. I could come too.

On the next Tuesday I drove down. Eight young doctors sat in his living room, cutting slices of Stilton cheese from a large slab and sipping wine or coffee. On the wall over the mantel hung the original Blake painting that Gregory had inherited from his father, "Satan exulting over Eve." The woman lies in the coils of the snake. Satan, with large bat wings, stands over her; his exultation looks at the same time like a mourning over evil. Under this cosmic ritual, our host was speaking to us of another ritual, of trance dance in Bali. How the dancers, reporting messages from the dead, talked in metaphors different from those of schizophrenics: their metaphors — leaving to one side that, in the context of Bali, these reports were "literal reality" — their metaphors are clearly labeled. Those of schizophrenics are not. The schizophrenic asserts, metaphorically, something about relationship, but he flees from defining it. I pricked up my ears. I had never before heard anything of the structure of schizophrenic language. I was accustomed to ideas like "the unconscious overwhelming the ego," but that told me nothing about the pattern of communication I faced. Had Wayne's "dance" with me contained metaphors that he hadn't known how, and I hadn't tried, to identify? Statements, symbolically enacted, about freedom not being given to him: he can "break out," but doesn't believe he can be "let out"? Gregory, meanwhile, was likening schizophrenia to runaway imagination. "You need a balance. Too much imagination, and you land in the booby hatch. Too much rigor, and you're dead." His guests asked him about Russell's Logical Types, which confused them. He gave examples. *Crime*, for instance, is of higher logical type than punishment. It is a way of thinking, a *spirit* of breaking the law. Punishment concerns acts, the *letter* of the law. With serious criminals, the inefficiency of punishment is simply that you can't change the spirit by dealing with action. You can lose a life, of course, to incarceration. But in briefer punishment, you are more likely to challenge the spirit to cleverer lawbreaking. Another example: *Exploration* is on a different logical level from *items of behavior*. Rats are explorers. You can't discourage a rat from exploring by consistently reinforcing its failures in a learning experiment. *Failure*, to an explorer, is useful information.

His listeners were struck by the reasoning. He cautioned us, however. That's well and good, but don't let logic get too pretentious. It's a small part of our inward circuitry, which in turn subtends a small segment of phenomena. Then he quoted Whitehead's words of praise to Bertrand Russell after a brilliant lecture on quantum theory: "'And especially *he left unobscured* the vast darkness of the subject.'"

Later, he and I stood in his driveway as his other guests drove off. I told him my tale about Wayne and my predicament at Langley Porter. Wayne's behavior intrigued him for its paradox: the refusal to be given what one wants to have. So did the way our game of "catch" seemed to transform into play. "'Never a more serious word than one spoken in jest,'" he added with a wink. I said: "So perhaps he was starting to feel free to get out." "Well, he started to play with the problem, playing with you. He was beginning to put quotation marks around the problem." "That's what made it a game?" "Of course. And made him bigger than it. As big as you." "I might have suggested accompanying him on his ramble," I went on, in Menlo Park thinking the unthinkable: a doctor on call at a hospital does not leave the premises. I asked Bateson about his relations with Dr. Ruesch. With a lift of the eyebrows, he said, "A trace derisive on both sides." He appeared to be enjoying how I had thumbed my nose at conventional psychiatry. Was he, too, I wondered, an incorrigible explorer? "But at the Langley Porter they do take themselves very seriously," he continued. And suddenly I saw what I had plainly missed before. What I still was missing now, thinking of a night on the town with Wayne. I had totally ignored a real context. I, a first-year resident in psychiatry, had mistaken a conservative mental hospital for a center of experimental therapy. Of course that wouldn't do. But in addition to a clear criticism, this English gentleman was giving me something else; his enjoyment showed it. He was, in a way, proclaiming me a friend of Huck Finn. The virtue in my rashness had been imagination.

We talked for another half hour. When I drove away, the deepest friendship of my life had begun.

For Gregory, himself, imagination always centered on "general principles." Collecting the data he needed, he was genial, hospitable, a model of therapeutic warmth. He could reassure the nervous family of a schizophrenic about his tape-recording equipment. "May I use it?" he would ask. "I feel naked without it." They smiled, relaxed; yes, the taping was all right. And for me personally, he had been a model therapist quickly: he had seen things my way, and then enlarged my perception of what I saw until I saw what I hadn't seen. But therapy was no more his concern, during his years at the Veterans Hospital, than ethnographic field work had been before that. "I am looking," he wrote an associate in 1964, "for examples of formal relations, which will illustrate a theory." The theory was to be a new system of order. It should embrace the most separate formal relations in nature and culture: organismic structure; biological evolution, the shaping function of context; the grammar of a sentence. To think about such diverse matters in a unitive way must mean to think *transcontextually* — leaving the varied data untouched, in Taoist fashion, while a few basic principles illuminate them.[10]

For example:

The fertilized egg itself is a sort of microscopic *Wunderkind* engineer, which already has the plans drawn up, coded in meticulously detailed relational signals, for all the organ structures, with all their interconnections, that will unfold in its later development. These structures will turn out to be internally self-regulated in a cybernetic feedback system. And the wonder traces back still further: to the parental chromosomes and their genes that were waiting in the wings, with their messages, to give the *Wunderkind* its encyclopedic information. They provide, at times, not only for the predictable differentiated organism which is to come, but also for the potential of what is *not yet* predicted: for the change in organismic structure which we call evolution. There the genetic code allows for *random*, or *stochastic* change (from the Greek, *stochazesthai*: "to shoot at; to guess"); the appearance, that is, of mutant genes. This is Nature's imagination. In this regard she is sporting. The genetic flexibility is of *higher logical type* than any one species, with its established blueprint, since the flexibility allows for development beyond the species. I shall come back to this point later.

At the same time, stochastic change means *selectivity*. Only certain new genetic outcomes endure, those appropriate to the environment. Gill breathing, for instance, will not suffice on land. The right environmental fitting of anatomy is an instance of communication-in-a-context, just as grammar is: a noun and verb are not adequately definable apart from their relationship. Therefore anatomy "must contain an analogue of grammar, because all anatomy is a transform of message material, which must be contextually shaped. And...*contextual shaping* is only another term for grammar."[11]

So the correlations of his thought proceed, moving, we see, always a step beyond species, beyond anatomy, beyond grammar. To use the Greek root, this step is *meta* to its subjects, and evokes a special language of its own. *Transcontextual thinking* leads to *metadiscourse.*

Students of Gregory were often confused by his discourse. "Is it all a sort of example?" he was asked. "An illustration of something else?" Of what? They felt that he was not "on the level" with them. And in a strict sense they were right. He was on *more than one* level; a Western song, "The Ballad of Two-Level Bateson" would be just. His essays and books, though full of metaphor, aren't typically poetic either, as Blake is, and Lao-tzu, and Buber at his most eloquent. Nor are they simple prose, in the sense that Kafka wrote about the "perfection" of his own prose in the sentence: "Two friends went for a morning ride." In place of that sentence, Gregory could have written, "When two friends go for a morning ride, what criteria must be met for us to call the action 'sacramental'?" The fact is given, and at once the speculation beyond the fact. And in his writing, quickly the ground floor is being seen only, so to speak, from the balcony; then, the first balcony from the second. He acknowledged the difficulty himself. "Some people say they have read my book of essays[12] straight through," he said to me once. "*I* could never do that."

But he wrote also in another vein. *Meta* to his own structure of thinking was the inquiring mind in which science, philosophy, and religion unite. That unity of concern lay, *par excellence,* in classical Athens.[13] And following Plato, Gregory wrote dialogues. The question I made up about *sacrament* is, after all, typical of him, and it is a Socratic question: it reaches from fact to value. Coming from his own life, his dialogues are between Father and Daughter; for Mary Catherine Bateson, called

Cathy, was the child of his first marriage, with Margaret Mead,[14] and very dear to him. It can hardly be a coincidence that the first dialogue was written in 1948, the year after the marriage ended, when Cathy was eight. Five more were published in the next six years. Being Gregory Bateson, he called them Metalogues.

Though they are not much attended to in critiques of Gregory's work, he was himself proud of them; they appear — a series of seven — at the beginning of his collected essays; and a final one is the epilogue to his last book, *Mind and Nature.* They are all vivid, witty, arch. The craftsman is at home in his own workshop of ideas, improvisationally free. If in fact the conversations are rather too *meta* for dialogues, lacking the offhand charm of Socrates digressing, they have instead a sort of offhand formality, in which the wit sparkles. The reader moves from one conversation to the next as from one stone of a Japanese garden to the next, the subjects always in graceful connection and pointing to all the major issues of Gregory's formal writings. I shall discuss five of the Metalogues, bringing in the more formalized ideas as the conversations tap them.

From the start, Daughter is a lively young intellectual. One easily senses her to be the daughter of proverbially articulate Margaret Mead, for whom the world is *sayable,* as for Lao-tzu it is not; as for Father, here, it is not. But Daughter is also a girl, with her own kind of Alice-in-Wonderland charm, impetuous, impatient, a little roguish and stormy. She plays with Daddy sometimes as Alice plays with her kitten; and Daddy, droll, crisp, self-assured, both formalist and fantasist like Lewis Carroll himself, enjoys the game, follows her, or makes her run after him. All the big issues, after all, are in their play; he knows it well as he joins in. After a while, then, they rest and settle back again on the river bank. Let us listen. Socrates is sitting down with Alice.

The titles of the Metalogues are themselves almost all Socratic questions. The first: "Why Do Things Get in a Muddle?" Later: "How Much Do You Know?" "Why Do Things Have

Outlines?" and the lyrical fragment, "Why a Swan?" At the end, the sharp, down-to-earth "So What?" In each case, our Alice begins with the question, then disputes or adds to Father's gloss on it.

The opening Metalogue asks the question most central to the science of order. Daughter explains herself at the start. "People spend a lot of time tidying things, but they never seem to spend time muddling them. Things just seem to get in a muddle by themselves." She agrees that things only muddle "if anybody touches them....But [why] do people *always* muddle other people's things? Why do they, Daddy?" "Now, wait a minute. It's not so simple." The Socratic probe begins. Father isn't, in fact, concerned here with people's *meddlesomeness*, but rather with the *inevitability* of muddle, which turns on the narrow limits of un-muddle, or tidiness. Narrow, first of all, in Daughter's view. For *tidy* to her means a paint box "on the end of this shelf...in the right place *and* straight;...[or] very *few* places [else:] if I move it a little bit, like this, it is still tidy." But probability, Father points out, favors its moving *many* places. Things happen "that way in which there are most ways of their happening....*And all of science is hooked up with that [fact.]*" Science, that is, subscribes to the data of probable outcome. Even more, by the Second Law of Thermodynamics, it describes how all patterns tend to randomness, which is a sort of muddling of order. It takes effort — the term in physics is *negative entropy* — to resist disarray.[15] Nature's tearing things down — storm, fire, flood — is manifestly much quicker and easier than its building things up: growth, harvest, evolution. All order must always work to shore itself up against the probability of its extinction. And always, within very narrow limits. Ten degrees' change in body temperature, and we're dead. A millimeter's lateral movement of an intervertebral disc and we're thrown from health into excruciating pain and disability.

At the same time, too much order is another death. Who wants the living room to stay just as it was before the guests arrived? In a later Metalogue, Father observes to Daughter, "If we didn't get into muddles, our talks would be like playing rummy without first shuffling the cards.[16] Take no chance, have no adventure, discover nothing.[17]

Daughter herself shows how the odds favor muddle, popping up quite untidily with her own remarks. Father has emphasized that there is only *one* way, which therefore makes it most improbable, of putting six letters together to spell DONALD. She replies, "But Daddy, the same letters might spell OLD DAN." Yes, but that's not his point. The point is that probability favors the "infinitely many muddled ways of anything." And now it's her bedtime. She, then: "Is what you're trying to say true about [tossing] pennies?[18] And about my paint box?" "Yes, that's right." "Daddy, why do grownups have wars, instead of just fighting the way children do?" "No — bedtime. Be off with you. We'll talk about wars another time." But her digressions aren't just muddling. There's a liveliness in them — if only the wish to stay up later — that has its own kind of order. Or rather, a mix of order and freedom — the very thing requisite for any new learning to occur.

But how can one think about this strange reality — order combined with disordering freedom — that brings about new knowledge? In another conversation Daughter begins discussing the subject as innocently as possible. "Daddy, how much do you know?" He, then: "I have about half a pound of knowledge": that is, a two-pound brain working at a quarter efficiency. She keeps it up: "Do you think we ought to measure [knowledge] by the yard?" Of course he doesn't. But the schools do just that "with examinations and tests and quizzes...You throw a lot of questions at the student, and if you find that you hit more places of knowledge in one student than in the others, then you think that student must know more." Surely knowledge, or learning, is more than *an amount*, is of different *kinds*. But the notion of quantity still intrigues her. "Daddy, why don't you use the other three-quarters of your brain?" "Oh, yes — that. You see, the trouble is that I had school teachers too. And they filled up a quarter of my brain with fog. And then I read newspapers and listened to what people said, and that filled up another quarter with fog." "And the other quarter, Daddy?" "Oh — that's fog that I made for myself when I was trying to think."

Light talk. But the joking, and the error, turn on the idea of knowledge as a mere sum. His serious point, developed eleven years later,[19] is that learning is hierarchical, like the logical categories. And like them, too, it integrates larger contexts.

Schoolteachers, newspapers, much of one's own internalized fog, stand for the smaller context of cultural conditioning, with all its prejudices and punishments which can lead one to seek psychotherapy. But there is a larger, unconditioned context of direct and unimpeded relationship to one's changing needs, moment to moment. The unconditioned is the context within which conditioned learning has occurred. The newborn child is filled with it; it's a genetic legacy. But to reach across to it in later life — so to speak, from Caesar to God — is no easy step. One must go through a profound darkness of self-doubt, of questioning all the premises of one's life, of feeling denied one's reality, as though the Tao itself had been disrupted and had disappeared — in short, the full thrust of double-bind experience. And one may get stuck in the chaos. But if one can emerge from it, it is into a world where "personal identity merges into all the processes of relationship in some vast ecology of cosmic interaction. Every detail of the universe is seen as proposing a view of the whole." So his mature thought spoke. But it was nascent in the metalogue. Daughter had been wondering: "*Really* do we only have one big thought which has lots of branches — lots and lots and lots of branches?" And Father replies, "I think so." They are both looking ahead toward Taoist selflessness.

The next dialogue continues the theme of learning, with a new specification for it. "Daddy," Daughter asks, "why do things have outlines?" The question is certainly his kind, with its touch of the Mad Hatter. He then, Socratically arch: "What sorts of things? A flock of sheep? Or a conversation?" But she is sensible Alice. "Don't be silly. I can't draw a conversation." "Do you mean," he persists, "that things have outlines, whether we draw them or not?" "I don't know, Daddy." He goes on with the idea his own way. Without hard edges, clear boundaries, thought itself melts (he gets angry thinking of it) into the "general mushiness of how people act and think: undiscriminating, liable to pick up on their fuzzy surfaces any social stereotype or prejudice: "sneaky Jew," "dumb Pole," and the like. Muddle again: too much of it! He remembers the total muddle of Alice's game of croquet on the Queen of Hearts' croquet ground, where the mallets are flamingoes and the balls hedgehogs. Daughter: "And the hoops walked around, too, because they were soldiers." "That's right." "Did everything have to be *alive* to make a complete muddle?" "No." But he pauses. "That's interesting. Yes, it had to be that way. Wait a minute. It's curious, but you're right." His excitement gathers momentum. "If the man who wrote Alice muddled things any other way, the players could have learned how to deal with the muddling details" — bumpy balls, or wobbly mallets. "But once you bring the *live* things into it, it becomes impossible...It's just the fact that animals are capable of seeing ahead and learning that makes them the only really unpredictable things in the world."

But how do "good outlines" and boundless freedom" fit together? And as learning theorist, he has a further question: Can the unpredictability itself *be trained for*?

Sixteen years after the talk about Alice's flamingoes, he found his answer at Sea Lion Park, in Hawaii, with dolphins. He had gone to Hawaii to study cetacean communication, and a trainer for the shows at the park told him of a curious discovery:[20]

Bored by the predictable learning skills of the animal, the trainer had tried a new tack. A female dolphin was trained at first, with a whistle, to expect food each time she raised her head above water. This was the usual thing. But in her next performance, the trainer made her wrong in her expectation: head up, no food. After a while, she made an accidental annoyed tail flip; and then she was fed. This new training was now reinforced. Then, in the following performance: tail flip — and no food. After many such learnings and frustrated learnings, in the fifteenth session her head came up and the dolphin at once "put on an elaborate performance, including eight conspicuous pieces of behavior of which four were entirely new, never before observed in this species of animal." The trainer had achieved the result: "I've taught her to do "I-don't-know-what."[21]

As Gregory described it, the training worked successfully with a double bind: Each time, the right thing became wrong: nothing predictable was right. Then in the end the dolphin learned a strange thing: *only the unpredictable is right.* Her success with the learning (rather than mere confusion or withdrawal) had several crucial determinants: 1) the recurrent, well-outlined learning context; 2) her good relationship with the trainer, who was a very benign double-crosser: many reinforcements of the single pieces of learning were provided each time before the rug was pulled out from under her; 3) perseverance of the dolphin and trainer, beyond her repeated failures to do something different; 4) the intelligence of both.

So all human learning, too, struggles with disruptions — the new obstacle, the new exception — and may finally come to accept novelty as the thing most to be learned. It is the goal of therapists who want their clients to have increased options, and, therefore, more unpredictability as to choice. Like the dolphin facing frustration, clients need dependable context and support from therapists. And they must both persevere, with sufficient intelligence, to reach the goal.

But the need for stability isn't outgrown, no matter how free we are. "Daddy," Daughter says at the end of the metalogue about outlines, "I'd rather have you unpredictable — sometimes." Honesty, we feel, can say no more. And also the shape of things is never so well defined as we want it. Perhaps in completed achievements, like a work of art. But in life, in a relationship, even in a conversation, it's our very freedom that leaves us with unrest: the yearning to finish what can't be quite finished, to be more than it is possible to be. "I don't understand," Daughter goes on, adding: Anyhow, "we can't do anything about it." "I don't understand it myself," Father answers. But he has his Taoist last word. "But...who wants to *do* anything about it?" Instead, we can yield to the paradox as it is given.

It's more typical of him, however, to look for the resolution of paradox in a wider scheme of harmony. The field broadens, as it will for the rest of his lifework, with the question of the next metalogue.

"Why a swan?" Daughter asks.

She gives us, charmingly, the swan-woman of Tchaikovsky's ballet. "Is she human? Of course the *dancer* really is, but on stage she seems inhuman or impersonal." "A 'sort of' swan," Father agrees. But with "no webbing between her toes." Daughter persists: "But what's really meant by 'sort of'?" "A relationship." "Between what and what?" "Between some ideas that I have about a swan and some ideas that I have about people." "What sort of a relationship is that?" "I don't know." And then he finds his key word: "A *metaphoric* relationship?"

In the metalogue (this one is the briefest of them) the word stays tentative. Father contents himself with one significant contrast to metaphor: a sacrament. "Which is emphatically *not* 'sort of.'...Men have gone to the stake for the proposition that the Communion bread and wine are *not* 'sort of' Christ's body." But this idea, too, is just touched on. And yet *metaphor* and *sacrament* will be cornerstones of his later thought: the search for an inclusive theory of all life that will increase for us the intelligibility of our own living. Not, he was always careful to point out, that human beings aren't uniquely different. But if it is true, in our fullest understanding that "every detail of the universe is seen as proposing a view of the whole," then Nature must, beyond the mere fact of evolution, be consistent and interwoven throughout. There must be (to take a word from his own first field of study) *kinship links* in the whole system: so that our bonds with the animal world, as displayed on Indian totem poles, are literal, not just symbolic realities; and one can just as well say, of the Catholic sacrament, that God becomes the bread and the wine.

What does metaphor tell us about biological linkage? We come here to Gregory's skill with illuminating definition. For his "metaphor," as he developed it later in his life,[22] is not what we learned in high school: "making unlike things equal." For instance, the Biblical image: "All flesh is grass."[23] The power of this image is the *actual likeness* of its elements: flesh, grass are both really frail; both really die. Gregory emphasized, "A metaphor is an isomorphism, a correspondence of form between one thing, and another." Words, indeed, are not the requisite thing; nor does an esthetic form — the dancer as swan — go far enough. "The whole of repetitive anatomy," he said, "and the whole of evolution — each of these vast realms is within itself linked together by metaphor." We see it in the bilateral symmetry of animals; we see it in evolutionary homologues, like the correspondence between the pectoral fin of a fish and the wing of a bird. *Metaphor provides the kinship system of comparative anatomy.*

When we come to the functioning of an organism — how the living metaphor works — we face a network of interacting parts: nerve receptor, brain, blood nutrients, voluntary muscle, all responding to the right adaptive environment. This is obvious enough. But then Gregory made one of his extraordinary generalities. The mind itself, he said, like any organism, is an aggregate of interacting parts, internally coherent, and transforming and responding to external events according to its own laws. It is a Kantian category of organic existence, coterminous with all life.[24] Consider mind, in its cybernetic self-regulation, at different evolutionary levels:

1) A male paper wasp in a Costa Rican forest dries his rain-filled nest by drinking up the water and spitting it over the edge. When the sun warms the nest too much, he cools his brood by vibrating his wings rapidly to make a current of air.
2) A woman in New York City watches a television news report on warfare in the Middle East. She gets angry. Then she telephones three friends, to suggest that they all send petitions to their Congressman for economic sanctions to protest the war. She grows calm again.

We may name the dissimilarity in the patterns here "instinctual" and "learned" behavior (the edge of greater effectiveness lying with instinct).[25] But for both, the pattern of internal self-correction is the same. *Mind provides the kinship system of comparative physiology.*

Two correlations of significance follow:

I referred much earlier to the "higher logical type" of mutant genes. They take off in a new evolutionary direction and, when successful, implicate a greater complexity of context: compare prehuman primates in their habitats with mankind in its cosmos. But human learning, too, moves from lower to higher logical type, from smaller to larger context: compare a restrictive life of thoughtless routine to the woman I've mentioned, roused to social action, or the Blakean grandeur of "One thought fills immensity." Learning, like evolution, is a departure from the habitual, a move into the unknown. But also, in neither case, is the development preset. Both learning and evolution are stochastic. The mutant change occurs by chance and may fail. A man or woman may waken to inner freedom, or may lose a freedom they have had. "It's...learning," Father said in the metalogue, "that makes all animals the only really unpredictable things in the world." Finally, then, it is this prevailing freedom, as well as the mental balance throughout living things, which led Gregory to the title of his last book: *Mind and Nature: A Necessary Unity.*[26]

"So what?" Daughter begins the dialogue which concludes this last book. It's a funny, laconic retort to Father's vast structure of intellection. And also, a new voice. Twenty-five years, it's true, have passed since we last heard from her, but it isn't just that she's grown up. The vivid little girl with the drawing box has faded into the alter ego of the speculative thinker. In the intervening years, Gregory's thought had in fact grown more full of esthetic concerns, but it's as though, ironically, he had paid a price for it in a hazier sense of the other person.

His own ideas, however, remain vivid. "I wanted clarity," he tells her. "You could say that faith and surrender were necessary to maintain the search for clarity. But I have tried to avoid the sort of faith that would cover up the gaps in the clarity." Faith, then, first of all. And with him, Socrates-like, *faith in clarity*. Then, his own particular domain, clarity about the large ecological stabilities of life, and about how they change. His word for "stability" comes, typically, from logic: he calls the organic world *tautological*. When it does change, with evolution, the tautology tears, "breaks up like the surface of a pond when a stone is thrown into it. Then it immediately starts to heal. And the healing may be ruthless. Whole species may be exterminated in the process." "But Daddy," Daughter says, "you could make consistency out of the idea that it always starts to heal." "So the tautology isn't broken, it's only pushed up to the level of the next higher logical type." We hear a logician's echo of Blake: "Without Contraries is no Progression." And this basic clarity about the organization of all life is needed, he says, to ask the next, the more specifically human questions: What is consciousness? What is beauty? What is the sacred? Indeed, they can only be clearly asked, without reduction, if they are placed in sequence with all the other ideas, which they will both reflect and develop. For everywhere in organic life a connective pattern glows; from the simplest organisms in cybernetic balance with their environment, through species' constancy and their evolutionary linkages, through levels of learning and their ascending complexity of context, to consciousness, beauty, and the sacred, each of these connected to the other, each in cybernetic bond to the cosmic context.

He did not live to answer the specific human questions, those new building blocks for the structure of his ideas. At least this work is not yet published.[27] But already his own wide consciousness inheres in the very form of his thought. In the levels he can see and discuss. In the levels he can foresee that perhaps he cannot discuss: those reaches of Mind of which "the individual mind is only a sub-system."[28] And in that perspective lies his strongest reply to "So What?" "'Always,'" he quotes from e. e. cummings, near the end of the last dialogue, "'the more beautiful answer which asks the more difficult question.'" Not to simplify; to keep the question wide and difficult: so a new hierarchy proceeds into the unseen, into the larger system of which his talks on order, knowledge, metaphor, have been parts. From where he is standing, on his lower balcony, he has already paid it tribute, his formed words for that which is unformed. Metadiscourse is sacramental.

Gregory liked to tell this story: a spinster lady dreams that, while she is lying in her bed at night, a handsome young man, elegantly dressed, climbs through her open window. She sits up as he approaches the bed, clutches the bedclothes around her, and asks hoarsely, "What're you going to do?" Whereupon he pauses, bows to her, and says, "I don't know, Madam. It's your dream."

Here is the taste of Gregory's wit! A dream expresses the uncontrollable unconscious, a wider field than conscious purpose and *meta* to it, a higher logical level. But the woman's mingled fear and wish, to give herself over to uncontrol, is brought up short. The higher level literally bows to the lower: the young man not only discomfits her with his reply; by putting her in charge of the dream he robs her of its autonomy. As its master, then, she can do nothing in it that isn't wrong. He has double-bound her. Or has he? For, on the other hand, the dream also presents relaxations of control: an open window, a charming intruder. The lower level of self-management reaches out, or up, to that of the unexpected and the unknown. Perhaps too far; the management returns to the dreamer. But this, too, is unexpected. So who, or what, in the end, is in charge?

The paradox of the dream is apparent; and Gregory's own answer to its riddle is his great contribution to human understanding. Not the unconscious by itself, nor the conscious by itself, is in charge, but the dance, *the system* which they comprise together.[29] In the dream, the system creates a witty ambiguity, about itself. But the system includes the ambiguity; is of higher logical type than it. And so too, with the systems all of us are in with the environment: with the air we need to breathe; the love we need and the struggles we face from one another; and more broadly, in wider contexts, one society with its collaborations and its conflicts, and interacting countries with theirs. In each case, the system controls; its members are subordinate and bound to it. Recognizing the system we are in can bring us a measure of control,allows for corrective learning. One might, for instance, improve the air by decreasing pollutants. But one cannot, as the metalogue has said, ultimately "do anything about" the system's supremacy.[30]

Systems thinking is radically different from the atomic thinking that separates the world into self-contained substances: "that person," "your problem," "my history." Of course individuals exist; but in the systems view, they can be most tellingly described by the response of others. Henry James, in his novel *The Tragic Muse*, says of a minor character: "It was her peculiarity that people were always saying things to her in a lowered voice." The systems point, further, is that the woman *keeps* the peculiarity because other people continue so to address her. Similarly, the English psychoanalyst Winnicott speaks of the "good-enough mother," who supports not too much, not too little, her infant's need for holding and handling. Winnicott's point *is systemic*, between mother and child. But in the manner of atomic thought, he then says he will "turn his subject inside out,"[31] and describe the effects on the child. The subject, however, isn't really "turned" at all. The good-enough mother is so defined by producing *the child who feels good enough* — feels both secure with mother, and free to venture forth on its own, to fall down, pick itself up — and who, in all this, then confirms the mother's sense of adequacy.

Thinking along these lines, fifty years ago, Harry Stack Sullivan revised the role of "impersonal" therapist to that of "participant observer," interacting with the patient in the field which he also observes.[32] But Sullivan's idea still suggests a kind of observational purity which cannot exist. The therapist's observing will reveal the systems both of his own formative life-experience and of his training; they join in the new system he makes with his patient: how, together, they pace things, talk seriously, joke, interpret, are silent. In this view, no particular therapeutic approach is being invalidated, only its objectivity.[33] The one requisite is what therapist and patient agree on, and that is only partly conscious and always culturally set.

Thus the psychoanalyst Sudhir Kakar, in India, describes the cure of an 18-year-old Hindu woman who for a few years had severe body aches, and had raged and grown violent against her good-natured husband.[34] It was agreed that a malignant spirit possessed her. For a cure, husband and wife went together to a temple of the Goddess Devi, and the young woman began to feel calmer, possessed now by the benevolent spirits of her dead father and mother-in-law. The decisive day came when she, her husband, and another couple appeared before the temple idol, the Mother Goddess. While the others chanted, "Victory to the Mother," the Goddess took possession of the young woman, and in a voice of thunder commanded the husband's respect for his wife, which he gave, bowing down to the ground abjectly three times upon divine order. When his wife came to herself, her aches and her fits were gone. Here is short-term family therapy with an irresistible therapist, whose lasting protection and support of the woman the couple accept.

In the Americas and Europe, family therapy is only some thirty years old, and has developed in the atmosphere of Gregory's systems thinking. A therapist, for example, meets together with a suicidal 17-year old girl and her parents, who are anxious "to save her for a happy life."[35] But parents and children harmonize more than they know. The parents' dark view of life, expressed vividly in their very fears of their daughter destroying herself, really promotes her depression; in effect, within their system, to which she is bound by profound emotional ties, it is *their* depression which she carries, and then reciprocally reinforces. The therapist intervenes with her own values, in a new system with the daughter. She appeals to the girl's desire for an independent life; supports her wish to live away from home with an admired friend from her college. The parents had formerly opposed the move out of ostensible fear for the girl's welfare. Deferring to the therapist, they accept the change. But now they must face, as never before, the drudgery in their marriage. This, in turn, may yield to further interplay within a new system of therapist-with-the-couple.

A system, we see, bows to the subjective: the attitude, the values of the subjects who make it up. In Gregory's case, his own biases have had striking effects on therapists who adopted, or rejected, them.

For one, his attitude toward time.

Early in his first book, the investigation of Iatmul culture, he takes his stand on a *synchronic* approach: events are to be described as they are in the present. "In a synchronic study of a fire, I should say that the fire burns because there is oxygen in the room, etc., but I should not inquire how the fire was ignited." Then, at the conclusion of the book, in a charming aside on how personal bias affects data-gathering, he says: "I myself have so little appreciation of time that I omitted almost entirely to enquire into...Iatmul calendric beliefs." Characteristic concepts of his developed thought — pattern, double bind, ecology, mind as a category of living — also leave time out. It is evident enough that psychological systems have their own history, and also that an individual has belonged to prior systems before his current ones. But Gregory, tireless logician though he was, could ignore the fact. He adhered to the cross-sectional view: the present system in the present moment. In 1958, his second wife was in a hospital, deeply depressed, and he grew depressed himself. "If my work is right," he said to me, "then it is my doing." He knew his own provocativeness: a passivity that could leave a woman feeling abandoned. But when I protested, "She lived under other influences, before you," the point didn't signify. Nor was he thinking of how his guilt derived from his own childhood system, the son who wasn't supposed to hurt his parents.

And yet, as the theoretician of cybernetics and of learning, he could hardly ignore time. There is no corrective feedback without it: you need a *sequence* of events. The changes in learning require it: the *repetitive* failure of an old pattern. The human mind is itself pervaded with it, to its farthest reaches, as we face the loss of our youth and anticipate the approach of our death. (But even here Gregory's phrasing is concessionary: our ideas, he says, are located "only perhaps in an *idea* of space and time.")[36]

Had he lived to discuss consciousness more fully, he might have woven together his discrepant senses of the temporal. As things now stand, therapists who work with systems have inherited from him a rather fuzzy view of it, many of them scoffing at lengthy psychotherapy, or uneasy about how to acknowledge the time that therapy needs. Gregory's own words about new learning are altogether cautionary. "All learning," he said, "is aversive." Habits are self-reinforcing. Change is difficult. Clearly, then, it takes time. How many "*good-enough therapists*" are there, indeed, who can guide us, long enough, through the artful frustration of old controls and the judicious provisions of new rewards, to produce our own spontaneous new behavior, like the dolphins at Sea Lion Park?

He thought they were rare. And his own circumspectness about feeling distanced him the more from them. Tender and generous in person, still it was like him to flee from emotion to thought, from the pain of mother and schizophrenic child to the logic of the double bind. He liked recounting the time in his own life when he took LSD, a simulator of psychotic experience, and his guide put a rose in front of him, to suspend his intellectuality. He contemplated the flower a while and murmured, "What a lot of thought it took for the rose to make that!" When he himself brought feeling and thinking together — and his integrative temper couldn't avoid doing so — the scale always tipped one way. In all of Blake, whom he loved, he repeated most often the words:

> For a Tear is an Intellectual thing.[37]

And so, in turn, he alienated many therapists and seemed rather pleased about it, as though good riddance. "But why?" I asked him, with exasperation. This was in the early 1970s. I was myself well along in the private practice of psychotherapy and committed to its value. Why did he grudge his own contributions to therapy? And didn't he bind himself in a way, wringing emotions out of the systems view which is intended to give them a stronger-based life? "Well," he reflected with a wink, "the system reminds me not to. But all that affect!" He sighed at the picture of so much litter, the inevitable flotsam of the consulting room, and after a pause went on, "Anyway, cure usually ignores the good sense of the disease. It wouldn't hurt the therapists to think about that. On the whole, they're lazy, and righteous about their commodity, and under the guise of helpfulness they covet power. I don't like them, you know." Actually, I agreed. Come to think of it, why was he so forbearing with me? Out of personal love, which grants the benefit of the doubt? I didn't quite dare to ask.

And yet the structure of his thought gave not only the sense of disease; it provided a rationale — more than he cared to observe — for therapeutic cure.[38]

As an extreme example, I have in mind Milton Erickson's work with a chronic schizophrenic patient in a hospital.[39] For five years the man had spoken almost exclusively in "word-salad" (a flow of obscure, unidentified metaphors which prevent all communicative exchange). Through careful attention to tape recordings, Erickson learned the patterns of the word-salad. Then he sat on the ward with the patient, George, and fed back the same *non sequiturs* he was offered, maintaining, however, a courteous, responsive style even when George grew angry. Doctor and patient continued their nonsense conversations for several consecutive days, Erickson's replies always carefully measured to be of equal length. Then came his most taxing day: four hours of monologue by George, four hours' response by Erickson, two hours more by George, two weary additional hours by Erickson. The following day, after the exchange of a few sentences of nonsense, George suddenly went on: "Talk sense, Doctor." "Certainly, I'll be glad to. What is your last name?" "O'Donovan, and it's about time somebody who knows how to talk asked. Over five years in this lousy joint."

Here, clearly, is a *tour de force* in treatment. I delineate the, so to speak, therapeutic trap, or positive double bind, that seems to be at work:

1) "Let's 'not communicate' together, in the same way. (Just how 'incommunicado' are you then?)" 2) "We won't discuss this. But you know I've caught up with you, and though I may annoy you, I'm not hurting you." (3) "In the field we share, you know that I'm sane and that I'm assuming you are."

Sifting through George's soul, these messages make him "wrong," as every double bind does. Gibberish no longer protects his isolation the way that it did formerly. At the same time, his new nonisolation is not brought about with pressure. The doctor just falls in with his isolated ways. And also this sane doctor shows him complete respect, assumes they are equals. So isn't the protective gibberish pointless? His "Stop talking nonsense" is a request to himself as well as to the therapist. Erickson reports that they kept up a sprinkling of word-salad through George's rehabilitation and leaving the hospital. George's comment on the matter was: "Nothing like a little nonsense in life, is there, Doctor?" To which Erickson readily agreed.

Thus understood, the double bind itself is clinically reframed: it *adds to* psychotherapy, rather than opposes it. And so can another element Gregory speaks of in restrictive learning: how it "punctuates experience." For instance, optimists move through failure and put a period after success; pessimists do the reverse. A therapist, then, merely by altering punctuation, will affect the quality of experience. Erickson, once again, demonstrates for us wonderfully.[40] He suggests "merely a change in punctuation" to a woman terrified of hostile male sexual power. "Did you ever realize," he said to her, "that a man's aggressive, insistent, domineering upstart of a member — do you realize that all this is changed by what *you* do into a puny, limp, ineffectual, dangling thing?" So much for not putting the period in the sentence too soon! With this winning invitation to see herself as "better than equal in the battle," the woman began to enjoy sexual relations; and then to feel in love. Of course, more than punctuation is involved. There has also been a change, to utilize Gregory's language further, in the logical typing. "Controlled, victorious fighting back" has become *a part of play* in the higher logical type of "love, with its many kinds of play." (Love is *meta* to aggression because it is less controlled and its context of receiving is wider.) And the wider the emotional base, the greater the reaching out, the more connected all the disparate parts of experience. Gregory liked to make this point with a pun on Browning's lines that could set Alice's Cheshire Cat grinning:

> Ah, but a man's reach should exceed his grasp,
> Or what's a metaphor?[41]

His own elegance of thought did not have the last word in his life; many rough complexities trailed along with it. In 1971, when he was about to leave Hawaii for a trip with students to the Orient and to Africa, a lifetime of chain-smoking arrested him. Weak and coughing continually, he was hospitalized. His lungs were severely crippled with emphysema. He stopped smoking and slowly recovered. Meanwhile, his relations with his third wife, Lois, grew strained. His work and his life with students had always tended to displace family life. Now also, as he approached old age, Eros held on more tightly — a counter-claim of his own internal system to the demands of a rapacious intellect. He was drawn elsewhere, without wanting to give up his family. In personal relations, when the reach exceeds the grasp, "meta" can swing round, get underfoot, and be something one trips over. Lois separated from him on their return to California. She still loved him — he remained the one man she unfailingly found interesting — and after a while they reunited. But she did separate, decisively, from the Western scientific logician. She found a spiritual home with the Indian holy man, Sai Baba. The marriage system balanced precariously.

Then, in 1978, while he was teaching at Kresge College in Santa Cruz, Gregory began spitting blood. Hospitalized at the University of California Medical Center, in San Francisco, he was found to have an inoperable lung cancer, and given six months to live; with treatment, a little longer. The body faced its final chaos from the old assaults of his smoking. Wondering just what he wanted to do, he served wine and Stilton cheese to visitors from his hospital bed, presiding like a host at a salon. One of his visitors was a psychic healer. This lady looked at him, touched him, and said, yes, he had a terrible cancer from which people die, but that in his case, it was a *dying cancer*. The devotee of imagination combined with rigor was delighted by *her* imagination; he let it trump all the medical advice. He decided he would be well, refused devitalizing chemotherapy and radiation, and left the hospital to complete his last book. Six months later, he moved, with Lois and their daughter Nora, to Esalen, on the Big Sur coast, where he lived and taught for over a year and a half, symptom-free, with increasing strength. Against all the probabilities, mind was restoring order, both fruitful shape and extra time, to the collapsing body.

So, with a sort of weary serenity, he lived on. One can see it in his face, on the cover of the Esalen catalogue for autumn of 1978. He is photographed holding a baby and smiling down in thought. The long nose, wide cheek, high forehead, and broad shoulder are all gently rounded, as Blake drew his own serene figures. About this time, my wife and I visited him and Lois, and in the sulfur baths at Esalen, a shaggy old bull of a man seasoned now by the Pacific Zen culture, he looked to me like the ox of the Zen ox-herding pictures. The disciplining of the ox is said to represent man's training in the truth of Zen. This oxherder from Cambridge would always tame the ox by clarifying its mind. "What happens to the hole when a doughnut is eaten?" he quizzed us, droll-voiced. The answer: "It gets reincarnated in another doughnut." So much for the supernatural. Lao-tzu would have laughed his approval.

In the spring of 1980, over two years after he had left the hospital, he began having chest pains again. He had long been reconciled to death: "You wipe the slate clean. Ideas survive in others — when true. That's the chief thing." But he feared "the technology of death — spitting up and the like"; and in his case it was dreadful indeed. Pain soon took him back to the hospital. The cancer, in fact, hadn't progressed. He was diagnosed to have pneumonia, and treated with antibiotics. But then the pain grew so severe as to be almost unbearable even with continuous morphine. Finally the viral disease, shingles, was found to be its cause. One doesn't die of shingles, but Gregory's will to live had receded.

Toward the end, he was moved to the guest house of the San Francisco Zen Center. Lois and his children were with him. By now the pain had gone, or he had retreated from it. But he seemed to have passed into a coma and wouldn't talk or even respond when efforts were made to rouse him.

I visited him a few days before his death, just as I was leaving the Bay Area on a long trip. His large room looked out on a quiet street. A Zen student sat meditating cross-legged in one corner. In this way the people of the house kept a vigil with him, should he need anything, and offered him also their calm, attentive presence. It didn't seem strange to me that he was being cared for by a spiritual order to which he did not belong (he had told me more than once, "I am not a Buddhist." "*Thought Forms*," as the Buddhists say, were clearly too dear to him). And yet the similarity of his views to theirs — of transience in all experience, of the value of nonattachment, of unitive living — had made him a sort of honorary Buddhist. Perhaps the maverick that he had always been belonged most of all with them, where he was finding a final home.

I stood by his bed and told him of the trip I was taking to a Buddhist retreat. It would have interested him. But he stayed motionless, eyes closed. Where had he gone? In the past he'd said to me, brightly, "I'll live by what happens." But now he wouldn't live by it. For his mind, like his heart, was only nourished when he could himself be lavish; and so he had withdrawn.

Silent now myself, watching him, I recalled something else he liked to say: "We are made of stories." And I thought again that he was always, really, the Cat who walked by himself. Like Kipling's Cat, he had gotten into the human house — into the forefront of the intellectual world. With the depth of his intuition and the flair of his premises, he had built toward heaven, as far as he could before he died, his own special tower, full of recursive circuits and feedback loops, and showing us afresh, in his sense of profound balances to be accepted, Taoist acceptance and awe. Had he not, after all, found out something, perhaps even more than "a little bit, of the structure and order of the natural world," that "splendid and purifying purpose" his father had foreseen for him? Like the Cat, too, chiefly he kept his own counsel, and went back often to the Wild Woods, "walking by his wild lone." But through all his disillusion with human weakness, others and his own, he adhered to the piety of True Ideas. They are the larger context of the context of the individual's inconsiderable bits and pieces. They give to the eye of the dying, ineffectual mortal the enduring, Platonic light.

I had to leave. Thinking of our times together, of the sadnesses and joys we'd shared and of all I'd learned from him, I said, in one of my happiest exaggerations, "Gregory, I remember everything." To my astonishment, he opened his eyes, took a few moments to focus on me, and asked, "Where's the retreat?" I told him, leaned down and kissed him good-bye. And the pattern that connects glowed, as he had said.

Chapter 8

JIDDU KRISHNAMURTI: THE UNCONDITIONED

Questioner: I am intensely lonely....What am I to do?
Krishnamurti: This is not an individual problem only; the whole human though it feels lonely.[1]

This exchange has a form familiar to us: a seeker in distress asks help of a guru. But we sense at once a difference in the reply. The questioner is not receiving a guru's guidance; the response suggests nothing, overt or subtle, of "How to manage." At the same time, the tone of the reply has authority: the questioner's problem is that of "the whole human thought," a phrase lyrical and also, without any technical ring, precisely psychological. It points directly to a divisive source among mankind, the partitioning nature of our thoughts. The state of mind of the questioner that has led to his question — that itself is this problem of thought, is the *loneliness* of thought. Krishnamurti will discuss the problem at greater length:

> Thought in human relationship is always demanding pleasure, which it covers by different words like loyalty, helping, giving....Thought is the breeder of duality in all our relationships; there is violence in us which gives us pleasure, but there is also the desire for peace....Thought

> not only breeds this duality in us, this contradiction, but it also accumulates the innumerable memories we have had of pleasure and pain, and from these memories it is reborn. So thought is the past, thought is always old....The word "loneliness" with its memories of pain and fear, prevents the experiencing of it afresh.[2]

All his description leads to the invitation: "Experience afresh." Guidance of any kind, on the other hand, can lead just to further thought, like "What is right or wrong?" And this is, again, mere opinion, that divides us and quickly grows stale. Only experience is whole and fresh. Krishnamurti has brought us this freshness himself, with his first words, which departitioned the isolated questioner: *You are not alone.*

Immersion in direct experiencing, and fidelity to its description, are called today "phenomenological psychology"; and Krishnamurti's approach to living is always phenomenological. In a sense, he is polar opposite to Gregory Bateson's Man of Thought. But we recall, too, that Bateson was a type of modern Taoist, letting life be as it is, celebrating its natural balances and connections in his formal ideas, and using metadiscourse to point to an invisible grace beyond words. Krishnamurti's own life and teaching are a rare embodiment of that grace. In our customary vernacular, we would call such a state "sacred," and find it rather mysterious. But once again, that is talk, that is thought, and for him the central reality is not thought-made nor a mystery. As a thoroughgoing phenomenologist, to whom psychology and spirituality are indistinguishable, he is a modern Buddhist, with the radical originality of the Buddha himself, though we shall see too how he departs in some ways from the Buddha's teachings.

All the facts of his life conspire to make him a religious myth. He was born in southern India, in 1895, the eighth child of a Hindu family ("Jiddu" is the family name), and at once his horoscope foresaw that he would be "wonderful and great."[3] His father, an orthodox Brahman, belonged also to the twenty-year-old Theosophical Society, a universalist religious group with some 16,000 active members internationally at that time. After his wife's death, when Krishnamurti was ten, and his own retirement from government service two years later, the father tried to get a post with the Theosophists 180 miles southeast at Adyar. As recompense, he sought only free accommodation for his family in their Compound. He was turned down four times. Finally, in 1909, he received a secretarial job, and for Krishnamurti the move was fateful. A few months later, the Theosophist leader Charles Leadbeater, a former curate in the Anglican Church, noticed the 14-year-old boy on the beach by the Adyar River. He had been proving a dim-witted student at school. He was scrawny, dirty, malnourished, and vacant-looking, with crooked teeth. But Leadbeater saw him also to have a wonderful aura — as he said, "without a particle of selfishness" — and predicted that some day he would be greater than the great Theosophist leader, Annie Besant. He soon recommended the boy to her. The Theosophists had been looking for a World Teacher to educate, a new Christ for mankind. Leadbeater considered that Krishnamurti was the proper Vehicle. Mrs. Besant, meanwhile, on her world travels, had already chosen an American boy for the same honor. We can picture the two Theosophist leaders, on her return to India, reviewing the evidence — messages Leadbeater had received, from an occult master on the astral plane, about the youths' former lives — as to the true spiritual thoroughbred. It would seem the one way to do it; this is not a role with worldly credentials, to be decided by a plebiscite.

One smiles at the measures used. But a powerful human reality underlay them, a key both to Krishnamurti's unfolding and to his ultimate message itself. He, the chosen one, was profoundly loved. Mrs. Besant, a passionate humanitarian and crusader for social reform, and a close friend of Bernard Shaw before her conversion to Theosophy, was in her early sixties when Krishnamurti was "discovered." She took him to her heart; and to him, from the first, she was "my dear mother" — both the loving mother he had lost four years before, and a new mother with extraordinary worldly powers.

And so the mythical life assumes the pattern of the Buddha's own: physical luxuries, personal devotion given by grateful, disinterested friends to the Crown Prince in his protected palace. (For Krishnamurti, of course, it was, as we say today of certain universities, a "palace without walls.") Mrs. Besant took him and his brother Nitya, three years younger, with whom he shared everything, to London for their education with private tutors.[4] Titled and cultivated friends surrounded the boys: Lady Emily Lutyens, Countess De La Warr, the wealthy American Mary Dodge, the *bon vivant* barrister Harold Baillie-Weaver. A special organization within Theosophy was created, the Order of the Star, with Krishnamurti, the coming Christ, as its head. His teeth were straightened, his long pigtail cut. With good nutrition and exercise, his body grew strong. The slender young man was emerging, a romantic ideal of the god in human form: large, flashing eyes that seemed to see through you, straight nose, delicate lips, hair worn full and free, an air of noble intransigence.

He continued with private tutors, but he wasn't much of a student. In spite of his influential friends, he couldn't get into Oxford; its old high standards were unshakable. Nitya went to London University, but Krishnamurti couldn't meet the entrance requirements there either. Meanwhile, he delighted in material things: a motor bicycle of his own; golf (he became a scratch player and won a championship in Scotland); the best London clothes; exquisite shoes which he polished to a high shine himself; fine leather gloves (vegetarian scruples did not rule these out). The Vehicle was a regular dandy of post-Edwardian England.

Mrs. Besant was often in India, writing and orating powerfully for Home Rule. In England, Krishnamurti's mother was Lady Emily. He wrote to her from Paris, a young man now 24, but with the accents of a homesick youth: "You know my dream, mother, which is being with you....You must tell me *everything, everything* you do, you think, you buy...." He felt homeless, empty. "We all have our moments of depression. So excuse." Soon after, he fell in love, briefly, with a 17-year-old American girl whom he met at Castle Eerda, in Holland. But physical chastity seemed natural to him; he couldn't understand "beastly" dreams he was having; in the daytime his thoughts were perfectly pure. Meanwhile, he has been reading *The Idiot, Thus Spake Zarathustra* and accounts of the Buddha — a triumvirate of religious heroes. One day, "I was in such a state that I had to sit down and meditate. Think of me meditating. Extraordinary." At times, a prophetic voice clearly sounds: his is angry about ceremonialism in Theosophy. "Why are we like this?

Because we can't face the Bigness of life, and so create Little Bigness which we can see." But frivolity kept a place. He attempted to control the bank at the Casino in Nice by willpower; he won, then lost. Still, the Crown Prince maintained a sense of humor about himself. Another letter from Paris to Lady Emily: "I changed into Indian dress and [the de Manziarlys] went into raptures. (If I allow myself, I could be the most conceited fool on earth, but thank God and you I shall never be that.)"

In 1921, Mrs. Besant summoned him and Nitya to India "to begin his life work." He spoke at the Theosophist Convention in Benares. But Nitya, the year before, had been found to be tubercular; he should return to Switzerland for treatment. The young men toured eastward with Theosophist friends. They stayed awhile in the Ojai Valley in California, near Ventura. And there, at 27, on a new continent, away equally from the aristocratic idleness of his life in Europe and from the Theosophical bandwagon of India, away from both Mrs. Besant and Lady Emily, in the stillness of the Ojai orange groves and rich summer flowering, a shudder took place in Krishnamurti's inner life; a light entered him, and hit. His account of it, to Leadbeater and Mrs. Besant, reads like passages on conversion in James' *The Varieties of Religious Experience.* At first he has severe migrainous pain at the nape of the neck, the feeling of needles being driven into his head, sensitivity to heat and noise, a sense that his bed and bedroom are dirty. He is semiconscious. There are three days of this turmoil, alternating with periods of quiet. At last, urged by a friend, he sits under a young pepper tree near the house, with scented blossoms; then a great Presence slowly arrives and stays with him, and an unshakable calm in the soul. "As you well know," he writes to Leadbeater, soon after,

> I have not been what is called 'happy' for years; everything I touched brought me discontentment...everything bored me in a very short time and in fact I did not find myself....For the last seven years, I have been spiritually blind....Now I feel I am in sunlight, with the energy of many....Love in all its glory has intoxicated my heart; my

heart can never be closed. I am drunk at the fountain of Joy and eternal Beauty. I am God-intoxicated.

And to Lady Emily, he declared the labor that he sets himself for a lifetime: "I am going to help the whole world to climb a few feet higher."

So the new Buddha left his palace. But now the myths diverge significantly. For the original Buddha spent six years experimenting with ascetic disciplines before achieving his wisdom of nonattachment under the Bo tree. For Krishnamurti, this wisdom flooded him, so to speak, on the palace steps. But he was still in his royal domain, where occult masters held sway, where those he loved the most gave unquestioning obedience to them and were also prepared, any day, to turn all their allegiance to him. At the end, the flood of light consumed all his connections to the kingdom. But this end was seven years away.

A battle within him, however, began at once.

For two such imperatives — an inward immensity, pouring like a cataract, and the gigantic, unrelieved worldly expectations and commitments — these two cannot coexist in the mind and heart. They must take their turns onstage; and the one entering always traumatically interrupts and dislocates the one present. So began many episodes which Krishnamurti called "the process." It came on with paroxysmal headaches, the same as ushered in his great illumination, and signifying a similar pressure and upheaval at work in him. Then, amid severe pain, raving, exhaustion, and semiconsciousness, a dissociative state occurred: "the adult" left him, and he reevoked long-forgotten scenes from childhood, "such as when I was ill with my mother how I used to rest on her stomach!!, the beggars we used to feed & how I used to be waked up by her...." Sometimes the dissociation was in reverse form. The student of Theosophy was painfully taken over by "a kind of flame," like the mystic's light. Without any analysis of the experiences himself and never seeking medication for their pain, Krishnamurti accepted them as a kind of required preliminary to his freedom. He was also writing a prose-poem: "I have gazed into the deep pool of knowledge and many reflections have I beheld. I am the stone in the sacred temple, I am the humble grass that is mown down....I am the lover and the very love itself."[5] The tone is earnest...and rather lusterless. But in his Theosophical circle, his voice was sharpening. To Lady Emily: "You are like people in a dark room waiting for someone to turn on the light for you, instead of groping...and turning it on for yourselves."

Meanwhile Nitya, after years of periodic medical treatment, was worsening. Distraught, Krishnamurti was told, by an occult Master in a dream, that Nitya would be well. He was convinced; he knew that Nitya was essential to his life work. Then, in 1925, as he was traveling by ship from Italy to India with Mrs. Besant and several other Theosophists, a telegram arrived from Ojai. Nitya had died. Krishnamurti broke down; in delirium, he spoke the native Telegu of his childhood which he no longer knew in his waking life. But within a few weeks the pendulum swung, and his recovery brought him a new depth of root in himself. He was in fact leaving his old identity behind, and with that, he began to feel "like a shell — absolutely impersonal." The "process" now was occurring only occasionally, with much less force. He told Lady Emily and Mrs. Besant that he wanted to "give up everything," that he was waiting for the right moment with "an eager patience."

To Mrs. Besant's distress, he chose against the occult wing in Theosophy. But amid factionalism in the ranks, she stood squarely behind him and decided indeed that the time for her own public testimony had come. In her eightieth year, in 1927, she announced to the Associated Press of America: "The Divine Spirit has descended once more on a man, Krishnamurti....The World Teacher is here." She would love him, as she always had, however he chose to present himself; she who had raised him would be his "devoted disciple"; love admits of dissent, even from what is most precious to the one loving. And soon she was sorely tested. For to Krishnamurti belonged the aphorism of Gide: "We develop in an atmosphere of sympathy...we only come to know ourselves in opposition."[6] He will love her too; his love for all his inner circle is unshaken. But his own dissent has grown to the core. The World Teacher now began the Transvaluation of all Theosophical values. "You must become liberated not because of me but in spite of me," he told his followers at Ommen Camp, in Holland (and by now, internationally, the Theosophists numbered 45,000 people).

> You must not make me an authority. If I become a necessity to you, what will you do when I go away?...Do you think Truth has anything to do with what you think I am? You are not concerned with the Truth but you are concerned with the vessel that contains the Truth....Truth comes like a burglar, when you least expect it.

He, in fact, was burglarizing their Truth; he knew he risked losing everyone; but he had no choice. For he had seen to the bottom of the myth of God's authority, in which he had played the leading role. He had seen clearly as *something else* had grown quite clear, something the vacant-eyed boy long ago had dimly known, a primal, indwelling truth which all the layers of his later experience had not snuffed out:

> I may not hope from outward forms to win
> The passion and the life, whose fountains
> are within.[7]

Coleridge's fountains cut the last cord binding him to Theosophy. In 1929, at Ommen Camp, he dissolved the Order of the Star, and before over 3,000 of its members, heard by thousands of people more over the Dutch radio, he declared his first sweeping message, his own Sermon at Benares,[8] to be varied, amplified, and reapplied during the next fifty-seven years:

> I maintain that Truth is a pathless land, and you cannot approach it by any path whatsoever, by any religion, by any sect....If an organization be created for this purpose, it becomes a crutch, a weakness, a bondage, and must cripple the individual, and prevent him from growing, from establishing his uniqueness, which lies in his discovery for himself of that absolute, unconditioned Truth....You can form other organizations and expect someone else. With that I am not concerned, nor with creating new cages, new decorations for those cages. My only concern is to set men absolutely, unconditionally free.

Like the Buddha, he was striking down all external forms. Unlike him, he was not offering any "right path" at all (we shall discover his reasons); and the tone of revolutionary manifesto is his own. His language would grow more psychological; his audiences (which in fact increase with the years) would become more widely defined as Everyman seeking the truth. But the urgent, provocative tone will remain.

Only a few of Krishnamurti's texts have been written down by him: a slender book, *Education and the Significance of Life*; three short volumes, *Commentaries on Living*, which were prompted by his great admirer, Aldous Huxley; a *Notebook* that he began on impulse when he was sixty-six and kept for seven months; and a briefer *Journal*, twelve years later, suggested by Mary Lutyens, daughter of Lady Emily. The *Notebook* is exceptional for its many accounts of ecstatic emptiness. But the bulk of his printed work is recorded talks, given without notes and without mental rehearsal, always the fruit of the moment, *ex tempore*, he would say, in the literal sense. And their subject matter, which permeates too the books I have mentioned, is seamless. It is a portrait of how we rig our lives into a trap, and of how the rigging can be undone. We have already heard this theme in my opening quotations. We shall hear it more fully, with varied perspectives, in the seven short chapters I shall discuss from a collection of talks, compiled at his request by Mrs. Lutyens and titled by him, *Freedom from the Known*. I shall bring in, too, other passages of his which develop the points at hand.

There is a striking difference between Krishnamurti's style and that of our previous writers. We do not face abstract logic, as in Bateson; paradox, as in Lao-tzu; ambiguity, as in Kafka; philosophical subtlety, as in Buber. We face clear statements. "The man who is hoping is dying." "All thought leads to sorrow." Wait a moment! Did I say: clear? I have already called Krishnamurti "provocative." But isn't the first effect of these words something more — isn't it *offensive*? They lack entirely Rilke's tone of warm encouragement, or the winning jubilation of Blake, or the permissive grace of Lao-tzu. We are listening to a voice that, even as it enlarges what it has to say, deliberately and continually brings not peace but a sword to all settled convictions — our convictions about the nature of our troubles, about cure for the troubles. To hope is to die? Is this some kind of joke? — as though he has taken Dante's inscription above the gateway to Hell and reset it at the entrance to Heaven. At the least, it's a shock. And the man who shocked the Theosophists in the 1920s did not stop shocking audiences throughout his life.

I shall take this at face value myself and — what wasn't needed with our other writers — raise questions at once with his text when doubts or objections strike me. For how can one avoid the questions? "Freedom is not choice." "All effort to meditate is the denial of meditation." Is he exaggerating for effect? Am I being played with, or simply misunderstood? Just what does he mean? How does one make any use of it?

Freedom from the Known: the title itself is ingratiating and lyrical; the alliteration, the long vowels and the nasal consonants resonate. But still...I pause at the word *known*. "Freedom from the familiar" — a much less beautiful phrase admittedly — seems more apt. I recognize in it an obvious pleasure; in fact it's the slogan of profitable tourism. And yet even here — I know I welcome the sound of English when abroad; the sight of an old friend is especially piquant. Freedom from the familiar — this, too, only to a point. Wait a bit. Can the idea, freedom from *the known*, actually be realized? In remote western China, *I*, at the least, will speak English *to myself*. Probably I will think more often of my family than I do at home. The stranger the scene, the dearer the past. Really, I must admit: his attractive title has an overtone of dread.

And yet Krishnamurti has used the phrase precisely to say: "For freedom: no less than this." For when we depend on the known, he goes on, "we are second-hand people...the result of all kinds of influences and there is nothing new in us, nothing that we have discovered for ourselves; nothing original, pristine, clear....Is there not a different approach altogether?" Well, if I think of freedom as a journey, it will lie far beyond western China too. It is, rather, like wilderness retreats which Buddhist students and shamanic initiates undergo, an aloneness free of the tarnish of learning, inviting, instead, destruction — the "destruction of what has been," Krishnamurti says, and an austerity "not...of ashes and sackcloth but that casual and unpremeditated indifference to the things of this world, its virtues, its gods...."[9] Free of the carapace of morality, as free of censors as of guides. And just in this peril of aloneness, at the very edge of the dread that I have sensed, just there, he tells us, is energy. And "[I]s not that energy itself the mutation?...That energy itself produces the radical inward revolution. You do not have to do a thing about it." In its full nonaction, it is Lao-tzu's *wu-wei*, the collected energy of being just, and justly, attentive; of looking at one's experience with the neutrality of a camera; of being totally open in the moment, as once we were when small children. For it is the way a child says to a stranger a welcoming "Hello," without any expectation, or a friendly "Goodbye," without any holding on.

But how is this radical freedom — no strings at all attached — really possible? We have heard the logic before, at the start, in Krishnamurti's discussion of the problem of loneliness. It is worth hearing, at length, again:

> I see a lovely cloud, or a mountain clear against the sky, or a leaf that has just come in springtime, or a deep valley full of loveliness and splendor...or a beautiful face, intelligent, alive, not self-conscious....I look at these things with intense delight and as I observe them there is no observer but only sheer beauty like love. For a moment I am absent with all my problems, anxieties and miseries — there is only that marvelous thing. I can look at it with joy and the next moment forget it, or else the mind steps in, and then the problem begins; my mind thinks over what it has seen and thinks how beautiful it was; I tell myself I should like to see it again many times. Thought begins to compare, judge, and say, "I must have it again tomorrow." The continuity of an experience that has given delight for a second is sustained by thought.
>
> It is the same with sexual desire or any other form of desire. There is nothing wrong with the desire. To react is perfectly normal. If you stick a pin in me I shall react unless I am paralyzed. But then thought steps in and chews over the delight and turns it into pleasure...[and then] into memory and memory is then nourished by thinking about it over and over again.

So too, fear arises with thought, the fear of the loss of pleasure;
and then pain, when the pleasure is actually lost.

On the other hand, he continues,

> [T]o end pleasure...which is to end pain, you must be totally attentive to the whole structure of pleasure...not condemning it or saying it is right or wrong...not cut[ting] it out as monks do...never looking at a woman because they think it is a sin and thereby destroying the vitality of their understanding — but seeing the whole meaning and significance of pleasure. Then you will have tremendous joy in life. You cannot think about joy. Joy is an immediate thing and by thinking about it you turn it into pleasure. Living in the present is the instant perception of beauty and the great delight in it without seeking pleasure from it.

Yes, I feel the breadth, the challenge of his vision. To uproot pleasure: "no less than this." And I sense the surge of energy in him which sustains the vision, energy that is a "mutation." But this summons of his to look, attend, "be totally attentive," doesn't it face me with — a labor of Hercules?

I pick up on this mightiness, the range of it, in his special use of words. They have an expanse of meaning in which traditional usages are lost to view. "Joy," he tells us, "is something entirely different from pleasure." But usually we think of the two together. His own distinction, it's true, is plain. He has portrayed pleasure as "the demand for the repetition of pleasure." It is a kind of addictive "fix" that one constantly fears to lose and seeks to restore. Yes, I know that as a component of daily life. And I see how his own mind equates pleasure in sex, money, religious faith...Faith? Is this, too, only pleasure? Worse than that, he tells us; it is a disruptive pleasure. "Faith invariably breeds violence." Wait a moment! Fanaticism, yes: that leads to violence. And to corruption: there has been the grotesquerie of Holy Wars and of Bible Belt empires. But can he mean *all* religious faith? Where is the violence in St. Augustine's "It is my faith that calls to you, Lord"?[10] What is schismatic in Sir Thomas Browne's faith, embracing "wingy mysteries in divinity and airy subtleties in religion"?[11] What of Mother Teresa's "Faith, to be true, has to be a giving love"?[12] Surely these people, these usages, speak of an integrating force, not the covetousness of pleasure.

Again, Krishnamurti: "There is no such thing as freedom of thought. It is sheer nonsense." It is? How is he using words here? — for now his critique sounds only flip, dismissive. What kind of thought? Of course, when thought harnesses and categorizes our responses, in the ways that he describes, it isn't free. But what of the "free thought" that mankind values, compared with church-controlled or state-controlled thought? That isn't "sheer nonsense." And what of generative ideas? "All men are created equal"; or Gandhi's non-violent resistance; or Bateson's Double Bind to account for schizophrenia — ideas that have led men and women, for a while at least, to see, feel, and act in new ways. Well, yes. It is true: fresh ideas wilt quickly, like fresh joys. We know "the land of the free" to be the home of prejudice and exploitation. India, after Gandhi, is full of bloodshed. Schizophrenics, after Bateson, are buried more than ever under drugs. I see a central point after all in his description. The sheer tonnage of 19th century genius, from Goethe through Tolstoy and Nietzsche, did nothing to avert the wreckage of the 20th century. Wisdom, alas, isn't transmissible, like cultural customs and the learning of a language.

And even if great thought has availed "for a while," that is not Krishnamurti's concern; he would raise us, as he has said, a few feet higher "completely," "totally." In fact, we make him wonder if we are "serious" as we listen to him; he uses this word often. If we were *serious*, we would be sweeping out our Augean stables — and yet, I know I am serious; though, admittedly, I'm not *single-minded.* I'm at times fearful, confused, irresolute, impatient, and stamped with the seven deadly sins. And isn't all this our general problem? Far beyond matters of word usage lies the question: How, with hands that our mortal frailty is always dirtying, do we wash ourselves immortally clean?

Christianity has named this frailty Original Sin. "Original" not only as it stems from the myth of origins, our ancestors in Eden, but because it begins afresh with each new Eve and Adam of us. Out of curiosity, defiance, and greed, we disobey almost as soon as we have caught our first breath. We can be, at any age, benevolent and tender, and yet always, with all its partialities and flaws, our self-concern comes first. As we mature, we understand that each new moment is brand-new, but somehow our home, our friends, our freshest tasks and dearest ideas manage to get old. We sense a great depth in us, and are often impervious to it. The loftiest motives and feelings mix turbidly with trivia. As we grow older, we console ourselves that it is never too late to realize how late it is, but still we remain slothful. With God's grace upon us, the best that we can say (in Auden's lucid verse) is:

> Though written by Thy children with
> A smudged and crooked line,
> The Word is ever legible,
> Thy meaning unequivocal...[13]

Buddhism, it is true, doesn't accept this inescapable human defect. The line need not be smudged and crooked. For a permanent self, with its permanent deficits, doesn't exist in the first place; it is a fiction. The truth we live with is that of a body and a mind subject to impersonal laws of desire and satiety, and to continual change ending in death. And the Buddha, out of his own discovery, gives us a psychological "middle path," avoiding extremes both of self-indulgence and self-denial, and advocating a practice of meditative awareness to ripen inner peace. The "middle path" is the best use of our mind and body as they have been impersonally designed. Not, through it, that we "rise above" confusion, attachment, and uncleanness. But when these arise in us, we simply let them go. That is our freedom, our "original virtue," beyond the stain of original sin.[14]

And for Krishnamurti, in the same way, awareness is freedom. His Buddhistic phrase is "choiceless awareness." For choice means selectivity, and this awareness is complete. But for him, there can be no path at all, precisely because a path followed is an authority obeyed, and all the meshes of conditioning lie in that landscape. He will only say: "Behold!" And at once, when we do, the divine "otherness" (a word he uses often)[15] is seen *not* through a glass darkly. It is face to face. His vision — the vision he means by "Look! Attend!" — is always that of epiphany, the clear revelation which illuminates the whole scene as by a lightning flash; which, dispensing altogether with faith's "I believe," exclaims, "I see!" It is as epiphany that we know immediately the truth that makes us free; the unconditioned truth that shows "the whole structure" in which pleasure, which is fleeting, leads always to fear of its loss and pain at its loss. Who, grasping this, could want that state of entrapment and sorrow? We hear Blake echo: "Truth can never be told so as to be understood, and not be believed."

Yes. But this epiphany: how will I, within my conditioning....? — Krishnamurti's hand rises in warning. To all objections, he has a simple phenomenological reply: "Don't believe me. Please, just look. Let us look further at your fear."

And fear is perhaps the best thing to look at now. For unlike pleasure, we want to draw away from it. Perhaps, then, from a little distance, we can also turn and observe it — observe, perhaps, even with fearless dispassion. Very well. I am afraid, then, of what? Of everything that endangers my security. Physical threats to survival naturally will cause fear, but in our daily life we suffer more from something else, from *Angst*, a pervasive psychological fear, which in turn can imagine physical threats that don't exist. "What we are really seeking," Krishnamurti observes, "is a satisfaction in which there is no dissatisfaction at all." But each new moment is literally an unknown, ending in the assured obliterative unknown of death. We've already seen how fear arises from the prospect of the loss of pleasure. But the canvas of potential losses is much larger: the success and acclaim I want in the world, the control over others and over myself. Only a moment ago I was nursing a particular fear: that "depth of conditioning" must intercept the fullness of epiphany. But wait! Isn't this, again, my *thought about* conditioning? Does *thought* perhaps enter, each time that I am afraid? "Suppose, tomorrow..." "What will I do if he, if she...?" "How will I ever solve...ever see clearly that...?" And am I not seeing clearly now: how all my fear is bound up with "all the mutterings of yesterday," as Krishnamurti puts it; how it arises, as he says, in "the movement from certainty to uncertainty," since it is *certainty* that I would cling to? Isn't my awareness illuminative now just because it *isn't* "full of thought" — because, rather, moment to moment I am staying in touch with myself? "Such awareness," notes Krishnamurti, "is like living with a snake in the room; you watch its every movement, you are very, very sensitive to the slightest sound it makes." There is no interval open for fear when you are wholly watching; no place for the demand of answers when you continually "live the question," as we have heard Rilke say. You stay, rather, with the Negative Capability Keats saw in Shakespeare: "when a man is capable of being in uncertainties, mysteries, doubts, without any irritable reaching after facts and reasons."[16] Krishnamurti's own dry sentence, to the same point, is: "The moment you have a conclusion...you are finished."

"A snake in the room" — here is one image of epiphany! And obviously it keeps us from speculative thought: who cares about where the snake came from or whether it is a good symbol for the Unconscious? And certainly it keeps us in the present: who cares how old the snake is, or what it may do tomorrow? "Thought," Krishnamurti points out, "is of course necessary for daily living. It is the only instrument we have for communication, working at our jobs, and so forth." But for inner freedom, is it any different from "quaint metaphysical opinions," which, Coleridge observed, "are like playthings by the bedside of a child deathly sick."[17] Time and memory, too, are required in the plans and schedules of daily life. And practical advances develop through planning — technological improvements, control over diseases, and the like. But biological growth over time, and spontaneous conversation, and time in drama and music — all this is time by a different measure, it is always moment to moment. One cannot with these, as with the worries and scheming of psychological time, jump several steps either backward or forward, recalculating the past, replanning the future. Further, Krishnamurti notes, thought *creates* psychological time. For this time is only "the interval between idea and action." When there is no idea, the interval disappears. And then the action of the moment is timeless; it is in no way a "canned product" from the past, a rehearsed speech or calculated maneuver. It comes from an emptiness to which nothing but death compares. And so he says, "You must die, not physically but psychologically, inwardly...To die is to have a mind that is completely empty of itself, empty of its daily longings, pleasures, and agonies. When there is death, there is something totally new." This vision leads, finally, to his title phrase. For death, the unknown, and life come together. "Freedom from the known is death, and then you are living."

As he speaks, I feel again the expanse of the words, his openness to the moment, the abandon in which self and its seekings have no place. It is the state that he calls love, passion — "but passion without motive — passion that is not the result of some commitment or attachment," love that is "the innocent mind, and the innocent mind can live in the world that is not innocent." There is great purity here, the purity we have already heard in his sense of nature when he evokes "a lovely cloud," "a deep valley," the purity of a fire in which, like Siegfried's sword, love is smelted and shaped innocent forever. "Can't you fall in love and not have a possessive relationship?" he challenges us. "I love someone and she loves me and we get married — that is all perfectly straightforward and simple, in that there is no conflict at all....Can't one have that without the other, without the tail, as it were, necessarily following?" Can we? For here we deal with the mix of experience we know in all those hours that we live between a pure dawn and pure sunset, amid the noise, the insults, the pressures of daytime. In that mix we're often foolish and indolent and base. And love, when we feel its immensity, comes to us all the more with its fragility, so that in honor we're bound to say: "Exactly at our best, we don't mate like fireflies on the wing, but with a pledge of hearts. And disloyalty to the pledge by one person will be felt by the other as hurt, treachery, loss. Yes, the tail necessarily follows. It's with the tail that the kite really flies."

And yet, also, this mixture is no grounds for turning meanness into a virtue. Love doesn't become productive through jealousy; nor can it be claimed as a right. Its freedom, the benediction of otherness, isn't to be "had" at all. It comes about in all that we give up: authority, demand, the claims of reason and pride. The benediction is destruction, and therefore new. From the *Notebook*: "As a terrific storm, a destructive earthquake gives a new course to the rivers, changes the landscape, digs deep into the earth, so [the benediction] has levelled the contours of thought, changed the shape of the heart."

Yes, I follow him. But my heart...what earthquake...just how...?

But again he warns: "Don't ask. Observe. Observe, in the first place, where your own observing leads you. Where 'you' go."

And here Krishnamurti reaches the central point of his vision. "When you give your complete attention — I mean with everything in you — there is no observer at all." We have heard this point before, it is implicit in his "Behold!" and "You must die." But now he will make much more of it. For epiphany dispenses not only with the "I" of "I believe." It dispenses too with the "I" of "I see." There is only "Seeing." Of course, a separate "I" exists, made up of the selections and judgments I place on experience; and like thought, like memory, it has practical uses. I do not interrupt you when you speak; you and I communicate and cooperate as daily life requires. And it can seem, from the nature of our grammatical forms, that the separate "I" is an ultimate reality. We have subject, predicate, and object. We say, "I see the tree," as though the observer and observed are distinct. In this case, once again, the *phenomenon* does have separate components which we can analyze out, as we know that a symphony uses many musical instruments. But the *phenomenology* of the moment, of hearing the symphony, seeing the tree, is different. My ears are only "symphony-filled"; my eyes are only "tree-ing." So, too, when in passion "I forget myself," I am no longer at all separately there to "remember myself." Certainly, in orgasm "I" don't "own the experience"; only the experience exists. "There is only the state of attention which is total energy," Krishnamurti says. "This awareness is not," he goes on — lest our minds tumble into a familiar groove —

> This awareness is not a process of identification with the observed. To identify with something is fairly easy. Most of us identify with something — with our family, our husband, our wife, our nation, and that leads to great misery and great wars. We are considering something entirely different and we must understand it not verbally but in our core, right at the root of our being. In ancient China before an artist began to paint anything — a tree, for instance — he would sit down in front of it for days, months, years, it didn't matter how long, until he *was* the tree ....That total silence in which there is neither the

observer nor the thing observed is the highest form of a religious mind.[18]

Yes, I see: oneness made plain, and named the "religious mind." But, again...just a moment. I was speaking, a few minutes ago, about Krishnamurti's sense of purity, compared with the turmoil I know in everyday life. Isn't the real point that there are *two* levels: the category of conditioning that Bateson speaks of, the basis for my standards, my continuity in experience, my personal honor, where awareness is always partial and, in the Christian sense, "fallen"; and this other level of the unconditioned, where one eats when hungry, sleeps when tired, and "I" am as variable as circumstance? Yes, here one can say, with Krishnamurti, that the truth has no path, no more than a butterfly in its flight pursues a path. Like him, one can say that this awareness is a meditation which "is not following any system...has no technique and...no authority...The meditator is entirely absent, for the mind has emptied itself of the past."[19]

But what of the mind at the level of "I"? Not the mind of epiphany but the mind that runs in streams of consciousness, fragmentary, digressive, reticulated? The mind of "free associations" which are, precisely, the associations of one's conditioning. And here is a curious fact. I glimpse this mind in its full nature, "its whole structure," as Krishnamurti calls on us to do; I glimpse it during just that kind of methodical meditation that he warns against.

Meditation, as formal practice, is indeed the extraordinary psychological discovery of ancient India, comparable in its facilitation of self-knowledge to the advance in culture made by man's discovery of the wheel. Indian yogis long ago found out that, by letting the mind be quiet, for instance through watching the flow of thought, feeling, and sensation, it can fully open to itself, and with "onlooking equanimity" one can see all things, within and without, come and go of themselves, in their natural impermanence. So Buddhist meditation teaches, utilizing practices of sitting and slow walking. But ordinarily the initial experience of these is far from one of calm. In my first hours of a Buddhist retreat, during one-half to one hour sessions of sitting and walking, my mind reveals itself as a multilevel freeway system jam-packed with cars at every level. (Thus, so to speak, on piers of reinforced concrete, "the whole structure of desire.") In a few days, I become a thick book to myself. Panic even may supervene, a terrible concentration of all my normally diffused self-doubt, so that the simple instruction, "Just pay attention to your breathing," turns wildly into, "But my God! I don't know *how to breathe*!" Surviving that (for I notice that I am only failing to exhale; when I let the air go out, breathing takes care of itself), surviving all the inner congestion of thought, slowly I begin to settle. In several days I begin to see themes in the book, my personal catalogue of preferred worries, judgments, demands. I can actually follow my breathing for a while without distraction, one breath at a time. I think: "Meditation is training in doing one thing at a time. What intravenous drip is to the body — moment-to-moment continuous nourishment — this is to the mind and heart — a sort of intraneuronal drip." The freeway traffic starts to flow a little and to clear a bit. I grow amused at my usual overvaluation of my problems.

Clearly, for me this kind of meditation, though a prescribed discipline, is not the "isolating, self-enclosed activity" which Krishnamurti cautions me against in all discipline. I confront, rather, what I often avoid, and in the acceptance move toward that uncultivated life in flower which is his own way of defining meditation. For so he speaks of it. It is the mind being open, unstructured, still, "neither resisting nor avoiding...capable [then] of perceiving what is true, and it is the truth that liberates, not our effort to be free."[20]

Yes, once again now, I hear him. Is it because I veer so much between mental congestion and stillness, between "I" and self-abandon, that his own stillness seems at times to come from a great distance? Well, even so, he is audible and clear. "You cannot invite the wind but you must leave the window open." So his book reads in its last pages. Yes, method in itself will not free me, even the best method of meditation. Receptivity will. He adds at once: "Which doesn't mean that you are in a state of waiting." Yes, I understand that. Passivity will not free me. Passion will. He adds again: "It doesn't mean you must open yourself to receive. That is another kind of thought." Yes, I understand. *Premeditation* (ah, there's a nice pun!) — yes, premeditation can't free me. But...but...again I pause. I notice my pun, don't I? *Thought* has gone into my noticing. And don't I *choose* to open the window he tells me to leave open? Don't I choose the meditation practice that leads me to understand what he means by "choiceless awareness"? So, naturally enough, the self-acknowledging mind, the mind of choice, the conditioned mind aware of its alternatives, comments and judges, reasons and asks. And, again, I hear something from a distance, audibly, clearly, but not, this time, his phrases; for his gift, most of all, is to evoke my own words from the deep tone of his that resounds. Of course there is a vital freedom to choose. But at the level of the unconditioned, there is the freedom *from* choice. It is the freedom to be undesigning. So I let go the known, and the closure of the known. Then living — it is no longer even "my" living — is new. Then, moment to moment, just in its being not known, it is disclosure.

Krishnamurti is a *naif*, in Schiller's sense: a man of "tacitly creative life, serene spontaneity of activity," great by "inner necessity [and] eternal unity with [himself.]"[21] We ourselves now see why hope, to him, is deathbound: it trails away from the one life which is in the present, just as the middle-class slogan, "Let's make wonderful memories," unmakes life as full presence. We see, too, how "thought leads to sorrow"; thinking, we pine for what is not. We see how freedom is *not* choice; freedom is just Schiller's "inner necessity." And we sense the immaculate clarity of human development as Krishnamurti envisions it. One moves toward one's talents, powers, and wisdom as one physically grows and becomes sexual, with a kind of hormonal certainty. One is in fact always at the point that Kafka always was seeking to reach, the point where "there is no longer any turning back." So, too, one disengages at once from all retarding and irrelevant claims on one's attention. One disengages explosively, breaking away all surrounding husks; Krishnamurti's typical words, "explosion" and "destruction," harken back to the violent experience in 1922 that began his spiritual life and that always give a fiery sweep to his accounts of "stillness," "ecstasy," "meditation."[22] But it is in the abandon to these, finally, that one is moving in one's natural element. The picture, on the whole, is like the one Thomas Mann's fictionalized Schiller draws of Goethe: "deft...blithe, and carefree..an effortless and gushing spring."[23] And, of course, it's a picture that challenges all our customary notions of human life, of ineradicable conflict, of ambivalence and anxiety and the ambiguity of motives, of the sadness of change and the constancy of folly, of the need for striving, effort, and ideals. In all these ways it is, exactly as he intended, revolutionary. And yet, for all its divergence from our world of frailty and labor and compromise, we find him also astonishingly apt in psychological analysis. The sense he makes is the sense we use. And he alerts us to a wholly new significance in it.

For his vision is not, with all its purity, an idealization. Or rather, he sees the ideal, the perfection, in our actual predicaments. As an infant, in a spasm of discontent, will relax at once in an embrace, so our hand, clenched in conflict, loosens when we give our loving attention to it. We can discover this in a moment; it is "actual fact," as he says over and over, "not a philosophical or mystical affair." His own language, it is true, begins in philosophical concepts. But he develops these into the psychological shape that we see our lives to have. *Thought*, as he discusses it, is the straitjacket which promotes *anxiety*, as we use the term: the sense of inner menace that dogs our restrictive acceptance of ourselves. The *security* we seek through thought, as he describes it, is the same *compartmentalizing of inner life*, familiar to us in obsessive work, in escapist pleasures devoid of heart, or in narcissistic self-inflation, by which we cut ourselves off from our vulnerability. The same *drive for security*, sealed, as he says, by knowledge, memory, tradition, involves us in the *mechanisms of defense* that psychoanalysis portrays: repression and regression, called forth to control anxiety, and superego strictures, the condemning judgments meant to subdue the flow of experience we refuse to permit in ourselves.[24] The *observing ego* he speaks of, "half alive," merely the storehouse of knowledge, memory, tradition, is the *conditioned personality* we know, which attends only partially to the present and carries past habits blindly into the future. And as to his very word, *thought*: haven't we too found that *analytic thought, conscious rationalism*, never brings integration? That moving to the level of preconsciousness — as he says, "dying to memory...[to reach] something the brain can't understand" — that then we are free from known conditionings; in the timeless arena where life regenerates? Isn't all therapy, in the sense we get of it from him, *crisis therapy*, occurring only in the present where the crisis is? Effective only in the present, with that "total energy...of attention" which loosens the clenched fist? The fist "should not" even be different. No "should's" apply to living. It asks only, like a beggar at the door, to be accepted as it is.

Krishnamurti takes another step. He calls this attention of acceptance "religious." It is religion in no sense doctrinal and in no sense "transpersonal." For doctrine is the partialness of conditioning; and there is no one "personal," in the first place, to transcend. There are only moment-to-moment phenomenological states. Unlike Lao-tzu, he gives us no cosmology. There are only the moment-to-moment states. And unlike both traditional religions and interpretive psychology, he accepts no symbols. When the observer and the observed fuse in one energy of attention, what reality is there, for instance, to dream interpretation, which depends on the observer analyzing, through the distance of memory, his observed dreams? The dream symbols may be verifiable from other recalled dreams and from correlations with waking experiences; but how will any of that help with changing moment-to-moment states and their ever-new crises? "When the house is on fire," he typically asks, "do you argue about the color of the hair of the man who brings the water?"

So he challenges us; and his clarity has evoked respect from various psychiatric groups. In the summer of 1946, Dr. Ben Weininger brought Krishnamurti to Washington, D.C., where he gave a series of four talks to forty mental health professionals, including Harry Stack Sullivan, Frieda Fromm-Reichman, Edith Weigert, and David and Margaret Rioch. Sullivan liked his analysis of ideologies, cults, and obsessions as self-damaging attempts to control experience; Sullivan himself called these defenses "security operations" and saw them as the glue of neurotic structure. He found Krishnamurti to have a very strong sense of self, and agreed with him that "personality," as a substantive entity, was a myth.[25] In the 1970s, Dr. David Shainberg arranged for several meetings between Krishnamurti and Freudian therapists, neo-Freudians who followed Karen Horney, humanist psychologists in the style of Carl Rogers, and the interpersonal disciples of Sullivan. Time and its "I told you so" had left these disparate approaches with a sense of common need; and the therapists found Krishnamurti's call for "instantaneous" change refreshing.[26] For in all its various schools, psychotherapy may be described as a kind of supervised transition. The client needs to make a change in his life, and feels stuck. Or else he is tossed pell mell by change, and feels chaotic. The supervision he is offered by the different schools is a form of "getting things under control." But often enough it fails. Krishnamurti pointed the therapists toward an opposite kind of supervising, toward a boundless uncontrol, awareness of the novelty of the moment, immersion in the timelessness of the moment, so that the client could move through his transitions, free.

And yet, and yet...therapists have questions left to ask him. Granting the overuse, in treatment, of a gradualism that may settle for too little happening over too long a time: hasn't nature a conservative side too? People have an aversion, as Bateson says, to learning, even to learning that their house is on fire. The flame has to be almost singeing their skin. Doesn't it make sense for insights to develop reluctantly and assimilate slowly? For fears and hurts of the past to need a prolonged "working through," as the analysts say? Don't we require, in the language of Gestalt, a strengthened sense of security, both inward and in relationship, in order to stop judging and fighting ourselves and to take productive risks? Why should a human being move to a place of new freedom with less caution than an insect that carefully probes the environment with its antennae? Aren't psychological symbols, as in dream interpretation, and personal ego-ideals, such as integrity and social conscience — aren't all these useful lighthouses and buoys across the straits of living? For that matter, why not consider Krishnamurti himself, who insists there must be "no religious experts," "no religious specialists"; why not consider him, with his unusual equation of religion and psychology, to be just such a specialist? Aren't his warnings about the dangers of authority an expression of expertise? Is not his "pathless way" a clear directive to us?

In 1946, as a young man, I heard him speak for the first time. As his custom was, he invited discussion from the audience, and a man asked him to comment on the idea, "The mind as the slayer of the real." The idea is central to Indian religious thought. Krishnamurti replied: "What do you mean, Sir, by this question?" At once he addressed the problem central to him, the motive of the questioner. For is there not a "mental slaying" in our very absorption in mental slaying? Can the questioner see how he loses himself in the question? Can he watch himself, can he follow his own inner movement so closely that he stays, in a sense, still? Krishnamurti's words cast an intense light; his singleness of mind was like the widest embrace. I felt the deceptions and restrictions of the conditioned mind — the door we shut — while at the same time he held out to us the accessibility of the unconditioned — the door we can open. I saw him standing at this door with us, assured, showing us, in our own uncertainties, shutting, opening, shutting it. But his own certainty seemed to leave him less than empathic, less than trusting, about our uncertainty.

It takes, in fact, a man of just his adamant singleness to teem with contradictions. He tells us, "Die to the past"; and he asks Mary Lutyens to write his biography: perhaps his past, he thinks, might explain his inner peace. He tells us, "Live beyond conditioning"; and his continual response to many words, "faith," "thought," "ideals," "duality," "authority," is as conditioned as any middle-class American's to "Communist" and "queer." He tells us, "Face the actual fact"; but invariably he changes the "actual fact" of his questioners' words into the patterns of his own language. Apostle of nonauthority and compassionate love, he often sounds like an oppressive authoritarian. In 1968, during an interview with Huston Smith, then Professor of Philosophy at the Massachusetts Institute of Technology, the dialogue between the two men took a controversial turn. "There is *no* duality," Krishnamurti contradicted Professor Smith. "We are talking of *the one* — one energy. You and I are *not* different — clothes, the surface, yes. But..." "That is a half-truth," Professor Smith broke in. "There is multiplicity *within* unity." "No!" Krishnamurti exploded. Then, with more and more heat, silencing their conflict as by imperial decree: "Sir, you and I *are one*!" And all this without a shade of humor about the irony involved.

Are we, to put the matter at its most extreme, are we, perhaps, dealing in him with a kind of *idiot savant*? Such people, otherwise retarded, do one thing to an uncanny perfection. For instance, the neurologist Dr. Oliver Sacks described mentally retarded twins in a state hospital who can give, in a flash, one six-figure prime number after another (a prime is a number that cannot be evenly divided by any other number except itself or 1: "7," for example, or "11). Dr. Sacks gave them an 8-figure prime that he found in a mathematical table. They concentrated for something less than a minute, then smiled at him, and within an hour were swapping, presumably, 10-figure and then 20-figure primes: no books existed to confirm this, and a sophisticated enough computer wasn't available.[27] The twins, apparently, *see* the property of numbers. It is a kind of epiphany. Is Krishnamurti an *idiot savant* of the religious life, clear, so to speak, on its factors and sequences — the ending of thought, the disappearance of the observer, the unending innocence of love — but one-tracked in his gift, dulled to what lies outside of its domain? Disgruntled at audiences which, again and again, did not understand him, he would say, "Are they deaf?" It was as though they did not recognize, as he expected, his prime numbers. To him these were so clear. Was the audience, perhaps, not really interested, not serious? We have already heard him ask the question, and it was never a taunt. He *wanted* to communicate. His failure to get across frustrated him.

At the same time, he seemed to take a somewhat perverse pride in his ignorance of other religious masters. He read Rex Stout mysteries and *Time* magazine, but "to protect himself against belief," had avoided the Gospels. What artist would be reluctant to look at great paintings by another? And composers, of course, often write variations and adaptations on each other's themes. Was his view a sign of some defect? We recall the vacant-faced 14-year old boy who was below average at school. In adult life, he totally forgot his childhood. He relearned it from the stories of others, and came to speak of his remote past as though it had happened to someone else. I heard him talk this way in Gstaad, Switzerland, when he was 75; I had the opportunity to be with him at lunch. He was warm, vividly present, with shining eyes. Then his gaze grew abstract. He began recounting his boyhood life, in the third person: "the boy," he said of himself, and "he." It took me some minutes to realize I was hearing about his own experience. This was clearly no affectation. And therefore, in fact, it seemed the more odd — if not a mental defect, certainly not a normality we know. But how, then, was he to communicate well with many people who feel continuous with their own pasts?

Krishnamurti was himself quite aware of his enigmatic nature. At 25, he wrote from Paris to Lady Emily: "I am a *lusus naturae* [freak of nature]"; and the question of his being a freak preoccupied him all his life. Who else could say, "People marry because they are lonely. I am never lonely." Who else could speak, continually, of "the tremendous reservoir" within him, "but you cannot come to it, you cannot invite it." Freakishness, of course, raised a big question: perhaps, then his message of epiphany and freedom could have no general application? But he knew too — it belonged to his gift to know — the psychological scope of his message, which gave it always its clear, broad relevance. "Anyone can accept the teaching, see the truth of it," he said in his old age. "If you make 'the freak' important, it rules out everything else." As to his "vacancy": is not this a virtual prerequisite for spiritual revelation? — the "less and less" of life in the Tao; to be poor in spirit, "empty of all knowledge," as Meister Eckhart describes Christian blessedness.[28] And if Kafka, the brilliant estranged man, speaks with his ambiguities to us all, why not "vacant" Krishnamurti, with his supernormal freedom? The comparison is instructive; often enough, the two sound as one. Thus, Kafka: "The fact that there is only a spiritual world robs us of hope and gives us certainty."[29] Again: "You are the problem. No scholar to be found far and wide." The great difference between them — their differing grasp of their gifts — was the difference in their history of relationship: Kafka deficient in love, Krishnamurti abundant in love. Assuredly, his freedom has as its premise much security of love. But Kafka's wisdom of sufferance could often have stood Krishnamurti, the frustrated teacher, in good stead: "One must not cheat anybody, not even the world of its triumph."[30]

In fact, beyond his single-tracked sense of wisdom, he did have other sides, full of playfulness, warmth, charm. Seeing a queue of people around the block from Town Hall, in New York, where he was scheduled to speak, he observed drolly to Mary Lutyens: "That man on the platform must know a great deal." For if he knew anything, he knew how little knowledge had to do with wisdom. The lightness of his early days — which led him to write Lady Emily: "Everybody is very anxious to see me and talk to me and take my advice. Lord only knows why. I certainly don't" — never left him. After the publication of his *Notebook*, in his 82nd year, he decided to write, "for fun," an anonymous review of it. His piece has a Shavian sparkle; no jot of a "defective mind" here:

> I have read this book very carefully. I am familiar with the Upanishads and have delved deeply into the teachings of the Buddha. I am fairly familiar with the psychological studies of modern times....I have not found [elsewhere] the phrase, "the observer is the observed"....Perhaps some ancient thinker may have said it, but one of the most important things that Krishnamurti has found is this great truth which, when it actually takes place, as it has occasionally happened to me personally, literally banishes the movement of time. Let me add...that I am not a follower nor do I accept Krishnamurti as my guru....[31]

Sometimes his lightness was all child-innocence. In an Indian forest, he put his hand out of the car to stroke a wild tiger, "this great energy of the forest." His host quickly pulled his arm back, lest the tiger tear it off. But was this impulse of his, idiocy? Perhaps his fearlessness and ease would have cast a spell on the animal, to keep him safe. As for the childhood he had forgot, which returned in dissociated fragments during the first bad years of the "process" — didn't he, finally, with an intuitive wisdom (never mind his pronouncements about the "dead past") — didn't he give the long-ago that was still alive within him a desired hearing, when he asked his biographer to retrieve it? The "process" itself, over the years, had grown mild. It recurred as headaches that accompanied, like a background drumbeat, his illuminative states. These were with him to the end and lit up his warmth. Dying in February 1986, in his 91st year, just weeks after his first symptoms of pancreatic cancer, he kept, so a close friend said, "an exquisite, lingering tenderness."[32]

What he does not allow, in freedom from the known, is the shuttling backward. For Schiller's naif, the spring never ceases to gush. But most of us live with our earliest conditionings ineradicable; they are, so to speak, our pre-verbal mother tongue; and so the movement between conditioned response and the unconditioned remains two-way. I recall Goethe's words: "God, if we stand in a high place, is everything." That is the unconditioned. "If we stand in a low place," he continues, and here we are conditioned, "God is a complement to our wretchedness."[33] The same distinction for freedom. Unconditionally, freedom is *not* choice, as Krishnamurti says. It is the perfect peace of God's will. It is oneness with the Tao. But at the level of conditioning, to be able to choose another condition, to transplant oneself physically at will, to speak or not to speak, all this *is* freedom. And "choiceless awareness" is only the compulsive craving of the drug addict.

As to his constant insistence on the limitations of "conditioned thought": isn't he speaking, rather, of how thought can be *misused*? Clear and probing thought certainly illuminates our lives. His own thought shows us this in action...thought that challenges and stimulates us deeply. And doesn't he too show the limits of thought, when he pontificates or sounds obscure and we must wrestle hard with his meaning? We can go still further, along with him, about the limits. All thought is a form of control, partakes of Buber's *It*, has elements of manipulation and connivance. On the other hand, one cannot connive at all at *Thou*, at artistic inspiration, religious insight, or faith in another. These are "unconditioned." So the shuttle in us moves, to and fro, like shade and light, violence and beauty, death on a battlefield and the recurring song of nightingales.[34] But the shuttle is not in Krishnamurti. He is always with the nightingales.

And yet we can only admire, today, his steadfast refusal to be an authority, amid our plethora of gurus and avatars, and our glut of "8-fold paths." We know that it was Theosophy, with its occult masters, its "stages" of spiritual advancement, and its bitter internal feuds that gave him his dour attitude toward any adult religious education. But he had a definite concern, too, with the liberal education of children, before they are trapped in social conditioning. And the schools founded in his name are meant to promote and foster individual freedom. They are as much as he would offer in "right spiritual training."

For the rest, as his message echoes in our heads: "Don't settle for half. Accept. Attend. To live so is to loosen conflict and to love," we feel he has the best of things to say. And in our own vernacular we dare to add: Often, in his saying it, he has shown poor communication skills.

The problem seemed clear to me when, in 1984, for the last time, I heard him speak. He was eloquent, as ever, about our crazed attachment to pleasure, our fearful imagining of death, our actual forfeiture of life. At the end, the audience applauded. He recoiled, as though he had been shot. "Please! No!" His eyes flashed reproach as he walked quickly away. "You are applauding only for yourselves."

I wondered: Were they? Was he a pure psychoanalyst here, showing his audience its idealization of itself in him? Or were they showing him a real gratitude which he wouldn't accept?[35]

And then, a year later, at the close of a conference on psychotherapy with many leaders in the field, I noticed something. The men and women leading the conference, really fine authorities on the value of human autonomy, were giving their autographs to adoring fans. It seemed harmless enough, these mementos, small "transitional objects," as ego-psychologists say, by which we stay connected to our heroes. But then I got embarrassed. Weren't these heroes promoting their own worship? Harmless objects? And I saw, in waves of images, a little epiphany. Relics of the saints; a piece of the True Cross; Holy Wars; a dress worn by Marilyn Monroe, sold at auction for $10,000; the dress stolen, the owner ready to murder the thief. Turn the knob of veneration a little, and you kill. And then another set of images came to me. A bard chanting anonymous folk ballads, the writer unknown; Artur Schnabel performing Mozart "whom," Schnabel liked to say, "one cannot play as well as he writes"[36] — the achievement not to be mastered; Karen Blixen speaking of "ideals higher than those that can be reached"[37] — the ideal not to be possessed; a body being cremated, the form of life disappearing with life. Nothing, in these images, to venerate, to own, to keep. Six months later the newspaper carried a story: "A War Stops for Soccer." Each night, in Beirut, Shiite Moslems stop fighting Palestinians to watch on television the World Cup soccer games in Mexico. I read the story and recalled my epiphany. I thought: So the True Cross or a mere dress can cause murder. And a game can stop it. Between the relic and life winging past, isn't it obvious which is higher? And doesn't the suspended war show us what sanity we're capable of; as, in the continuing warfare, what insanity? Yes; that day of Krishnamurti's "poor communication," wasn't he saying quite clearly: "Be sane. Don't applaud a transitional object or an ego-ideal. When you hold on to these, you only aggrandize yourselves. And then come factions, rivalries, one ego storming another in conflict. Sanity lies beyond the self."[38]

Yes, he is demanding, with an insistence that may seem idiotic. But with his demand, we glimpse the vision, and it is credible. Sanity lies in life in itself, in its self-presentation of its own boundlessness, if we let it be, if our wishes do not scare it, like a shy squirrel, away. And can this message be told fully, from his own place of un-compromise, and not come to us full of dissent, challenge, difficulty? For such purity of intent a man we know of was heard, then crucified by his fellows, then worshipped, then ignored and distorted in the worship, and then, sometimes, again heard. That is another of our alternations.

Certainly we feel in Krishnamurti something exemplary. A youthful rebel at 90, with a natural and vigorous elegance like that of the young Keats, he still knew, like the poet, how to "burst Joy's grape against his palate fine..."[39] He had, we sense, absolute pitch for living. It stirs us, and we corroborate it where we can. His last request, two days before he died, when asked by a devoted friend what he wished for, was, "Don't let anyone spoil the teaching."[40] It shouldn't be spoiled; we have urgent use for it. It is a measure of our integrity in the world. And of course we will spoil it, again and again. He is caught in that human alternation. The wish itself, in its purity and its helplessness, is godlike.

Chapter 9

CONTEXTUAL THERAPY

To turn now from the therapeutic insights of our texts to therapy itself: I shall give vignettes from brief therapy, or from pointed moments in longer, ongoing work.

The phrase "contextual therapy" takes its adjective from Bateson's view of what is most relevant in all communication, and lights up a host of concerns important to me. It accommodates both developmental needs, for which therapy provides a *context of nurture*, and existential meanings, for which it provides a *context of values.* When I think of "a good life," I think of one richly nourished in its development with love, so that it can use its own resources to go its own way. We have seen how Krishnamurti's life reflects this course. But I think of "a good life" too, apart from its development, as imbued with certain values: integrity, compassion, readiness to persevere with tasks and to challenge limits. Thus, Kafka, in his incessant struggles and rare perceptions. These values in turn inspire continuous self-nurture, in harmony with Blake's faith in desire, Rilke's confidence in inner wholeness, the fulfillment of one's nature, or Taoist *Te,* and unrestrictive presence with others according to Buber's *I-Thou.*[1] Contextual therapy, as I am defining it, establishes standards of nurturance and of meaning, to the end that the person takes better care of himself.

Nurture, as one offers it to another, has a special quality of discretion. It is like the gentle shake that rouses a sleeper without frightening him, so that he awakens receptive rather than guarded. I am always relearning, in this respect, the power of the minimum. To begin with Ron:

Thirty-eight years old, he came to see me troubled that his life felt flat and stalled. The good-looking son of wealthy, reserved parents to whom he was close, he had worked for years in the family business and wanted now to strike out independently as a business consultant. But he couldn't get himself going. He was affable and accommodating with me, always and only reasonable. For several weeks I tried to evoke an emotion in him, any at all. I asked him how he felt about his parents, about a former girlfriend with whom he had been in therapy and who had leaned on him too much, and about his present, empty life. He gave brief, dry opinions about everything, his eyes candid but a little blank over his trim, black beard. "This is all intellectual, I know. I'm really not aware of my feelings." Finally I suggested a trance state, to help him recall scenes of significance from his past. He was afraid that he would go to sleep. I said, "You might be interested. Just listen." Then I encouraged him to relax muscle groups from head to feet, letting waves of heaviness roll down over his body as tensions ebb and his eyes close...In a few seconds his eyes did close. And he began snoring loudly. I stopped talking. He awoke at once and apologized for falling asleep. "I'm so unemotional," he said. "It feels natural. That's my real problem — that it's so natural for me to show no emotion. Many therapists have told me that." Was I fatigued by my own steady failures with him, or especially responsive myself, after attempting the trance induction? I had my moment of *wu-wei*. I said, "I've been telling you the same thing. But I've just realized something. It's natural for you to be rather level about emotions, and that's what's important. It's all right with me. Be as intellectual as you please. You needn't be at all different." He blinked, and looked at me with a new intensity. "No therapist ever said that to me," he replied. And his eyes suddenly swam with tears.

The connection here is striking: the validation of reasonableness became a validation of the heart. It is also, of course, the validation which Buber calls *I-Thou*, the acceptance of another's existence as it is. For *wu-wei* — letting things be as they are — is just what Buber is speaking of about personal relations. But he brings in another element that continually challenges all therapists: the necessity for anyone in a teaching role "to imagine the other"; that is, to feel his way into the existence of the other person more than the other does himself. "Reasonableness" is the *horror vacui* of many therapists, Gestalt therapists especially. But if a patient has lived by it, a therapist won't die of it.

I-Thou, also, gives us what Bateson calls a *system*, the dyadic system that so much of therapy is. For the "boundless acceptance" of *I-Thou* is a boundlessness that, in Gestalt terms, is "nonconfluent." The two persons don't merge (though this may at times be a client's, or a therapist's, fantasy). The communion of *I-Thou* remains, unyieldingly, a system of two persons, each with his own boundary. And so therapy has this further range of a double context: the patient brings, from past systems of his or her life, an inner biographical context of need and self-deprivation, which the context of the therapeutic system is meant to correct.

Of course, there is some struggle between the old and the new, or the therapy, as a sustained deliberate force, wouldn't be necessary. It would produce change at once, as the sun brings light. But not so.

Mona, an attractive woman in her late thirties, was forthright in managing her successful business career, but almost mute about her personal wishes. Divorced from an abusive husband she had stayed with for years, she longed to be married again and to have a family. For several months, since her unwanted isolation first brought her into therapy, she has been involved with a man she loves. "I know he loves me," she said to me. "He's mentioned marriage. But I can't get him to make any plans for it." "Do you ever bring up the subject?" I asked. "No, I don't want to push him. That's humiliating. Though he always says what *he* wants. He wants to travel to India and live in Italy. I don't know that I fit in at all." She paused. "I was like that in high school." "What do you mean?" "I said what I wanted. Then in college I faded." I thought over her words. "In college, wishes get more serious. And anyway, this is more than 'saying' what you want. It's asking for it." She shook her head. "I don't like to." "It's harder. Since you can't control what you'll hear." She paused. "I can't see anything to do." "Well, imagine asking him, 'Will you be here for me?'" She shook her head again. "*That's* the *future.*" I smiled. "So it's the wrong question. You want to be married *now*. Then imagine saying to him '*Are* you here for me?'" She looked at me blankly. "I don't know what that means." I persisted: "Never mind. Say it anyway." For the power of the therapeutic system is its new supply to the patient's old repertoire of response, always provided that the therapist imagines well just where the supply is needed. Mona had corrected my wrong idea: though she might think of "plans," her real question to the man wasn't about the future. Then, out of the power of her old self-censoring, not asking for what she wants, she didn't at first comprehend how she had corrected me — that she had a present wish. But she took my insistence in good grace; she repeated to me several times the words I suggested. And then, with great care, over the next months, she began to ask the man for things in which future plans clearly mixed with present intentions: where he and she might live (for he worked in another city); just how they would live (*not* together, she told him, if they weren't married). She became confident about expressing herself and she stopped seeing me. Six months later, I heard that she had moved to his city, married him, and was expecting a baby.

Therapeutic nurture invariably deals in a "Never mind! Do it anyway!" It cultivates Blake's "Persist"; Kafka's "No longer turn back." And the push is necessary because of the famous "resistance" to which psychoanalysis has called attention since its first days. Resistance sets the limits of emotional safety for the person. Here is where trust in the therapist, and in the system established with him, acts as a sort of *Arabian Nights* genie to make resistance permeable. Or to alter the fairy tale (and fairy tales are seemly here; for if therapy is enchanted in any respect, it is about resistance), the therapist insists gently, like the friendly woodbird that leads the perplexed Siegfried just where he wants to go.

So my attempt with Jim. He was a successful lawyer in his late forties, long very depressed about his isolated life. A bright and appealing young woman in her mid-twenties, Terry, was in love with him, and wanted to marry him. But prohibitions from his cold, dominant father in his childhood, "Don't waste your time on girls"; "don't talk back to your mother" — kept him always negative about marriage. His struggle against feeling dominated, combined with both genuine goodwill and guilty respect toward women, now reemerged with Terry, whom he took care of as a needy child, giving her a car, finding a job for her — but whom, in her request for marriage, he steadily warded off. He had a catalog of objections. She was too young for him. He wasn't sure he wanted children, as she did. He wasn't enough in love himself, and often he was indifferent to lovemaking — though he knew he "stopped himself from feeling sexual." At the same time, he was afraid of losing her. His varied complaints seemed rather like misleading clues in a treasure hunt. What wishes of his own, I wondered, were lost to view? And what did he want of me? For a few months, his tone with me had stayed clipped, his manner abrupt. "You're keeping me away too, I said." "I don't want to," he answered. "But I'm afraid." "Of what?" He began to sob violently, his mouth drawn back in the deepest grief. "You'll leave me." I said: "Tell me you want me to stay." More sobbing. "I'm afraid to." "Try it." "I can't." Then, after a moment: "All right. I want you to stay." I said: "I intend to, so far as it's in my power. You know now that I've said that, forever. Even if a car ran over me tonight, you'll know forever that I said that and meant that." He continued crying quietly. I went on, "How about inviting me to sit beside you?" "I'm afraid." "You could still do it." "I'm afraid to," he repeated. And, after a little pause, "All right. Come over." I did so, and put my arm around his shoulders. A flood of tears. "My father never did that." "Yeah. Take it easy." After a few seconds I asked, "How are you feeling?" "All right," he said. "I'm relaxing." "Do you like this?" "It's all right." "Tell me if you like it." "Yes," he said, smiling, "I like it."

He came in the next time smiling again, looked at me for a moment, then grew solemn. "I feel I'm avoiding something." "Are you?" "I don't know. I thought you thought so." "No. But you seem to be assuming something devious about yourself." "Yes. That I'm avoiding the cause...." He paused. "It's just occurring to me," he resumed. "Do you thing — no, it's hardly likely. But — could I *create* my own gloom? I always assume that I have to discover the lost key to what makes me gloomy. But is it possible that I just *create* it each time?" He was smiling broadly now. "You look much lighter," I said. "I wonder, though," he went on. "Maybe this is a way of fooling myself. So that I can avoid looking for the key." "You're a bit stuck, aren't you, with the question 'Which one is wearing the wig? Which one is the real Jim?'" "Yes." I went on: "That question too could be part, as you say, of your daily re-creation of gloom." It didn't occur to him that the key which locked him into his gloom — the prohibitive father whose love he wanted and doubted and compulsively obeyed, at the sacrifice of his own initiative — that this was one and the same with his daily creation. Nor did I care to point that out now; it was too full of thought, and he used thought against nurturance. I just wanted to turn the key the other way. I added, lightly: "Your daily re-creation is ingenious. It's your perversely neurotic approach." He smiled again. "That's good. 'Perversely neurotic.'" "Sure. They're your middle names." I went on: "What if you 'did' your 'days of gloom' another way? You know what I mean? What if you just considered, each day, what you want?" He kept the banter up. "And what will happen to my being 'perversely neurotic?'" "Nothing very promising. Tell me: How much longer will you be 'perversely neurotic' with depression?" "Three to six months," he said, smiling again. "And how do you arrive at that?" "I want to stay within the calendar year. What do you think?" "Fine," I said. "Naturally, you have to start now. If you're to have 'the new way' really *take*, in so short a time. You may want to see me a bit next year too. To assure yourself: 'Have I really done it?'"

During the next weeks his tone with me stayed warm. He thought of something new for his career: consulting to an ecology organization. Then, two months after our banter, he suggested that we focus more intensely on his relations with Terry. He knew that he loved her, but not as a soul mate. The love had begun to feel to him like a father's care for a daughter, and this wouldn't do in a marriage that, after all, he would like to have. But it was very hard to disappoint her. These matters were weighty and sad, but not depressing as he had felt before. During the last month, he said, his depression had cleared.

My banter with him had been a deliberate attempt to promote his self-nurturing. The question, "How long will you be depressed?" challenged his helplessness by assuming his authority over the course of the depression. Then the actual estimate which I asked for instituted his authority at once. I took no chances with him, and made this point explicit: "Of course you have to start now." At the same time, it didn't escape either of us that the power I credited him with lay in the context between us: his question, "What do you think?" wasn't casual, but a wish that his power be confirmed, and I was determined to confirm it. In fact, the personal path that he sought for himself was to unfold, not within a year, as I had glibly suggested, but over several years. He found another woman, much more a companion, with whom he began to assert his wishes much more freely. I remained with him the kind of father who, staying present, puts the son's interests first.

Long-term therapy is based on the depth of a patient's self-nurture that is blocked and yet sought.[2] Then the instances of the therapy must be prolonged and cumulative. And yet, too, Krishnamurti's observation applies: any moment, when it is fully enough felt, contains the whole scope of the therapeutic work. In a seminar I conducted with a Jungian analyst, I was especially struck by the accessibility of unconscious data — or rather, of the analytic interpretation of this data[3] — for immediate conscious use, though its assimilation took a few more years.

Using a Navajo Indian drum, the analyst, Don, struck an incantatory drumbeat for twenty minutes. The participants in the seminar remained awake but in a mild state of hypnotic trance, and while listening to the drum evoked from their unconscious a wealth of visionary experience, which we subsequently discussed. Jung has called this conscious mining of the unconscious, "Active Imagination."[4]

Antony, a tall blond 28-year-old dancer, described three visions to us. "In the first, a snake points a direction for me to take in the desert, which I love. The vision ends abruptly; then in the next vision, I am flying over the desert, with a sense of great power. The rocks and valleys below gradually look like men's bald heads and faces. They have power too, and I fear it. They threaten me. I think: I gave away my power to them."

Don: "Often the snake is a symbol for unconscious wisdom."

Antony: "This was a good snake. It was like the friend of the Little Prince."

Don: "But you didn't take its advice. You didn't walk on the earth. You flew over it."

Antony (firmly): "The advice of the snake ended the first vision. The flying in the second vision was a new thing. Then I felt my power. I knew just how to have it."

Don (again): "The snake in the first place told you 'just how' to have it."

Antony (slowly now): "You're suggesting something quite new to me. I hadn't thought of that. It's very interesting."

I: "I wonder what you're doing with Don's suggestion."

Antony: "I'm thinking it over."

I: "But how? There seems to be a resemblance between your fears of the earth people, in your second vision, and your way of taking in his words."

Antony: "What resemblance?"

I: "It's as though you feel powerful as a flyer, and you might lose some of that power if you don't keep Don at a distance. That he's powerful, like them."

Antony: "It's true, his idea seems to be only intellectually interesting to me."

I: "Yes. Only remotely interesting. You don't go out to it, or down to it. You flew over his head." (Antony smiled slightly and swallowed. Pause.) "How could you keep your power and let him, too, have power with you?"

Antony (guardedly): "That's a good question."

I: "Well, what answer do you have?"

Antony: "At the moment, none."

I: "Maybe the only answer is to *do* something. Perhaps, to say something. Like: 'I have power. And I'll let you have power too.'"

Antony: "I'll try." (He turned grimly to Don.) "Don, I've got power. And I'll let you have power too."

Don: "How does that feel?"

Antony: "It isn't easy."

I: "I believe you. What if you said the same to the earth-figures in your vision?"

Antony (pausing): "*That* feels very shaky."

I didn't insist. Powerful persons from his past probably are involved, whom he can't very well confront so quickly; and he is busy enough confronting Don and me. "All right. Let's go back to Don's suggestion. I'll restate it. 'Only by walking on the earth yourself can you learn to use your earth power.'"

Antony (after another long pause): "That makes more sense to me now."

Don: "It came from your first vision."

Antony: "And it explains the third vision. I try to leap from one mountain in the desert to another, across a lake. But I fall instead, into the lake and crash down through the water to the rock bottom. It's only after I hit the rock that I bounce back up and fly again. I had to be on the earth, in contact with the rock, to have the power for more flight."

Don: "I see."

Antony: "It's a lot."

I: "It is. You notice you dealt with Don's power at first by a pseudoagreement with him, the intellectual agreement that really was a dismissal. It was the only way, at first, that you could keep your flying power."

Antony to Don: "I'm getting clearly now what you said. It's upsetting."

Yielding oneself, as Antony did, to the dream-message is another instance of *wu-wei*. *Fusing* oneself with the message takes *wu-wei* a step further — to the identity of the observer and the observed of which Krishnamurti speaks. But for Antony this identity was clearly a troublesome thing.

He began to see me privately, and also a few times together with his wife, Kim. She is a physiotherapist, and like him, a dancer. She had been my patient before their marriage three years ago. They made a tall, slender, handsome couple, both with intent eyes and regal tilt of the head, his blond and her dark hair setting each other off. They were deeply attached, but often got embattled. When he was remote and abstracted, she grew critical and bossy. He became enraged; she withdrew. He placated her; she got stubborn. He sulked; she moved toward him; he pulled back. In this medley of distress, they came to see me, and I gave them an assignment for the next week: to write down, each day, a few things they were appreciating in each other. "For," I said, "you don't have any relationship without that." I was thinking of Rilke's "two solitudes, which protect, border, and salute each other." I wanted to establish with them, from the start of our meetings, this basic context of relevance.

They arrived the next time, written assignments in hand and full of mutual goodwill. They had kept their lists secret, and Kim listened with delight now to his appreciations. "She didn't pressure me to talk this evening. I like her smile." And so forth. Then he listened to hers: "He fixed my lunch. He stayed in bed with me an extra hour this morning." And so on. At the end he said, "I like hearing her list. But it's hard for me to accept the appreciations." I asked him: "Can you tell her, 'I like you appreciating me'?" He: "That frightens me." "What's frightening?" "I don't know." I persisted: "Can you say: 'I don't want to lose you'?" He nodded and suddenly was in tears. He whispered the words to her. She too started to cry. "I feel let in," she said. "And I'm so sad. I don't know why." "Maybe," I reflected, "because of the times you *don't* feel let in?" "Yes," she said. "So often I don't. It's as though he's on another plane. Or behind glass." "How about telling him: 'I want to be let in'?" "Oh yes!" She turned to him: "I *want* to be let in." He, now: "I'm afraid to. I'm afraid you'll see how unworthy I am." He paused. "But I guess I have to risk it." Another pause. He went on: "And sometimes you blame me. If I let you in, you could do that." She was looking at him with a sort of helpless perplexity. I said to him. "Sometimes she will blame you." "I don't want that. Then I feel no good." I asked: "Who says so?" "I do." "Yes, that's your Little Devil's Syndrome — your LDS" (a play of initials I had used with them before, reversing the initials of the drug LSD, which each of them had taken years ago). "You know," he said, "my father was always right and I was always wrong." I went on, more strongly: "And so therefore, now, you can't be criticized *at all*? That's as crazy as saying you're Napoleon Bonaparte." "Wait a minute, Stephen! Sometimes I accept criticism." "Yes. But then you don't have this problem together." "That's true." "She'll criticize you at times. I'm sorry. It can't be helped. You're not perfect for her, just like she isn't for you. You've no choice, either of you. You accept each other in As-Is condition." This was all my fatherly context-of-values talk. "Wait a minute," he repeated. "You mean if I criticize her less, I'll also criticize myself less?" I hadn't been thinking of that, but I said, "Sure." "I'm only occasionally impossible," she said. They left in good spirits, and after one more visit, stopped seeing me together.

A month later, alone with me, as he was speaking rather desultorily about his friends and his job at a city museum, I asked "Just what do you want of me?" He looked startled. "When?" "Antony! You know I'm trained in Gestalt therapy! What could I be thinking of but the incessant Now?" He laughed, but still looked perplexed. "Want — from you?" "Yes." "Well, support." I pushed a bit. "Be more specific." "What do you mean?" "That's up in the air. Support — of what?" He thought a long time. "Well, I've started kayaking. I'd like you to support my sea kayaking." "All right. That's specific; and easy for me to do. Of course I support your doing it." "I have a hard time asking for what I want," he added. I said: "And I get impatient with you." "I know. I don't like it. But sometimes it encourages me." He left, looking preoccupied.

The next time he began: "It isn't my kayaking I want you to support. It's something else." "What?" Long pause. "I want — encouragement. I *know* I'm not being specific again." But I was remembering the last time. My impatience, and his wish to see the good in it, were the flick of the whip of my countertransference and his transference. I wanted him to be, in my view, a "perfect patient," who would be as specific as I thought he should. And he didn't want me to be wrong. Kafka's words came to me: "There is one cardinal sin: impatience." Well, Antony had just mentioned "encouragement," and he'd used the word the last time too, at the end. Let *wu-wei* take over. "You're being specific enough," I said. "Keep your own words. Don't be concerned with pleasing me." "O.K." He went on slowly: "Encouragement — to be myself. To express how I feel." "I'm glad to do that." He took a deep breath. "God! That was so simple. It's simple to the point of stupidity." "It's simple — when you're in touch with it." "Yes. Usually, as soon as I have a wish for myself, I have a doubt. 'Is *that* what I want?' It's like a flash fire, and I go up in smoke." "But not now." "No. I'm walking straight ahead." I added good-naturedly: "So keep it simple, stupid." He smiled. "Now there's a mantra to walk with."

The following week he told me he had gotten a long-requested raise at his museum job. We had spoken often of his grievance at not receiving the raise much sooner, and of how he could persist with the request. It had taken a year from his first mentioning the subject to his boss to carrying through all the needed paperwork; but he had kept at it. "Next time," he said, "I'll move faster. I'll go directly to the Board of Trustees and the Department Heads. Oh, by the way. I made a special call, too, to my father in Arizona, after I got a long letter from him. It was full of his evangelizing about his Born-Again Christianity. I told him to lay off. I've always avoided telling him that, and I just came out with it. I said I had different religious ideas from him, and I'd like him to hear them some time. Do you know? He actually listened to me — I could even *visualize* him listening. And it was like one of those bald heads in that vision, only now the face *looked up at me.* It's interesting, I hadn't been thinking of my father then." He paused a while. "I think I'll come to see you every other week. It's time to let the seedling out of the greenhouse and into the weather." Two years had gone by since his visions in the seminar, and he had worked a great deal on his flightiness and his earthiness. The power of his own nature, the *Te* of Lao-tzu, had grown. I said to him: "Right. For planting in a landscape you like."

He continued with appointments during the next year. Meanwhile, he became the chief lighting engineer at the museum. Overworked, he got the administration to hire an assistant to help him. He spoke out when he felt unappreciated, and received new recognition from his colleagues for an excellent job. On his final visit to me, he said that he wanted to leave the museum and the city and establish himself as an independent lighting consultant. Then he and Kim will have a baby. "It's amazing," he went on. "I used to work so hard, years ago at school, then when I danced, then on a series of jobs: to prove that I was worth something. To show my father, of course, and of course I couldn't He has no eyes for it. I used to count on you to feel grounded and freer."

I was thinking how far he had come from needing to be treated with care. "You've changed," I said, "from being tentative to assured."

"Yes. And it isn't completely new to me. But what is new is the sense of accepting everything in my life. I don't feel compelled. For instance, I don't feel a compulsion to leave the city now. It can happen later, when it works out well. I enjoy myself here. And I'm not working in a compulsive way." He paused for a moment and then thrust both hands downwards. "It isn't just *part* of the old structure that's gone. It's been dismantled."

In Antony's therapy, I paid a lot of attention to his self-awareness, which, as Krishnamurti has said, is always awareness in the moment. The essential requirement here, the essential value, is one's full presence. In a gambling casino in Las Vegas, there is a sign which reads: "You must be present to win." This is the one standard that a casino, Gestalt therapy, and Krishnamurti have in common;[5] and it points out the special value, in therapeutic practice, of Gestalt work. All my suggested sentences, to Antony and others, were intended to enhance present awareness, though of course the sentences only succeed when, as Buber says, they "imagine the other person" well. But a second value basic to Gestalt therapy, that of adequate contact, is as fully imbued with presence and seems to me deeper even than awareness. At any rate, to my mind and taste, "awareness of the physical environment and of others," can be understood as *good contact* with them.[6] And "awareness of self," when it is full of life and not just intellectual, is precisely a heightened sense of *being in touch with oneself.* I have often been impressed by the primacy of contact in therapeutic change. A chronically depressed man of fifty, for instance, whom I had long encouraged to pay attention to details of his physical surroundings, said to me one day, after months of negativism: "I feel better. I came home from work the other night, depressed as usual. But I listened to music on the radio after dinner. That was unusual. Then I suddenly decided to take a walk. I felt the cool air. I noticed for the first time the buildings I walked by. I saw stars. It was wonderful." In the face of outward contact, when one musters it, the little devils of depression seem to withdraw. As to self-awareness, if an individual is not intellectually prone, is more the Sensation Type that Jung describes, his sense of greater presence is chiefly the sense of better contact with himself.

I saw a disorganized man in his early forties whose checkbook never balanced. He was always late to his job as a carpenter, always had too much to do, overate, and chased after young women as though he were a teenager. "You think I'm chaotic now?" he said to me, grinning. Our therapy had been underway for a few months. "You should have seen me when I *was* a teenager. But with the father I had! Can you believe that he wouldn't let me cross streets alone, when I was in high school? He still won't, and I'm 43. He has to take my arm and protect me. I hate it!" "Maybe you're still waiting for him to show his faith in you." "What do you mean?" "Maybe you're holding out and fucking up a lot, waiting for him to say, 'You can do well on your own. I trust you.'" "Of course I'd like that. But I'll never get it." "You could be holding out for it anyway." "Maybe. I doubt it. It doesn't seem the point." He continued uninterested in the point. And the therapeutic problem here, it seemed to me, didn't have to do with a poorly timed interpretation. A psychological idea didn't really engage him. But then I took it up in another form. "You keep waiting for a bus to run on a street where buses don't run." "Yeah?" he said slowly. "Maybe I do." The image captivated him. He could see it, touch it. And he liked my own faith in him: that he could bestir himself, so that his own life did "run."

He began getting to work on time. He dieted. He dated, mostly one woman. He felt a little more balanced with money. Years ago, a friend had introduced him to T'ai Chi, and very irregularly he attended classes in it. "Balanced — like this," he said to me one day. And leaping from his chair, he drew himself into the T'ai Chi position, Single Whip. He couldn't talk about the balance very well; he felt it in his body as he stood there, alert, poised, right arm extended to the side with the wrist loose. Really, he was becoming a "single whip." He took new action, too, with his physical environment. "I've changed around the furniture in my bedroom," he said to me soon afterward, his eyes shining. "It's hard to believe how much better I feel since I rearranged the bedroom furniture."

The carpenter's name was Jeff. With his shock of curly black hair, broad open face and smiling eyes, he looked in perpetual readiness for fun. Years ago, in fact, in the spirit of a prolonged party, he had conducted a six-year affair with his wife Susan, while she was still married to her first husband. Then, after her divorce, when they were spending a night together on LSD, she had said, "Let's get married." He answered, "Sure." And, since Jeff is Jewish, they drove from San Francisco to a rabbi in Reno. The rabbi looked at Susan's snub nose, suspected, correctly, that she wasn't Jewish, and inquired in detail into her family: her mother's maiden name, her father's Hebrew name. Jeff supplied the names of his aunt and uncle, and they were married. They stayed together for ten years. He went in and out of small businesses — hardware store, florist, door-to-door housewares selling; she raised children from her first marriage and worked in a dress store. Then three years ago, they separated; and with global questions in mind — "What do I want? Can I find the right woman? Have my own baby?" — he began seeing me.

By now our therapy was ending its second year. He had settled into his own business, and had one new woman in his life, Jan, a former customer whose house he had helped to remodel. He savored with me the physical details of the job: "I did a platform for her new wood-burning stove, and a quarter-circle wall behind it, using bronze Briar porcelain tile. It's fabulous. You should see it." Brief pause. "Jan is nice. She's smart and level-headed. And she's wonderful to make love to.

She's making all kinds of changes for me. She's started wearing nylons and garter-belts. It's wonderful — on the freeway, at the movies, in a Chinese restaurant. No more panty hose — where she's packed in netting like a goddamn sausage. The chemistry between us is fantastic. But..." He closed his eyes and moved his shoulders around. "There's something about Susan. She's so cute. It's special. I still love to take her dancing." He sighed. "But she makes me crazy. She belongs to this nutty Japanese Buddhist group that know nothing about politics and the real world and spend their time chanting for world peace. It's what drove me away from her. And she's absolutely sold on them. She evangelizes constantly. This group takes advantage of innocent people like her and exploits them. She's supposed to spend her little bit of money soon on a trip to headquarters in Japan. She has no idea about what they're doing to her. And she's totally dumb about the real world. She thinks Bangladesh is a rock group. I don't know what to do. I want to bring her in to talk with you." I had seen Susan a few times, at the end of her first marriage, and we had gotten on well. "If she'd like to," I said, "we can try it."

She came in with Jeff the next time. At 50, she was herself still youthful, with quick, birdlike movements, and eyes, like his, that looked ready for fun, though now they were clouded with hurt and reproach. "We've got to talk about the Buddhism," he said. She turned to me: "He's always bringing this up, more than I do." "Susan! You eat, breathe, and wallow in this crap every day!" "Do you hear how he talks to me? Just go on, Jeff. Go on. Let Steve hear it all." "I'm just trying to talk some sense into you." He turned to me himself without a pause, waving his arms. "Really, Steve, you should see them, singing their songs together, like Nazis. She's invited me to a meeting; that's how they evangelize. It's the most incredible stupidity I've ever seen." Yelling now: "And then she'll tell me how some woman in her group chanted for money and the next day she stepped across a $100 bill lying on the sidewalk. And she got it because of the chanting. That's the brainwashing they're constantly exposed to." She, to me: "This is the respect I get." "You get the respect you deserve." "Jeff, I feel very, very sorry for you. You mean a lot to me, and I wish you well. From the bottom of my heart. But you're vicious. And there's nothing left. You've trampled on everything between us."

He turned to me, tears in his eyes. "The thing is: I love her."

I asked her: "What do you make of that?"

She sighed: "He means it. That's the worst." She, too, moved with sensations moment to moment, and almost all that they could do together now was to storm. I suggested that she come and see me once, alone. Was he willing to pay for that? Yes, by all means.

She came in fact several times; the expense didn't trouble him. And she told me, more than I had heard from her in the past, about her early years. Her unmarried mother had deserted her when she was ten years old, and she grew up in a foster home, taking care of another woman's children. She had searched in her first marriage, and then with Jeff, for a sense of belonging and of peace that had never occurred. In her Buddhism she had found it. She had had recurrent hopes of a new life with Jeff. She had never wanted a divorce and in recent weeks he had been more attentive, while Jan was away. She knew she was scattered. She drank too much. She should learn to take better care of herself.

Then, during her fourth visit she said that she couldn't continue with me. Jan was back. Jeff had disappeared from view. She had no money to pay me, and she wasn't comfortable with him paying. He would only scream recriminations at her if she didn't change in the way he wanted her to. "He's been sneering at me already over the phone about my chanting more. And I know it's the best thing for my head." I said to her: "Of course you can't go on with me under the circumstances. But how about once more, in a few weeks? So we don't have to finish so abruptly." She agreed.

The next time I saw Jeff, he began: "So Susan is going to stop seeing you! Just when she was getting a little reasonable." "She can't come on your money, Jeff; not with the distance between you. And she feels there are strings attached." "She mentioned all that to me, in passing. Mostly she talked about feeling good chanting more, chanting *two hours* a day. Instead of coming here. There goes the craziness." He paused. He was sitting up straighter than before; he appeared to be more a

Single Whip than ever before. "I'll do something about the money," he said.

Then, at our next meeting: "I did it! I gave Susan $2,000.00 cash. I had it, extra." He sighed. "And I know now that I should get divorced from her. It's hard. I love her. But it's the only way, I just sense it, after our scene with you here. We can't live together. He paused. The impulsive young man seemed to have new reins. He went on, with unusual deliberativeness: "Then I thought more about money. She's much too impractical to ask for anything in a divorce settlement. But she should have something. And this is the first time in my life I have spare cash myself. Of course I want her to use the money for you. But like you said, no strings attached. I know she wants to go on this ridiculous trip to Japan. It would cost half as much if she went through a travel agency. But she has to go with her Buddhist group. Well, it's not my affair. I want to give her something, right? I said to her, 'Take the money and do whatever you want with it. It would be good if you went to see Steve Schoen. But it's yours. Take your trip if you want to.' And what does she do? She bursts out in tears. I take her to a restaurant for dinner, and she can't stop crying there too, she's so grateful. The waiter is worried, 'I'm all right,' she tells him. 'They're tears of joy.' I say to her, 'Just do me one favor. When you go to your Buddhist meeting, *don't* tell them, 'I chanted for money and I got it.' Tell them *honestly* how you got the money. That I'm offering you an advance on your divorce settlement. *Please,* be honest, for once.'" He paused. "I was glad to give it to her. But I don't know if she heard anything I said. She just kept weeping for joy."

On her final visit to me Susan looked reflective, with a quiet happiness I hadn't seen in her before. I told her so. "It's true," she said. "And I want Jeff to be happy. I feel *very* good saying that, though it's hard to lose him. But we can't be together. It's clear, I sense it. I wonder if he'll be happy with Jan. I don't think he knows what he wants." She paused. "I've been a Buddhist now for five years. It gets to you slowly. And it proves itself, more and more. Did Jeff tell you about the money he gave me? Something about a divorce settlement; I don't think about those things. But you do get what you chant for. I told them all about it at my last meeting, with the money in my hand. I've chanted so much for this trip to Japan. And now I can go. I'm chanting two hours a day now. Our big aim is world peace." She smiled warmly. "If this miracle could happen through Jeff, world peace will happen too."

It is hardly possible to speak of "awareness" here in the usual psychological sense, such as "perceiving how reality is different from one's projections." And yet clearly, in Jeff's and Susan's contact, delicate antennae began to disentangle. Accusations subsided. Each, more than before, said *Thou* to the other. Each came to wish the other well, though they faced a darkness in their loss of each other. And the therapeutic system — when I dealt with the two of them separately — promoted their *I-Thou*. It did so through strange events: she gave me up; they, each other. But such a system makes its own rules. Who can say, in this case, that it wasn't a part of the system of Susan's miracle?

Jeff's therapy continued years longer. Jan broke off their affair, and he remained for a long time caught in his pain at losing her. Eventually he settled down with an extremely pretty young woman whom he married (a small family wedding), and he has his first child, a little girl now one year old whom he adores. But his gift to Susan, as I've described it, was a specially high point in his life of which he remains proud.

The use of a psychological theory — whether one stresses awareness or contact or both or something else — is the use to which the therapist puts it. There is always a personal factor here. A few years ago, I bought a cervical pillow. It was made of foam rubber, and shaped to hold the neck forward and let the head fall backwards in an anatomically natural way. It did support my head and neck, but a little uncomfortably. Then I noticed that I could double over, roll, press, and mold into shape any ordinary pillow, so that it would conform each time to just the right shape of "cervical pillow" for me. And each time, I shaped it a little differently. That depended on just where I was lying down, at just what angle, and also on something that felt a little different each time in my head and neck. All the diagnostic and therapeutic models current in psychotherapy — for example, the analytic theory of narcissistic wounding and of character defenses to protect the wound; Sullivan's concept of a self delimited by a zone of anxiety; Bateson's idea of a balanced system with its internal coalitions; the device, in Neuro-Linguistic Programming, of accessing appropriate sensory channels in the client, visual, auditory, or kinesthetic — all these are preformed cervical pillows. They support the therapist's head and neck, but a little roughly. He must himself mold the pillow each time to just the right shape, trusting that his own head and neck each time, in the moment, know best. This trust is a Blakean leap. It establishes, in a stroke, its own authority, and its own morality. "Always be ready to speak your mind," the proverb says, "and a base man will avoid you."

I had to trust myself in this way with Ron, whom I described briefly at the beginning of this chapter. In time, his rationality had softened with me into a warm, placid friendliness. Meanwhile, a consulting job he sought fell through. A woman who interested him got involved with someone else. He spent more and more evenings alone in his apartment, watching television. He had enough money from family investments, but he seemed stagnant, and content to be so. With me he chatted amiably about the newspaper headlines of the week.

"Why are you seeing me?" I blurted out one day; "I want to work with you. But I've lost the sense of it." "Your support is definitely important," he said with his usual placidness. "But nothing else is important to you these days." "Not now. The tube has me drugged." Should I suggest he cut out the drug? I didn't feel like suggesting anything. I felt under wraps myself. Suddenly Blake was perched on my shoulder. "Those who restrain Desire, do so because theirs is weak enough to be restrained." I said to Ron: "You're so passive, and I'm so depressed with you. You have talents and appeal and what do you do? You stay drugged. It's like you're sitting in a broken-down car, and you won't get it repaired or exchanged, and it's not taking you where you want to go." His eyes clouded over. "Don't give up on me," he said. Not thinking of anything, I said, "I won't." "It shakes me up to hear that you're depressed." "How so?" "As if I should do something for you." "Oh, you needn't take care of me. I'll get over it." There was a silence. "I'm always passive underneath," he resumed. "Even when I'm active, I follow others' leads." I replied: "When you said just now, 'Don't give up on me,' you didn't sound passive at all." "No. I wasn't. "So you aren't 'always.'" He watched me, motionless, bearded, manly, and looking swaddled. But as I continued to look at him, something felt fresh between us. "I won't give up on you," I repeated. "I trust you not to" he said. "Actually," I added, "I'm feeling better now." "The tube really is stupefying," he went on. "I wonder where I've been after six hours of silly programs." He stretched. "I think I'll join a health club and work out every day." "Well, good."

He did join a health club in his neighborhood. He exercised daily and took a renewed interest in his career. "That comes first," he said. "Before I get serious with a woman." I heard his decisive tone; he was beginning to steer his life. He looked forward also to a visit from his parents, who lived in the East, and he told me for the first time how much he had felt his father's disapproval when he had left the family business two years before and struck out on his own. I suggested that we might talk about it all together. "That's an interesting idea," he said. "But the timing isn't good. They're having it very rough with my brother. He's in psychoanalysis in New York and he's full of hostility toward them now. They had a terrible scene together, with Tim's analyst. I tell them to consider that Tim's in a phase. It's especially hard for Mom. She likes everything to be 'nice.'" I thought of the depression I had felt with him when he was keeping everything "nice" with me, and also of his harassed concern to take care of me. "That's all very well. But what about your own needs? You're the one who's troubled by your Dad." "Maybe I'll ask them to come," he answered after a moment. "It'll be my birthday. It can be a present to me."

And so we met together. The father was gray and stout, the mother slender and chic. They both looked a little haggard. Ron took a jocular, host-like tone with them, and they in turn praised his loyalty as a son. "We've always been able to count on him," the mother said. "They think well of me," Ron echoed with a contented laugh. It was difficult for me to sense doubts among any of them on the subject. "But you did have a question," I finally said to him. After a long pause, he turned to his father. "It seemed, a few years back, as though — at the time it wasn't quite comfortable — my leaving the business didn't appear the best thing — to you." "No," the father said. "Do you mean," I asked, "that it was all right?" "Yes, certainly." There was another long pause. "I mean, at the time," Ron said at last. "Well, it wasn't clear what you had in mind. I want you to feel good about what you do." "But my leaving itself, that was all right?" "Yes, that was perfectly all right." "You had seemed upset." "I had other worries then. I was already troubled about Tim. But not about you. It's your life, for whatever you want to do." Ron wrinkled his forehead and sighed. "You look happier," his mother remarked. "It's my birthday, Mom." "Could it be something more?" I asked. "Well, maybe." "Good," replied Mother, in a tone that concluded discussion of the matter. "It's nice here," she added, relaxing in her chair and looking approvingly at the Chinese silk brocade on my office wall. "Our son Tim worked us over last week in his doctor's office," the father said to me, grinning. "It's a pleasure to be having some relief." I nodded to them, wondering: How much of Ron's unvoiced anger at you both has Tim pinch-hit for?

In the next month, Ron got much more active. Suddenly it was hard for him to keep appointments with me; he had so many business meetings on his calendar. "I might stop coming for a while," he said, six months after my day of depression with him. "All right," I answered. I was thinking of his unresolved problem with his parents; but with his new decisiveness, that seemed out of place now. "Come back when you've a bride in mind and tell me about her." "It may be a lot sooner. About business decisions. I haven't got the job I want yet." "Come when you like." But he didn't show up soon. I phoned him four months later to find out how he was doing, and he sounded lively and vigorous. He was going into a clothing business with a friend. He would invite me to the opening of the store.

With Ron, the context of nurture was one of slow and only partial weaning to independence, facilitated by his asking for and receiving his father's consent. The obedient older son began to go his own way, to get the support from his father that he desired, and also to be independent in business. The further step, of setting up his personal life more fully, he wanted to take later, after having tried his wings with his new career. It wasn't clear how free he felt for an intimacy with a woman. He hadn't yet stood up to his father as an equal, nor to his resolutely agreeable mother: he was all too much the Unprodigal Son. But for now, my own sharing my depression with him had, it seems, weaned him from a relentless inertia which appeared to derive from his attachment to her. It had, I think, mirrored and magnified something irritating to him in the inertia, a muffling, Blakean "restraint of desire" that, *perhaps,* needn't be endured. The therapeutic system presented him with this "perhaps" of protest. "Don't give up on me," he said at first. It was a call for support, to be more fully addressed as *Thou,* so he could get free of his most locked and cloying place. I didn't give up. He took a step to break loose.

I could make a maxim: "Trust that unreasonableness is therapeutic if it helps the patient break loose." But how do I know, in the moment, that I am anything more than self-indulgent, or a prey to my own impatience? I don't know. I only want to believe it. I look as well as I can, and then I leap. "What is now proved was once only imagined." Or to adapt Blake: what I now imagine may come to be proved.

With Bryan, whom I saw only twice, I imagined in part poorly. Then I stood corrected.

He is a thirty-five-year-old high school teacher with large green, worried-looking eyes. He had known me in a therapy workshop I conducted in San Francisco. In the workshop he had been shy, but appealingly open about his recent happy marriage after years of solitude. Three months later, he phoned me for an appointment "just one time, two Fridays from now, in the evening if possible. Thirty minutes will be enough." I don't usually work in the evening, but something in his urgency and precision won me. I agreed.

"It's about cocaine," he began as soon as he came in. "I'm not addicted. But I know that I'm depending on it. I started using it with friends, about a year ago. But the problem really is with Sharon, my wife. She's been leaving me, for a week at a time, in the last three months. Her mother is very ill in Portland with a stroke; her dad died last year; and she and her sisters rotate taking care of her. It's remarkable devotion by all of them, and very much like my wife. Well, when she goes away, I feel calm enough. I don't even notice that anything is happening to me. But then at night I suddenly can't stand the loss; and I take the stuff without even thinking. The first night is the really bad one. And also the last, just before she comes back. It's like, at the end, I can't stand waiting any longer. She left again, today. I knew what the date would be when I called you. I thought if I talked with you, I could get through the night."

"Does Sharon know about your problem?" I asked.

"No. What's the use of upsetting her?"

"What's the great thing that happens with the cocaine?"

"I forget everything else. I don't miss her — until afterwards, coming down. That's awful. But somehow I seem to bear her being away better."

"It's *so* good?"

"You have to *know* how good cocaine feels. Do you?"

I waved my hand. "Drugs and I: minor leagues."

"But in a way," he went on warmly, "it isn't all that good. It grabs you and holds you; it's a sort of monotonous stereotyped pleasure." He paused. With his wiry body and tense, green-eyed look, he looked to me like a sort of constrained devil. And then he took me up on my image; "I think the greatest pleasure to me is feeling I'm doing something *absolutely wrong*. Even more than the effect of the drug, just the action, just the gesture of taking it. Or the effect and the gesture — they go together. I watch myself snorting it in the bathroom mirror, and I feel wonderfully, wonderfully wicked. I'm doing the thing that I absolutely shouldn't do, that I know is crazy and wrong, I'm a total rascal, and no one is going to stop me." He smiled. "I was brought up very morally. Could you guess?"

I smiled too. "I see you aren't hesitant about telling me everything."

"I felt I could, after we played with devils in the workshop."

"Good. Do you see your wicked look in the mirror *without* cocaine?"

"Well, no. Then I'm not looking for it."

"Let's practice."

I fetched a hand mirror from upstairs (my office is in my home), and he quickly warmed to the task: the raised eyebrow, the wink, the smirk, the delighted smile at wanting to cause endless mischief. We both played, watching our faces in the mirror. I was thinking: "Imagine being paid to outdo cocaine! And of all things to nurture, what's better than nurturing the forbidden? A pretty folly to persist in.[7] Is Blake smiling?" I kept my thoughts to myself.

"You can practice at home, too, during the week," I said, putting the mirror down.

He roused himself as from a hypnotic trance. "I'm feeling much lighter now. I want to get over the stuff completely. If I didn't have it around when she's gone — so I had some time to think —"

"When she's gone, you are, in a way, on a trip too. Of course, there's no way to make being lonely not feel lonely. But consider this about your own trip. You are in a quite different place without her. And you could enjoy it more." I paused. "If you flushed your supply down, wouldn't you make things simpler for yourself? The freest devil is without props. An immaculate devil." We hugged one another.

"I'm thinking," he said. "I'd like to come again next Thursday. It's the day before Sharon gets back. I'll pay you now for both times."

"All right. Sleep well, and you'll enjoy calling her in the morning."

He returned the next Thursday.

"The week went wonderfully," he said with his warm smile. "I couldn't believe it. I simply didn't feel the tug I was afraid of. Except for one, very bad time." He was silent for a few seconds, as if remembering. Then he continued: "It was early in the morning, just after I saw you. I'd gone straight home from here and fallen asleep easily. And then,at 5:30 in the morning, I woke up, feeling smothered. I threw off the blankets, and lay back again to sleep. But then a very big jolt came, like an electric shock. It was really strange — and unusual. I jumped out of bed, turned on all the lights, dressed, and walked up and down. I remembered what you said about being on a trip, but it didn't help. I kept wondering what I could do to feel better. Then, without even thinking, I drove to my dealer's house. I took a book along to read, it was still ridiculously early, and I had to wait for him to be up. But I was starting to feel better. Then I bought a large additional supply of cocaine. Of course I had some at home, and I was spending money now that I really didn't have to spare. But I had to — after you said that about flushing it down. I've kept some in each room of my apartment all week; I wanted to have it everywhere. And I've held it in my hand, each time I made faces in the mirror. *That's* been fun. I stood there and thought of new things: like cutting long hairs out of my nose — what the ads call 'unsightly'? Then I'd do it, winking at myself. It all sounds pretty tame now. But the thing is: I haven't used the cocaine *at all.*" He paused, and looks at me reproachfully. "This devil needs a lot of props."

I said: "I'm sorry."

"That was one weird tailspin. You were a little too fast for me."

"Yes." I was thinking, in a quick jumble: Stephen! *Immaculate devil* indeed! And he struggling with his immaculate childhood! He knows his own timing. These visits that he's calculated ahead so exactly. The way he pays me in advance. He's nothing if not meticulous. Why am I in such a hurry to cure him?

"But apart from that," Bryan went on, "I feel great. My body feels great."

"In As-Is Condition."

"That's right!" He sat back contentedly. "Now I've got to collect all the stuff and hide it from Sharon. Maybe I'm really through with it. I don't know. I may be back in a month. If not, I'll see you some time in another workshop."

He was full of plans again. I took them as a cue.

"Why don't you pay me for another visit now? You don't know when you'll be back. Maybe, as you say, in a workshop. But you like to stockpile. You have your reserve supply of cocaine. You can have another reserve supply. A stockpile with me."

He smiled thoughtfully. "That's a clever idea."

But after the last time I felt more circumspect. "There's only one thing wrong with it."

"What's that?"

"It's my idea. Not yours."

"But I like it." He was already taking out his checkbook. "I'm dating the check today," he said. "So you can cash it. And alongside *memo*, I'm writing 'Stockpile.'" As he left he shook my hand warmly — and rather devilishly, I thought. That was six months ago. I haven't heard from him since.

Something powerful had happened, in part adverse, but on the whole, it seems, beneficial. And yet, had I been too cautious — leaning over backwards from "curing too much" — not to suggest that he continue to see me a while longer? Perhaps the extra payment had only bought him out of therapy, with a sense of his staying in control. What do I know yet about the depth of his feelings of abandonment? For it was as though my suggestion about getting rid of the drug had turned into a horror he must defy; as though it had brought on a paroxysm from the past, a sort of acute attack of his childhood. And there were other questions about the present too. Beyond accepting himself as devilish, hasn't he more to learn about self-acceptance *in all seriousness*? As a devil, you're free to transgress restrictions; but also you're given to self-mockery. He could be more self-nurturing than this. He could accept the face in the mirror as *Thou*.[8] Well, he would appear again at his own timing and his own wish. Really, I trusted that. And we'd both seen to his having a reserved seat.

But it is obvious that two-session therapy has its limits. The therapeutic system has too little chance to influence all the problematic expectancies that a life keeps in store. And it is just that kind of influence that this system, over a sufficient time, exerts, gently but insistently presenting its own wiser expectancies. So I feel it, with a therapeutic optimism that suits my own temper. The system provides, to use an image from Buddhism, a large enough pasture in which the tension-ridden bull can run himself calm.[9] It "expects" that the bull can be calm, and wishes to be, and in that pasture will be. Tensions will return, but the pasture always allows for the return of the calm. And beyond therapy, the pasture belongs to the bull, forever.[10]

The system generates its own power, power arising from the unformulable source of which Lao-tzu speaks, and maintaining itself, between human beings, in the boundless acceptance of *I-Thou*. That source is the system's spiritual center, and in our immediate comprehension of it, it may feel both familiar and unique. In fact the events of therapy, as readers may have been noticing from my examples, sound rather like stories heard before. One feels stuck or confused or empty or driven; one finds an unfolding, a clarity, a fullness, a release. For in its content, therapy can no more be new than prayer can, or love. But in the same way, like prayer, like love, it isn't anything if it isn't new.

Chapter 10

TOWARD A NEW PARADIGM OF THERAPY

Contextual concerns lead us to considerations of a new paradigm for therapy. For "context," we have seen, refers to inner individual experience, with all its conditioning from past interpersonal contexts; and it refers equally to current outward contexts of one's life, with friends, family, society, and in therapy itself. The person, and the past and present contexts of his living, are indivisible; as his significant contexts change, he changes. But major theories of modern psychology, and the therapies following from them, have maintained a division. Analytic depth psychology has concerned itself with the individual, systems therapies with the interplay of individuals in families and other groups. And the proponents of each view usually call each other wrong. What is needed, I think, is a paradigm that embraces both views. This does not yet exist.

And yet the synthesis is implied by the very nature of human life at its outset. The infant, having left the all-embracing context of the mother's womb, moves into the formative milieu of its family, and something vital to its becoming a person begins at once with the bond of mother and baby. Here is the basic human system that Buber teaches, his receptive *I-Thou*. In time, the baby leans to feel confirmed as a separate *I*. It comes to recognize its voice as its own, to belong to itself in its own right. And precisely in being a separate person, it may enter and help to shape other systems, both of *I-Thou* and of control over the environment, Buber's *I-It*.

But from his description we do not learn what kind of person the person becomes. Buber's is an ontic *I*, not a characterological *I*.

The history of psychoanalysis is the history of how the characterological *I* develops, through the parental offerings of acceptance, permission, support, solicitude, and safety on the one hand, and, on the other, of disapproval, rejection, anger, indifference, and threat. These various contexts structure the child's inner life, anxiety within him or her being the great marker of the acceptable and the safe from the disallowed and the dangerous. The total inner structure, then, is what we call the character, with all its particular preferences and prejudices, its memories and hopes, its defenses, its mental intolerables and emotional untouchables. And psychoanalysis assumes the great stability of the separate character, its fixity, and relatively small aptitude for change. Here is the break with a continually molding environment. The psyche is no longer affected by its interpersonal milieu like seaweed in a current. It is firm as sea anemone when water flows over them, as constant in shape, though like them too, somewhat porous and expansive.

But how fixed are the character fixations? Or rather, just where does the fixating element, the anxiety itself, reside? Is it entirely within the person? Or is it, as systems thinkers would say, a movable fulcrum that includes the individual and his significant contexts?

But as soon as we put in the word "movable," we are dealing with something "less fixed," whose "fixity" is contingent on the system that presides.

Take a situation that may seem superficial but, I think opens onto depths. A man moves from Alabama to California, and by degrees starts to modify, or to lose, his southern accent. The environment no longer reaffirms it to the same degree. Or rather, the extent to which his significant environment evokes, or discourages, a change in how he speaks will affect his speech. If he attends acting school in Los Angeles and rehearses roles in Shakespeare, his accent will alter much more rapidly than if, a seclusive man in the first place, he lives fairly isolated with close Alabama relatives who have settled in Bakersfield. (I speak of one man, but in effect am now sketching two quite different characters, or personalities; on these grounds Harry Stack Sullivan was fond of remarking that an individual had as many personalities as he had interpersonal relations.)[1] The actor has reason to feel anxious if his home regional accent stays. The seclusive man, with his few close family ties, has reason to feel anxious if the familiar tie of accent goes. These effects, of course, depend on reciprocities. The actor, of his own, has chosen acting school; the withdrawn man, his family circle. But the actual change in the actor's speech, and active resistance to change in the family man, happen because of their new situations: before he left his eastern home, the potential actor had learned no new accent, nor had the seclusive man avoided learning one.

We recognize this same impact of milieu in cultural history. Samuel Johnson was a supreme literary stylist. But when, in conversation, he said, "Clear your mind of cant," and "Sir, we *know* our will is free, and *there's* an end on't," these sentences, and many like them, have been immortalized in *The Oxford Dictionary of Quotations*, not for being very grand themselves, but for the ambience they come from and which still lingers fresh in them: the rich coffeehouse world of 18th century London, in which a deep voice boomed.[2]

These ideas are not absent from analytic concepts: the very fact of therapy speaks of the shaping power of a new milieu. Because of the analytic work, old defenses — old accents of character, so to speak — are "broken through," "worked through," "dropped," or "modified," according to the analyst's language and claims. But the fixity of old structure is assumed. The analytic work of insight is a chipping at cement that encases integration and its further flow. Or, in Jungian analysis, the work is midwifery: one observes and presides at an autonomous psychic development. John Perry, for instance, describes a young woman's schizophrenic delusion. Her eyes are being used as television cameras by aliens in space vehicles. And so she cannot look at her friends without endangering and betraying them. Also, her inner world is divided between materialistic, aggressive, northerners and impulsive animal life, which is being compressed by the northern enemy to the South

Pole and about to blow up. It is her mission to halt the northern forces, but she can't break through a force field at the equator. And yet she can catch a glimpse, to one side, of "the clear light of God," which communicates with the northerners and can bring about a remedy. She has still another fantasy: of looking up through her own rectum, and seeing disgusting annular layers of internal organs. But all of these, way up inside, open on a view of herself at the age of thirteen, pretty and fresh.[3]

The young woman has a history of being punished at puberty by her mother for her sexual looseness. The loose behavior was just the mother's fantasy. And her father was coldly cerebral (at his top, "northern" end), and emotionally chaotic underneath. Taking into herself her parents' viewpoints, she had come to bury her own fresh feelings about herself, to compress her developing femininity, and to give over her own vision to the familial "destructive aliens." The Jungian therapy, in turn, assisted her spontaneous quest, through feeling and fantasy, to recover herself — to move through these traumata toward her own integration. The therapy in fact proceeded quickly, over a 12-week period. At its most active, the therapist's insight focused the psyche's course, but did not direct it. The psyche directs itself.

In the systems view, on the other hand, inner life is more impressionable from outside, can be affected at once by a significant new force, as the flow of a river can be redirected by an earthquake. Even a single event can alter the course. I have seen a cartoon of a psychoanalyst who rigged a guillotine over his couch. The reclining patient stares at the blade overhead; it is connected to a cord, the other end of which is in the doctor's hand. The doctor leans forward and says good-naturedly: "Makes all your other problems seem trivial, doesn't it?"

Here, for sure, is a sort of earthquake, a moment of shock therapy — and also, of crisis therapy. Krishnamurti, with his view of life as continual crisis, in which the psyche is always facing its life or death, would have appreciated the clear issue at hand. I can hear him saying: "That patient knows what counts." But how do we describe just what he knows? Is he seeing, insightfully, the truth of the doctor's words? Is he, beyond any words, reshaping his inner structure, for the time being, as the truth of the blade overhead flows through him? Is he contacting his own deepest imagery of self-preservation? His own deepest dread of a threat to it? And what about this new system he is in, containing doctor-cum-guillotine and conveying something about big and little problems...and something else, too: how one's sense of a significant problem connects to one's sense of relative powerlessness? The man will have, surely, a feeling about all that, a sort of insight into it, but insight without reflective thought (there's no time; that blade could fall now); and how do we speak of insight which is without thinking? As to what he will think, a little later: will he consider the analyst a sadist? Or a savior? Or, more moderately, an eccentric giver of insights himself? The cartoon shows us just the moment of crisis. The river flows on, we do not know just how. But one thing is clear: the system in the cartoon makes for a drastic reordering of the patient's immediate experience, without any conscious reflection about it. And the situation implies that any new system can make for some degree of this reordering. So a stubborn old miser opens his purse to his charming granddaughter. And a psychotically depressed man in a hospital smiles at the warm nurse on his ward whom he has come to like. Systems thinking often takes another step. In the writings of Don Jackson, Jay Haley, Paul Watzlawick, and Virginia Satir,[4] not only is character always affected, at once, by a system of which it is a part; character is *nothing but* experience systematized; a piece in a jigsaw puzzle which fits in and around it. Its shape comes from the thrusts, the pulls, the tensions and relaxations of significant systems in early childhood — systems of prevailing tenderness or rejection, attention or neglect, freedom or confinement, and so on. As life proceeds, the shape of character is maintained by reinforcements from new systems, or it may be altered by a significant new system. Thus Bateson's description of schizophrenic behavior — that it results from contradictory messages from another in the double bind — speaks of an ongoing system of enmeshment. It has nothing in common with the psychoanalytic concept of schizophrenia in which, as a fixed and relatively finished piece of individual sculpture, the unconscious has submerged the ego. The systems therapist, therefore, need only be clear enough about the reigning system, and with sufficient impact on it himself, alter it so that the pathology integral to it no longer is needed. And so we hear Salvador Minuchin speak to a depressed and withdrawn 15-year-old girl who is often psychotic. (She often hears a hallucinated voice. She assumes, of course, that it is quite beyond her control.) Her parents, also in the room, are, as usual, at each other's throats. Minuchin says to the girl: "Yvonne, I suggest you go quite crazy today, so that your parents can become concerned about you. Then things will be OK between them. You seem to be a good daughter, so you will go crazy, and you father will support your mother in taking care of you, and things will be OK" To the parents, he adds: "I think that your daughter is trying to save your marriage...I think that Yvonne has kind of perceived that you are at the deep end, and she is saving you by being crazy, so you will organize yourselves." With this exposing of the "demented system," from which everyone who is within it suffers, the parents begin to work on themselves ("We don't communicate," the girl's mother acknowledges to her husband); and the girl starts to feel off the hook, in control of herself, and newly interested in having her own school life and her own friends. What does it mean to Yvonne herself to have been told "to go crazy"? She may only think that the therapist is crazy. But something has stirred in her, something about her own capacity for self-control. Meanwhile, there has been no time-out from the ongoing system in order to understand the fixation of her psychosis from the past; that isn't considered relevant. All we need, for therapeutic impact, is clarity about the fixations of the present. The contents of Yvonne's hallucinated voice — to the Jungian therapist a rich source of information about her struggles to find herself amid the emotional tangles of her family — hardly concern Minuchin. He wants only to reinforce what is positive: "Is [your voice] friendly?...Is he wise?...That's nice. If you're going to have voices, it's nice that your voices should be interesting and wise." The simpler his acceptance of the voice, the less likely it is to keep its dissociated existence; it is being too well communicated with. "[H]is name is Alex?...I prefer Moishe myself. When I had a voice, I called it Moishe. It's more friendly. Alex has a ring of detachment in it. It's kind of too Waspy for me." As much as the Jungian therapist, Minuchin assumes that the basic roots of the psyche are healthy; but he does not examine its leaves in the same detail, and he is a much more active tiller of the surrounding soil. Yvonne showed the benefits. A few weeks later, she was out of treatment, busy at school, and content. Looking back, she said about Minuchin, in a kind tribute to his aggressive stance: "He drove me sane."[5]

Certainly he affected her interpretation of reality. And "character," Bateson wrote in his last book, or rather, as he says, "What used to be called character [is] the system of interpretations which we place on the contexts we encounter" — interpretations such as "I cast blame"; "I grow pessimistic"; "I get scared"; "I hear voices"; "I prepare to attack." Bateson's definition hews to interaction; and yet it is interestingly partial to the person also; in particular among systems thinkers, he does not forsake the individual, nor something singular and powerful in the individual's destiny. For, he goes on, "these interpretations...can be shaped both by genetics and by learning"; and "genetics" is the most inward of stabilities. Minuchin, too, speaking to Yvonne, implies her individual wish for a stable, nurturant family: her own need for her parents to "organize themselves." And *her own* need, too, that they grant her personal freedom.

So the individual's concerns, though tied to outward systems, are not to be dispatched in their own right. We must attend to both person and system. And beyond therapy, our attention from one to the other, from inward state to outward involvement, from autonomous psyche to the psyche of communication, sometimes shifts as rapidly as attention to the tennis players on opposite sides of the net. We hear a great musician; he is playing in a concert hall; the emotions he evokes command his audience. And we notice, too, how his listeners' rapt response is evoking, giving wings to the performance. Or we recall how the concentration camp victim was brutalized by his captors, who were obviously upheld by their own system-network. But out of their opposition, they could produce in the inmate a unique fortitude and heroism, the deadly system kindling faith in life.[6]

Sometimes, in our self-involvement, our attention stays on one side of the net. I go to a meditation retreat, to awaken my inner being. This is, I understand, a retreat into inwardness, where also I can reevoke my love for others. But what about the milieu itself? Haven't I found a "retreat into protective custody"? A short-term voluntary confinement, in which I agree to give up drugs, alcohol, sex, and even talk (what a set of pressures to be rid of!); where I may meet old friends, am given good food, good shelter, understanding companionship, and unlimited sanction to take care of myself. No wonder, quite apart from my meditation, that I emerge from the experience less anxious, more content, more loving. On second thought, it doesn't seem astonishing to me that I once heard a man say, at the end of a retreat, "I come here to meet people." He never speaks to them, except very briefly, at the close. But without words, indeed because there were no words but, instead, continual shared intentions of mutual acceptance, he met them more fully and intensely than at home, in the world of noise and cross-purpose. At the same time, my actual inward practice, in meditation, makes me, all the more, a person this man would seek to know, as it remakes for me all the systems of my own normal world.

Clearly the new paradigm that therapists need requires both person and system. And as things stand, clearly we do not know how to bring the pieces together. Initial attempts to do so, in their awkwardness, reveal the difficulty. The English psychoanalyst Wilfred Bion, for instance, has drawn up a theory of group dynamics that acknowledges constituent members, but without any reference to their individualities. He speaks of irrational assumptions that pervade a group and interfere with its overt task: assumptions of dependence on the leader, of fight or flight from the leader, or of intragroup pairing to bring about a savior for the group. His ideas are intriguing and demonstrable.[7] They go far to explain the forces that run pell-mell through mob violence, scapegoating, and cult slavery. But anyone who has participated in a Bion-structured group has the odd sensation of being a forgotten person — a sensation inevitably odd since each group members knows himself to *be* still a person. Bion acknowledges this fact once only: in his concept of the individual's *valency* for group dynamics. But the group itself remains, so to speak, one tissue; it has no differentiated organs. How full a picture can this be? What if one considers a choral group, for instance, noting only the members' "valency" for producing the required sound, with no regard for the color, the timbre, the strength and range of the individual voices? And what if the group's work called for solo passages, duets, large contrasts of harmonies and dynamics? The tone, in effect, could hardly be described. It is like not seeing the trees for the forest.

Buber himself, for all his finesse of thought, falls back on a comparably inadequate notion in *I and Thou.* He gives us *I-Thou* as the defining reality of the person: "In the beginning is relation." But he wishes to cross-reference this concept to the newborn infant itself, the single organism. What impels it toward relation? Buber says: the baby arrives among us with an "inborn Thou." Now, in some sense this must be true: other needs, the sucking reflex, for instance, are "inborn." But one thinks of the latter as belonging to a defined person, while the otherness of *Thou* is the condition for *becoming* a person. How can the newborn's existence, in the first place, incorporate this otherness, which it must experience outside itself? It is as though the child, in the womb, already contained the mother within it — as though it possessed not only the impulse to suck, but the milk. The concept is *ex post facto* and ungainly. It is meant to account for something unaccountable from the individual's side. And that is the point. The person and his twosomeness *are* discrepant ideas.

The discrepancy is as old, in philosophy, as that between Aristotle's concern with individual facts and their causation, and Plato's with systems of form. And it is as new as basic data in today's physics: those phenomena in electromagnetism and in light which are perceived sometimes only as discrete particles, sometimes only in the form of waves. Among the peaks of Western culture, this dualism is expressed psychologically in Tolstoy's grand essay, in the second part of his epilogue to *War and Peace,* about "the life of people and of humanity." He describes, on the one hand, an individual's inner sense of his free will, of the discrete, particulate, self-directed nature of his being (we have, in fact, followed Tolstoy's characters by this point through more than 1,000 convincing pages of their own choices); and on the other, the external web of fatalities that determines everyone's living, from the involuntary nervous system he is born with, to his physical needs for air, food, shelter, to all the shaping pressures of personal and social existence, all those systems which give one's life its deterministic form. These views, too, like Plato's and Aristotle's, like particle and wave theory, are fundamentally discrepant. But we can, Tolstoy suggests, look for a communality between them: this will be the laws that govern both views. In daily life, we may treat ourselves to Dr. Johnson's view: "I *know* I'm an individual, and *there's* an end on't." But we can also allow the wider question. We can ask: what general laws enter into our sense of individuality, as well as into the appreciation we have of our being system-determined?

And here we begin to perceive some pertinent groupings among the texts we have considered. Buber and Bateson have concerned themselves outrightly with systemic views of the individual: one is who one is by virtue of one's connectiveness to a context. Krishnamurti, too, though he speaks always from the side of an individual's personal dilemmas, brings us to the same place: the individual is nothing but his present phenomenological state, conscious and unconscious, and this state, in turn, is always in a weave with others. Therefore, he says, "Relationship acts as a mirror to reflect all the states of our being, if we allow it...."[8] But what of Lao-Tzu and his interest in the sage? What of our Western imaginative writers, who look at the individual and his destiny? But also, when Blake talks of energy, Rilke of solitude, Kafka of parable, Lao-Tzu of wisdom, their meaning lies clearly beyond what the psychoanalysts call "character." They are speaking of a consummate quality of experience by which to measure, value, and understand all specific experiences — the pure gold behind the currency of daily exchange. Their concern, like Bateson's, is indeed context. But it is not outward context. It is the placing of individual life within a frame larger than any single experience or set of experiences, within a *Gestalt* enduring beyond any momentary *Gestalten*; these become fragments of the greater one. For our writers, the individual separate from this larger truth does not fully exist, just as, for systems thought, he does not exist separate from the system he belongs to.

I shall be more specific. When Blake says: "Energy is eternal delight," and "He who restrains desire does so because his is weak enough to be restrained," and "Man is made for joy and woe," he gives us a vision of inner context which dethrones the constrained, partisan ego of character. At one stroke, life is impulse and exulting and lamentation. One does not take sides. One embraces all sides. When Rilke says: "Love your solitude...[Let it] grow wide about you, [so] your distance is among the stars," and "Perhaps all the dragons of our lives are [disguised] princesses," and "Life holds you in its hand; it will not let you fall," the vision, again, is of an inner boundlessness and of one's fidelity to it. At one stroke, life is a solitude to welcome, an enchantment to discover, a harbor to trust. One accepts its hardships as ingredients of its blessings. When Kafka says: "The positive is given; what is laid upon us is to accomplish the negative," and "There is one cardinal sin, impatience," the vision, again, is of a measureless wholeness we can intimate at once, here, through the veil of our conditioning. However little we see, we see enough to be challenged to see more, and to have faith that more is willing to be seen. In each case, the vision is, like Lao-Tzu's, of an infinite ever-present vibrancy flowing through and defining us. Like his, each of these Western visions is what we call "visionary"; each speaks of how we find ourselves in what is "beyond" ourselves, as on Prospero's island, "when no man was his own."[9] Or, in our usual psychological language, how we find ourselves in our unconscious source. And so defined, the person is no longer a "fixed personality." "I" am variable. The inner context of my awareness reveals me to myself as tied, more or less, to habits, old loyalties, old commitments, but changeable, within a vast field of possible responses.

And defined by outward systems as they affect me, within their panorama of possibilities, "I" am also not fixed, am also changeable. Outward and inward are equal in this inherent fluidity. The present moment as I sense it subjectively, and the outward situation it presents me to cope with, are both unique. Each moment has its own evanescent fingerprint. I must keep on the move if I am to locate myself outwardly, if I am to know myself within.

Let me refine this equality further. We recall how Bateson speaks of "the context of the context" in order to emphasize the hierarchical patterning of awareness; and how he sees in this abstractive patterning an instance of Whitehead's and Russell's Logical Types. We ourselves can use the logical typing to heighten our sense of both what is inward and what is outward.

The inward "context of the context" is the space within, the infinite circumambient moment in which all specific experiences cluster, all the infinite facts of my and your "10,000 things." The outward "context of the context" is the space without, the ecological infinitude which houses all the moments of unfolding experience, your "10,000 things" and mine, as they continue and as they change.

So, too, as "inward infinity" speaks of an unconscious fertile source in experience, the interpersonal systems that govern us trace also to unconscious sources. It is a commonplace of psychotherapists to think of motivation as beyond conscious control; and at the same time to invite the client, through access of insight, or by some directed experiment that the therapist suggests, to explore just this uncontrollable thing. We have heard Minuchin instruct 15-year-old Yvonne "to go crazy"; by his reckoning, she had the power to do so, and she might want to exercise the power because of her deranged family system. Perhaps, with a change in the system, her use of her power would be different; would be for sanity. This kind of constructive playing with unconscious forces is the therapist's *forte*. It allies him with the traditional *shaman*, and allows us to rank him, in this regard, as a religious figure. Among us Westerners, Milton Erickson was a special shamanic master, and at the same time the most homespun of men; it is pleasant to recall one of his cures — one in which shamanism wore the thorough disguise of an American village doctor's medical science. A naive married man came to him with a sexual history made up solely of drooling, unsatisfying orgasms, and almost no erections. Erickson, first of all, determined that there was no organic damage. Then he looked the man over, like Sergeant Cuff in *The Moonstone*, whose eyes "expected more of you than you were aware of yourself." He said to him: "You have never learned to get your secretions going right. You must, by daily masturbation in your bathroom for a month, practice getting them in correct order: those of the testes first, then the seminal vesicles, then the prostate. You need to teach yourself the right sequence."[10] By this wonderful pretense of biological reasoning (it has never been clear to me, actually, whether in this case the shaman didn't believe the reasoning himself — which, of course, would add to its power) — by this pretense and under its shelter, the man learned what he had to learn: how to expect and approve and officiate in a gradient of physical excitation moving to climax. Taking charge of the experience each day, and so accepting it in full consciousness, he could in time turn his attention, of his own, to the excitement he wanted the most — with his wife. In another way, too, his rather prolonged self-help was crucial to the treatment. If a condemning conscience wished to deter him, it had a lot of opportunity to interrupt the process: he could forget the assignment for days, or be prevented from it by a pain, or it could just fail to work. In fact, the man did his bathroom homework scrupulously for a few weeks. Then, one morning, he had had enough. He came out, picked the lady up in his arms, and took her successfully to bed.

The shamanic voice here tells us of a virtuoso access to the unconscious.[11] And granting that it belongs to the school of strategic therapy, of instructions to promote a specific result, it leads us to consider further the implicit strategies, and religious rites of a sort, of every school. I think again of the cartoon analyst with his serviceable guillotine, and of an eloquent point he has made for all clinicians: aren't analysts and systems therapists, alike, a tribe of strategists, seeking for the guillotine to constraints of character as for the Holy Grail?

But to most therapists these religious references are wild additions. Only a few would welcome them: the "transpersonal psychologists," so called because of their interests in "spiritual integration" beyond the ego. Here again, all the writers we have considered, both of system-life and of inward experience, have a fresh word. For to them "the infinite" and "the eternal" dwell in ordinary experience, are immediate fact. The secular is barren soil and "spiritual integration" a redundancy; there is nothing, in personal life as it is, to be "trans" to. For Bateson, the man of System, religious need just "affirm[s] membership in...life and environment," with their endless capacity for change. To Buber, it points to maximal Personhood: God is the relationship which never objectifies and limits; He is *Thou* unvarying, the Infinite Person. For Lao-Tzu, the eternal, unnameable Tao is the one reality, within and without; the realized man is fully open to it. Blake, Rilke, Kafka give us the limitless within. Experience is always enough. It breaks all bondage. Blake's voice is oracular: "Eternity is in love with the productions of time." Rilke speaks with a purgatorial ardor: we are preparing ourselves for infinite inwardness, for God, "the fruit of the tree whose leaves we are." Kafka's is incisive: "To be is to be His." When we invite it, "the world rolls in ecstasy at our feet." Krishnamurti picks up all these echoes, and throws them back to the four winds. To him there is no unitary person at all. The sense of our separateness and stability rests on conditioning. We need it for the basic traffic of life; but at the core, a stable, solid individual is illusory, and as the Buddhists say: "If there is anyone there to suffer, he will." For everything changes. The most rock-bottom experience is as permeable as clouds, as fanciful and evaporating as dreams. When we are aware of this clearly, then we experience infinite otherness.

We are hearing, through these texts, a language at once extreme, exalted, and worldly, both mystically lyrical and everyday. But we do not easily connect it to the therapist's daily thoughts and experience. Perhaps, when Erickson adjures us, "Don't put up limits where none are given," a sound like Blake's comes through; or when we see that the sexual powers his shamanism awoke are at play in Blake's eternal landscape: "The lust of the goat is the bounty of God." "The nakedness of woman is the work of God." Perhaps, at times, all therapists feel a discreet tapping of forces in themselves and their patients, so that without any fuss, with the "fine excess" Keats speaks of in great poetry,[12] they go beyond their own characters. Something in them suddenly stands still, like a deer on a path. They need to go no place, and all roads are open. They meet each other freely. The rare, this-worldly magic of *Thou* occurs.

That moment feels exceptional, and of course, it is. It is disentangled from usual conditioning. And yet it may really be that the two poles we have been considering, of inward life and systemic life, will only meet in the dimension of their infinitudes. That, in fact, is the message of our texts. Blake's inward, exultant: "Enough! or too much"; Rilke's fervent "Life is right, in any case"; Kafka's assured "There is only a spiritual world"; Lao-Tzu's infinitely yielding man of Tao, all connect with Krishnamurti's world-pervading "other"; with Bateson's "larger Mind of which the individual mind is only a sub-system"; with Buber's Infinite Person, by whom alone *I* am fully defined. The inflections, the emphases of each vary, but they speak as a unified group. Only in its nonfixity is our inner life at large, at ease, attentive to itself, and in its natural habitat. Only am I fully myself when, as myself, I am an open system, aware of my bondedness to the system of the world, capable of total bonding to another person, to a cause, to an ideal, and able also to detach from any one bond.

All this is fundamental tenet, a sketch of how the adaptive hand fits the changing glove. But in our partial and partisan living, we are less adaptive. We do not, in fact, meet others. We meet our projections of them, as they meet theirs of us. And the systems which we then make together are full of confused images, like blurred double exposures, and of bewildering echoes, as in large, labyrinthine caves. Here is where we need an embracing paradigm in detail. For if system and individual are so intertwined that we cannot, with justice, speak of them apart, we hardly yet know how to talk of them together. A system, as Bion says, reverberates with its own tone, different from that of the individuals within it, when they are taken separately, and yet it does, so to speak, unravel into just so many individuals. What transform operates between system and persons? In fact, these two must be continually modifying one another. But by what laws? And how can we transpose from the one clinical framework to the other — from the autonomous psyche of the schizophrenic woman whom we viewed in Jungian analysis, to the psyche of interaction in Minuchin's work with the teenager? And yet, do the systems that these therapists themselves utilize really differ so deeply? In Minuchin's manipulations of the girl and her family, one senses something powerfully permissive toward the girl; in the Jungian work, something directive to the woman about evaluating her family relations. But if the systems have a common denominator, it needs a lot more defining; and the difference in level of concern remains dramatic. Can a therapist learn to shift between these levels, in order to maximize his patients' awareness and contact with self? To maximize his own? As I pose all these questions, they seem still to speak of conflicts inherent and inbred. How can they be restated for mutual translation?

Meanwhile, we can say, with a smile, that our focus on the individual in his own right is good for our assertiveness; focus on his systemic determinants, good for our humility. And we can assume that science, with its usual insolent insistence, will come to reason all the data into a logical form.

In this pursuit, too, our texts offer a guiding spirit.

I am speaking of their constant espousal of Negative Capability: "when," as Keats said, "a man is capable of being in uncertainties, mysteries, doubts, without any irritable reaching after fact and reason."[13] There *are* answers. But they are provisional. And one can be free of an "irritable reaching" after them; or one can notice this reaching. Each of our writers, it is true, has a great assurance, but each one, also, has a profound conviction of not knowing, and even of readiness, of cheerfulness not to know. We have heard Rilke announce this most explicitly: "Try to love the *questions themselves...Live* the questions now. Perhaps you will then gradually...live along some distant day into the answer." There is no rush. To rush is to evade or to misstep. Lao-Tzu doesn't know why "some things are not favored by heaven. Even the sage is unsure." So, too, incredulous Blake, before the fearsome tiger: "Did He who made the lamb make thee?" Science-minded Bateson concludes his last book with the motto: "Always the more beautiful answer [which] asks the more difficult question." And Krishnamurti's whole freedom is freedom "from the known." Buber, among our writers the most dogmatic, stands with bowed head before an ultimate paradox: "God is the 'wholly Other'; but He is also the Wholly Same...nearer to me than my *I*."

And Kafka, above all, is our master paradoxicalist: one cannot "know" indivisible truth; to divide oneself from it, in order to know it, must be false.[14] As to final tests, humanity "makes the doubter doubt, the believer believe." Again, as to truth, failure in a worldly sense can be, in parable, success. In which realm, then, shall we live? One can imagine Kafka nodding with Donne about his grave illness: "I do fear the increase of the disease; I should belie nature if I should deny that I feared this";[15] and nodding equally to the words of the physician Osler: "To talk of diseases is a sort of Arabian Nights entertainment."[16] To be enough without inward fixity for both nods: that is his advice. It is, as he says, "to accomplish the negative" — to disengage ourselves patiently from any one of our too positive, always partial answers. And it is, with Rilke, to return to a love of the questions themselves.

The advice applies in all scientific search. And the search for the widest paradigm will not stop with the paradigm of person and system, of inward and outward contexts. It could, plausibly enough, lead these two into the organic substrate which joins them, the functioning of the brain. Freud's own large questions about mental life always included its physical basis; and we can ourselves muse on this afresh as we look ahead to emerging frontiers. In fact, some interesting data already exist.

The current work of Gerald Edelman on behavior of the brain points to *variable* neuronal groupings which categorize perception and adaptive motor response. For instance, an owl hears a field mouse, maps its location from the sound received through both ears, and connects this mapping to a visual map, then to motor response: the owl dives accurately to catch its prey. But owls raised with one ear plugged learn quickly — in one to one-and-a-half months — to alter brain mappings and catch their field mice too. The neuronal groupings evidently can change; there is no fixed storage place, as there is in a computer, where the internal mappings exist. And so too, Edelman says, with memory: a new experience reinforces connections to events in the brain, but the connections themselves are affected by ongoing life. My recall of my mother's voice is recast by the woman now who reminds me of her; recast, again, by whatever motives I have for holding on to the memory of her voice. In this view memory, also, isn't a matter of fixed storage, but is in part invented; Proust's monumental evocation of time past is a reality created, not only recalled.[17] We are, in fact, discovering here too a complex system, the brain not as a simple set of electrical and chemical reactions, but as an elaborate, interactive Gestalt. May it be that its own variable network mirrors the variable "I" which reshapes in therapy, and which, in systems thought, continues to reshape throughout living, as its systemic commitments change?[18]

So physical research suggests a path to new connections. But here, too, we are not at a limit. We only push the limit back to a new obscurity, to who knows what unexpected synthesis and, with it, what new set of problems. There may be no outlying limit. Or only the one which I quoted from Wittgenstein in the first pages of this book, and which now we can hear as an echo of Lao-Tzu. "What we cannot speak, that we must consign to silence."[19] In that silence, in fact, from its beginnings, lie the heart and the conscience of all human advance.

On this note, the note of Negative Capability, I conclude with the best affirmation. Ours is a time of rapid change, of gropings for stability, and of little faith in the human spirit. We are not naturally part of a group, like Medieval men and women in their guilds and church, where the shared life was *Thou* and contact within it signified a multiplicity of trust. Nor have we a firm sense of independence, a self-trust, like the Western frontiersman of a hundred years ago. In our need for community, we are easily prone to cults, with their repressive bonds and final answers. In our need for self-assurance, we are vulnerable to a quick-and-easy perfectionism: to "feel mental mastery," to "dissolve negative programs," to learn, in communicating, just "what to do when" and to get "on-target responses more quickly" (I quote at random from advertising flyers in my last week's mail). We flounder between zenith and nadir, between megalomanic peaks and abysses of depression; and mostly we live, with uncertain foothold, on the slope between. How do we connect again to the open acceptance of *Thou*? The wisdom to which our texts have witnessed points the way: to smile at both the heights and the depths, to see their coexistence as the paradox of our nature and to embrace the paradox; to keep all our conditioning but to wear it lightly; to be without complacence in good fortune, and with courage and resourcefulness in bad; to be compassionate toward all things, our mistakes and silliness too; and to be loyal to the always unfolding moment.

NOTES

CHAPTER 1

1. The more recent twist to the popular image of the psychiatrist is the "deranged doctor": with a light touch in "Dead Again," monstrous to the last degree in "The Silence of the Lambs." But these instances of Mr. Hyde don't devalue the reality of a good Dr. Jekyll. They just make his job more problematic and challenging.

2. Frederick Perls, Ralph F. Hefferline, Paul Goodman, *Gestalt Therapy.*

3. Paul Watzlawick, Janet Beavin Bavelas, Don D. Jackson, *Pragmatics of Human Communication.*

4. Stanley Keleman, *Your Body Speaks Its Mind.*

5. William Schutz, *Elements of Encounter.*

6. Milton H. Erickson, *Advanced Techniques of Hypnosis and Therapy.*

7. From *Seven Gothic Tales.*

8. This is the language of the science of semiotics. See Roland Barthes, "Myth Today," in *Mythologies.*

9. From *The Great Learning.* Quoted by Erich Heller, "Literature and Political Responsibility: Apropos the letters of Thomas Mann"; from his collection of essays, *In the Age of Prose.*

10. In "The Sermon at Benares." My comments on Right Speech follow Joseph Goldstein, *The Experience of Insight.*

11. From "Ali Baba and the Forty Thieves," *The Thousand and One Nights.*

12. From *The Sparkling Stone.*

13. In *Last Tales.*

14. From *Speak, Memory.*

15. From "Good Readers and Good Writers," in *Lectures on Literature.*

16. From "Characters," in *Pretexts: Reflections on Literature and Morality.*

17. From Joseph Conrad, *Typhoon.*

18. The theme of illness itself as an opening to greater awareness is an old one. See André Gide, *Dostoevsky*, and Joan Halifax, *Shaman: The Wounded Healer.* Among major Western novelists, the idea is central to Thomas Mann's *The Magic Mountain* and *Doctor Faustus.*

19. "Gestalt" is German for "shape." "Gestalt therapy" deals with the moment-to-moment shape and reshaping of experience, comparable to the in and out of respiration, or the flow and ebb of tides.

20. Perhaps, too, relativism comes easier for me as a student of literature, where so many differing voices have spoken of human vanity, illusion, unredeemed longing and loss, and even so, the persistent sense of a center, resolving and absolving,

> The still point of the turning world.
>
> (T.S. Eliot, *Four Quartets.*)

21. Goethe, "Maximen und Reflexionen," No. 1068 of the complete listing in *Goethes Werke,* Band XII, C. H. Beck, München. The English translation appears in *The Viking Book of Aphorisms.*

22. From "The Storyteller — Reflections on the Works of Nikolai Leskov." In *Illuminations.*

CHAPTER 2

1. From her poem, "Poetry."

2. From a letter to his friend Thomas Butts.

3. The opening lines of "Auguries of Innocence."

4. Marginal comment in Joshua Reynolds' *Discourses*.

5. From "The Rossetti Manuscript."

6. From "Songs of Experience."

7. From *The Varieties of Religious Experience*.

8. From "Auguries of Innocence."

9. From "The Four Zoas."

10. From "All Religions Are One."

11. Here, on the other hand, is how Blake disposes of Sunday School morality:

> He has observ'd the golden rule,
> Till he's become the golden fool.
>
> (From the *Rossetti MS.*)

12. From *The Idler*, May 19, 1759. To be fair to Johnson, his essay is ironic on the virtue of playing safe.

13. From "Absalom and Achitophel."

14. For Blake assumed that Isaac Newton himself, the genius behind 18th century science, had deadened the human spirit within the mold of physical laws. In fact, Newton the man had a sense of awe and humility before the cosmos that is Blakean:

> I do not know what I may appear to the world, but to myself I seem to have been only a boy playing on the sea-shore, and diverting myself in now and then finding a smoother pebble or prettier shell than ordinary, whilst the great ocean of truth lay all undiscovered before me.
>
> (from David Brewster, *Memoirs of Newton*.)

15. From Lynn Segal, *The Dream of Reality: Heinz von Foerster's Constructivism.*

16. In his essay, "The Transcendent Function."

17. From Jay Haley, *Uncommon Therapy.* I also heard Erickson tell this tale himself.

18. From Milton Erickson, "Hypnotherapy of Two Psychosomatic Dental Problems," in *Advanced Techniques of Hypnosis and Therapy.*

19. Pope's thought rings true here: "Good-nature and good-sense must ever join." (From "An Essay on Criticism.") But one can easily hear Blake snorting at it.

20. Throughout this book I use the word "patient" when quoting the views of physician therapists, "client" when speaking of the therapeutic process more generally.

21. In conversation.

22. From the Foreword, *The Viking Book of Aphorisms, A Personal Selection*, by W. H. Auden and Louis Kronenberger.

23. From "Auguries of Innocence."

24. From "Gnomic Verses."

25. From "Songs of Experience."

26. From "Gnomic Verses."

27. Most of Blake's poetry was completed by 1808. He engraved and painted during the remaining 19 years of his life, perhaps sustained in his work by receiving more recognition for it than for his verse. Even he must have been troubled by paucity of response.

28. My translation; to my knowledge, the book is not available in English.

29. From "Auguries of Innocence."

30. From his encyclopaedia article, "Psychoanalysis," 1922.

31. Kleist's essay, "Über das Marionettentheater." My translation; to my knowledge, the essay is not available in English.

CHAPTER 3

1. The publisher Kurt Wolff gives evidence for a physical love affair between the young Rilke and Lou, from his conversation with her in 1916. (Kurt Wolff, *A Portrait in Essays and Letters.*) But what remained important for Rilke was Lou's kindling of his creative life, not of his passion.

2. From *Advent,* 1898, in *Translations from the Poetry of Rainer Maria Rilke.*

3. From *New Poems,* 1907-08, in *Translations from the Poetry of Rainer Maria Rilke.*

4. From *New Poems.*

5. From *Sämtliche Werke,* Band 2, "Entwürfe, Paris, 1913-1914." The translation is mine.

6. From *Italian Hours.*

7. From *Sonnets to Orpheus,* 2nd part, number 4, 1922.

8. From *Sonnets to Orpheus,* 2nd part, number 24, 1922.

9. From "Uncollected Poems, 1923-1926" in *The Selected Poetry of Rainer Maria Rilke.*

10. Ibid.

11. Kappus was in his mid-forties, in 1929, when he published Rilke's letters to him. Rilke had died at the end of December 1926.

12. It is, of course, a reasonable guess that Rilke's change in tone was strongly generated by new concerns about sexual uncertainties and loneliness in Kappus' writing. All Rilke's letters appear to have been written as specific replies to Kappus, and the whole series may be understood as the "young poet's" increasing comprehension of Rilke's message.

From the continuity of address in the last two letters we have, spaced four years apart, it also seems probable that there were some other answers by Rilke in between, which Kappus didn't submit for publication.

13. Compare the poet W.H. Auden's differing candor on: "The physical tedium...of writ[ing]...out in longhand...a poem by

somebody else. [T]he hand is constantly looking for an excuse to stop." From his collection of essays, *The Dyer's Hand.*

14. Thus, for instance, the eighth letter concludes:

> Do not believe that he who seeks to comfort you lives untroubled among the simple and quiet words that sometimes do you good. His life has much difficulty and sadness and remains far behind yours. Were it otherwise he would never have been able to find those words.

15. So speak existential psychotherapists of our time — Ludwig Binswanger, in Switzerland, Rollo May in America: for a true picture of the inner life, subjective detail is everything.

16. Rilke's sense of the future that is already contained in the past is the exact inverse of Proust's, that we recover our past again at a much later time, through the action of involuntary memory. These two geniuses of literature and psychology, writing in western Europe at the same time, both famous, apparently never met or knew each other's work. But one feels that each of them would have accepted the other's insights as an extension of his own.

17. His letter is from January 1913 — nine to ten years after Rilke's letters. But he is the same age that Rilke was when addressing Kappus.

18. The inner quotation marks are Rilke's. Evidently he is quoting a phrase from Kappus' last letter to him.

19. This last, memorable phrase is from the sixth letter, Christmas 1903, written in Rome.

20. Quoted by Roland Barthes, *A Lover's Discourse.*

21. From the ninth letter, written November 1904, in Sweden.

22. To list them in order of priority that they speak — or rather, that I hear them speak — in my office: pride, anger, envy, sloth, lust, gluttony, covetousness. This listing may appear merely subjective on my part, but I believe it represents

a phenomenon of our time that modifies Freud's drive theory of neurosis. Pride, sloth, envy are significantly disorders of the ego as much as of the Freudian id. The distressed ego is swollen, tender, painful, self-protecting; in short, it is inflamed. It suffers, we might say, from *Egoitis*. Weak egos inflame readily. Strong egos are more able to moult into that "not repeatable being" which Rilke describes us to be.

23. From the ninth letter.

24. From the third letter.

25. From the ninth letter.

26. As a therapeutic standpoint, Rilke's is fundamentally noninterpretive. Confusion, sadness, loneliness are not explicable and removable. They are states of being. But a wider view of these things increases the factors in them, shows them at a larger base, as the fraction 16/32 has more factors in it than its equivalent, 4/8.

27. From the seventh letter.

28. From the eighth letter.

29. From the ninth letter.

30. Rilke's goal of invisibility strikes a further accord with Jung, whose therapeutic concern with the withdrawal of projections also moves toward a withdrawal from the external world. "In this way," he writes in the next-to-last chapter of *Memories, Dreams, and Reflections*, "the imagination liberates itself from the concretism of the object." But the question remains: how much of life does this liberation disavow?

In fairness to Jung's earthiness, however, he speaks in his last chapter of the wisdom of stooping low, "to fetch water from the stream." And he had his own critique of Rilke's refined sensibility: in a letter of 1957, he acknowledged the poet's depth and gifts, but added, "he doesn't have what it takes to make a man complete: body, weight, shadow."

31. According to Peters' biography of Lou Andreas-Salomé, this famous statement of Rilke's attitude toward psychoanalysis originated as a warning to him from Lou, during a conversation between them. As a psychoanalyst herself, she was evidently showing a profound distrust of her own profession.

32. I have amended Freud slightly. The quotation is from his first book, *Studies in Hysteria,* and at this point he is speaking of just one neurotic symptom, "hysterical misery": that is, emotionally induced physical suffering, pain, paralysis, and so on. But my generalizing to other neuroses — chronic anxiety, depression, phobias, and the like — is true to the spirit of his words.

33. See his essay, "Analysis Terminable and Interminable."

34. Rilke's pessimism has its moments too. For instance:

> We're not at one. We've no instinctive knowledge
> like migratory birds. Outstripped and late, we
> force ourselves on winds, and find no welcome
> from ponds where we alight.

(From "The Fourth Elegy," *Duino Elegies.* The translation, uncited, is taken from *The Viking Book of Aphorisms.*)

But Rilke makes a recurrent return to inward harmony; whereas Kafka gives us, we shall see, Himalayas of disharmony.

35. In 1916, as his military service, Rilke was at the Ministry of War, in Vienna. When the war began, he had heard a creative note in the reappearance of the "war-god," and written odes in this vein. But soon the sheer destructiveness of the war overcame him. In Vienna he couldn't produce the propaganda expected of him. A cultivated officer saw that he was left alone to do his own work — such delicacy within warfare still was possible in World War I — and soon Rilke was demobilized, and traveling again.

36. *Purgatory,* end of Canto 27, John Ciardi, translator.

CHAPTER 4

1. From his story, "Report to an Academy."

2. Compare Gogol, a month before his death, stoking the fire with the second and third parts of *Dead Souls*, against the pleas of the servant boy who was with him. Kafka did himself destroy some of his manuscripts, but, fortunately, only a small share. It was like a suicidal gesture, instead of the actual thing.

3. As to public affairs, Kafka was exempt from armed service during World War I because of his job with a government organization. Austrian defeats caused him anxieties, but his chief concern remained personal: whether in war or peace, how should he, how could he live?

4. From here on, I give the number of the aphorism in parenthesis. I follow the listing in the volume, *The Great Wall of China: Stories and Reflections*. The numbering is slightly different in the published German text.

5. The aphorism about the Tower is number 15 of the series. The "pit of Babel" comes from elsewhere. It is printed in Franz Kafka, *Parables and Paradoxes*, 1961.

6. A central theme of his *Concluding Unscientific Postscript*.

7. Six words, in Kafka's German: "Ein Käfig ging einen Vogel suchen."

8. Translation, for once, has an edge on the original: in the German, "Weg" opposes "Zögern" with no wordplay.

9. The opening lines, third stanza, of "Sailing to Byzantium":

> O sages standing in God's holy fire
> As in the gold mosaic of a wall....

10. Admittedly, Kafka's German is more fragmentary than the translation of Willa Edwin Muir that I have used. The imperative, "Let the face sink," isn't in the original, only an infinitive with its tone of speculation: "To sink the face...on the breast." But the vision of reconcilement is there.

11. From *Psychoanalytic Theory, Therapy, and the Self.*

12. This statement belongs to one of many Talmudic-like commentaries on a parable which K. and a priest discuss.

13. See Sigmund Freud, *Introductory Lectures on Psychoanalysis*; Harry Stack Sullivan, *The Interpersonal Theory of Psychiatry*. For the double bind, see Chapter 7 to come.

I am not implying that the good theorists are without therapeutic effect. But it is more sporadic, a shaft of light on obscure suffering, as when Sullivan was exquisitely gentle with a mute psychotic. But he was known too to be moody and remote with patients. Freud, on his part, ended a therapeutic pessimist. Bateson considered most therapy invasive, not liberating.

14. Kafka wrote another, briefer set of aphoristic notes, dated 1920, which speak of "He." Curiously, this third-person series sounds more private, more like a special case. For example: "Some deny the existence of misery by pointing to the sun; he denies the existence of the sun by pointing to misery." The aphorisms which I've discussed do have several "He," but more of "We" and still more "Du."

15. It isn't surprising that Rilke himself admired some stories of Kafka that he knew, and that he wrote to a friend, in 1917, saying he wanted to read everything Kafka wrote.

16. From *The Longest Journey*.

17. From his letter to George and Georgiana Keats, 14 Feb. - 3 May, 1819.

CHAPTER 5

1. From "Gnomic Verses."

2. A fine phrase from his essay, "Images of Good and Evil."

3. Buber's epigraph to *I and Thou*.

4. From the Anglican *Book of Common Prayer*. St. Thomas, the source of the words in the prayer book, speaks somewhat differently. "Our sacraments are signs of present grace." *Summa Theologica*, III: 38, 6, 5.

5. Maurice Friedman reports that Buber used this word with him in conversation about *Daniel*. In *Martin Buber's Life and Work*, Volume 1.

6. From Buber's preface to *Pointing the Way, Collected Essays*, 1957.

7. For her essay, "The Mottoes of My Life." She uses not the modern "Je répondrai," but the Renaissance French spelling; she got it from the words on the crest of the Finch-Hatton family.

8. From "Proverbs in Prose," *The Permanent Goethe*, Thomas Mann, ed. In the German, from "Maximen und Reflexionen," #1088, *op. cit.*

9. I use the translation of Ronald Gregor Smith, Buber's first and favorite English translator. The fine scholar Walter Kaufman has since retranslated the book, claiming to be more accurate. But what he has gained for Buber's pedagogy, he has lost of his lyricism, and the loss is major. His "I-You," for instance, simply doesn't convey the combined intimacy-and-loftiness of *I-Thou*, which is Buber's "Ich-Du." The same prosiness runs throughout Kaufman's version. Gregor Smith keeps the poetry.

10. Or *hers*. For Buber's own point about third person pronouns, see the next paragraph of my text.

11. Whitman, the free-verse American democrat, is a far cry from Buber, the cultured methodical European. Therefore the one lights up the other more vividly.

12. An etymological note on word-conscious Buber repays our attention here. The disyllable "*Gegen*" belongs to all his basic nouns. It is out front in "*Gegenwart*" and "*Gegenstand.*" It is contracted between prefix and suffix in "*Be-geg'n-ung*" and his neologism "*Ver-geg'n-ung.*" In German, "*Gegen*" often signifies *opposition*, as in "*I move against the enemy.*" But also it can mean, *in contact with*, as in "I lean against the wall"; and that is its function in Buber's words. "*Gegenwart*" means "presence," or "being in contact with"; "*Gegenstand,*" "an independent object which I contact." As to "*Begegnung*": the prefix "*Be*" generally signifies *empowering*; therefore, "fullness of contact," or "meeting." *Ver*" is at times a sign of *falsity*. And so "*Vergegnung*": "false contact," or "mis-meeting." All four words bear a kinesthetic sense, a tension of physical movement. They convey the solid muscle of relationship, precisely what Kafka missed in it.

13. Mahler's words, "object constancy" refer to the sense of "emotional constancy": for instance, Mother, as a recognizable object, is still a loving person to the small child after he is separated from her. (Margaret Mahler, *The Psychological Birth of the Human Infant.*) So goes a fortunate development, and

that is what Buber is describing here. In disturbed development, the object is "inconstant" "bad mother" irreconcilable with "good mother": *Thou* has left the child too soon; and so the story of *Thou* and *It* in his life becomes more complicated.

Mahler's theory of development begins differently from Buber's. It assumes that the child's earliest infancy is autistic, then slowly differentiates into a realm of relating. But another psychoanalytic theorist, Daniel Stern, has described self-development from birth by a series of concepts that align much more with those of Buber. (In *The Interpersonal World of the Infant.*) Stern's "emergent self" and "core self" (from birth to six months) are guarantors that I, from the start, am in a relational communion, not an undifferentiated oneness with the mother. However, the "core self" of Stern already has the "self-coherence" that Buber ascribes to separated-I. Later, beginning after seven months, Stern's "subjective self," the capacity to share and not share, and his "verbal self," with its abstractions from direct relatedness, definitely have the dimensions of Buber's I in *I-It*, "[s]hrunk from substance and fullness...."

14. From "The Garden."

15. Here for once the translator has improved on the original. Buber's German lacks the wonderfully repeated word.

16. My italics.

17. My italics.

18. In *Letters of Flannery O'Connor: The Habit of Being.*

19. My "his," for client and therapist, is a generality for the sake of style. It stands equally for the woman client and therapist. Buber's "his" has the same generality. See, too, footnote 10.

20. Reprinted in his collection of essays titled *The Knowledge of Man.*

21. From "Elements of the Interhuman," reprinted in Buber's *The Knowledge of Man.*

22. From "Elements of the Interhuman."

23. From *A Believing Humanism: Gleanings.* The middle sentence is also Buber's; its special brackets refer to its occurring before the other sentences in Buber's text, and in reference to a teacher and pupil. But for Buber the same point applies to the therapist and patient, so I've interpolated the sentence to strengthen the passage.

24. From "Dialogue between Martin Buber and Carl R. Rogers," Appendix to Buber's *The Knowledge of Man.*

25. I follow Buber's thought in "Elements of the Interhuman" and in the essay, "Healing Through Meeting," reprinted in his *Pointing the Way.*

26. Here I follow Buber's "Reply to C.G. Jung," published as a supplement to his book, *Eclipse of God.*

27. From a translation and recording by Rabbi Zalman Schachter.

28. In conversation with Jack Kornfield, the Buddhist meditation teacher. Equivalent words occur in her book, *A Gift for God.*

29. See, for instance, Arthur Young's diagrammatic book on the physical world and consciousness (*The Reflexive Universe*) or Ken Wilber's tabulations of spirituality East and West with ideas from psychological science (*The Atman Project*).

30. From *Between Man and Man.*

31. From "Objects," in *The Concept of Nature.*

32. From the essay, "Man and His Image-Work," in *The Knowledge of Man.*

33. From his letter to Louis Colet, August 8-9, 1846.

34. From A. E. Housman, *Last Poems.*

35. From "Proverbs in Prose," *The Permanent Goethe,* Thomas Mann, ed.

CHAPTER 6

1. Approximate pronunciation of the book: *Dow Duh Djing.* Of the man's name: Low Tsuh (the first syllable rhyming with "now.")

2. The traditional number of the verse which I quote is given each time in the parentheses just after the excerpt.

Serious problems of interpretation exist with the *Tao Te Ching,* as the text is obscure and no translation is unarguably accurate. But the sense of awe and the spirit of allowing are in all of them. I have chosen the translation of Gia-Fu Feng, liking the stateliness of his verse and the heightened sense it gives to the leaps of the thought. But what language, indeed, will convey the wordless truth of awe? We have climbed down a metaphysical rung from Buber's Primary Words. Here is the essentially inexpressible.

3. Generalities about art, as about religion, are always dangerous. One does see Eastern equanimity in Byzantine mosaics, in Fra Angelico, in Raphael, as one sees passion in Oriental art — for instance, the famous frieze of dancers at Angkor Vat. But even in these cases, there is a contrasting inflection: for Raphael, the theme of personal drama; for the sculptor at Angkor Vat, passion formalized beyond the personal.

One significant exception to the contrast that I sketch is Christian mysticism, which joins with that of the East in a sense of union beyond any sense of deity. Therefore Meister Eckhart: "I pray God that he may quit me of God." (From his 28th Sermon, on "Blessed are the poor in spirit.") And yet, once again here, Christian drama returns: for this is fervent prayer to a personal God.

4. From *The City of God.*

5. The phrase, derived from William James, incorporates what we mean today by the stream of the *unconscious*. James would not have liked this partitioning of mental life into two domains, but clinical work has taken us there. And our literature, of course, is rich in experiments with the unconscious, most elaborately, *Finnegans Wake* of James Joyce.

6. From his *Commentary on the Secret of the Golden Flower.*

7. From Eric Jantsch, *Evolution and Consciousness*. Jantsch makes a still wider parallel between the "pure process" of biological evolution, consciousness, and Taoism.

8. From Marguerite Yourcenar, *Mishima: A Vision of the Void.*

9. From Ssu Ma Ch'ien. In Lao-tzu's speech, I quote the traditional words in my first sentence, but adapt the rest, with equivalent images and ideas for today. For a standard translation, see Alan Watts, *Tao: The Watercourse Way.*

10. From the *Svetāsvatara Upanishad.*

11. From *The Wisdom of Laotse*, Lin Yutang, editor.

12. At the same time, we note a difference from Buber's view. For his *Thou* is a fleeting experience. But Lao-tzu's sage lives unbrokenly with *Thou*. When he turns to worldly affairs, he shifts his attention to Buber's *It*. But the shift is like the shift of weight in T'ai Chi when the distribution is 70%-30%: so to

speak, weighted forward on one foot in worldliness, 70%; rooted behind 30% on the other foot and grounded in *Thou*. When his weight re-collects, at 100% for the next movement, *Thou* moves with him.

13. From Shakespeare, *Henry the Fourth, Part I.*

14. The contrast in Western theology is obvious. Milton's famous resolve, at the beginning of *Paradise Lost*, is to

> assert Eternal Providence
> And justify the ways of God to men.

15. From his *Greece.*

16. Quoted in *The Viking Book of Aphorisms.*

17. Perhaps it is the permeating images which make the text (according to the last word of its title, *Ching*) "a classic": *Tao Te Ching: The Classic of the Way and Its Power.*

18. I heard this tale from the Buddhist meditation teacher, Jack Kornfield.

19. As told to Jay Haley; in his *Uncommon Therapy.*

20. From Heinz Kohut, *The Restoration of the Self.*

21. From his essay, "The Borderline Adult: Transference Acting-Out and Working-Through," in *New Perspectives of Psychotherapy of the Borderline Adult*, ed., James F. Masterson.

22. Kohut has died, but his stylistic successors continue, in print and in the consulting room.

23. From Ralph Waldo Emerson, "Circles." In its lucid imagery, Emerson's mysticism joins with Lao-tzu's.

24. From his talk in Jerusalem, April 26, 1990, upon receiving an honorary degree.

I selected this passage from Havel before the recent divisionof Czechoslovakia, when "an abyss" did open for him and in the "middle of being president," he resigned from office. He remains, in failure as in success, a man of Tao.

CHAPTER 7.

1. From *Just So Stories.*

2. Quoted in *The Viking Book of Aphorisms.*

3. From his book, *Mind and Nature.*

4. Quoted as a personal communication to the author, in David Lipset, *Gregory Bateson, The Legacy of a Scientist.* I am indebted to this book for quotations of Bateson apart from those given in other stated texts, or from my own conversations with him.

5. From Gregory Bateson, *Naven.*

6. During World War II, Gregory worked for the Office of Strategic Services in Southeast Asia, feeding Japanese propaganda back to the Japanese. "We listened to the enemy's nonsense and we professed to be a Japanese official station. Every day we simply exaggerated what the enemy was telling people...The enemy [was] probably telling lies as big as he dared, and therefore it [seemed] a good idea to have him appear to tell still bigger lies." Thereby rendering himself unbelievable. — This was a piece of symmetrical schismogenesis.

7. From Bertrand Russell and Alfred North Whitehead, "Introduction," *Principia Mathematica.*

8. So, too, we can explicate Buber's poetic statements: "Prayer is not in time but time in prayer..." etc. (Chapter 5, page 105.) Prayer is a higher, more inclusive logical level.

The image of nesting boxes indicates too how a higher level can comprehend a lower, but not the reverse. An ant crawling on a grapefruit can take no bearings as to the round shape. But a human being watching both is aware of the sphere. Similarly for any larger Gestalt: Kafka's "parable," as a higher logical level, includes "reality"; and the Tao, Lao-tzu's "ten thousand things."

9. The same for the data itself. For instance: a schizophrenic man in a mental hospital shows his spontaneous love for his mother on a visit by putting his arms around her. She stiffens. He blushes. She then says, "Dear, you mustn't be so afraid of

your feelings." In a few minutes he is too agitated to stay with her, assaults someone else, and must be restrained.

The double bind observed is: If he shows love, he is in the wrong. If he doesn't, he is in the wrong. And he wants her love. But he can do nothing to get it. In this case, the double bind seems dramatically clear; but after all, I *have presented* it dramatically. Gregory noted that the thing observed always depends on the observer: a *caveat* to all theorists of the mind. "You can't *count* the double binds in a situation," he once said to me. One can hardly imagine the number that Kafka saw.

10. This can be called the intent of all inclusive theorizing in science. But, as I've said about Western approaches to the Tao itself, fact and theory are often bent to fit one another.

11. From *Mind and Nature.* Of other contemporary thinkers, only the French essayist Roland Barthes reminds me of Gregory. Barthes speaks, for instance, of the *pheno-song* — a composer's intention and style, and the *geno-song* — the singer's voice in all its expressiveness. (From his essay, "The Grain of the Voice," in the collection, *The Responsibility of Forms.*) This bonding of anatomy and an art form is similar to Gregory's connection of anatomy to grammar. Both men delight in subtle, cross-disciplinary concepts such as these, which contain a certain irreducible exoticism.

12. *Steps to an Ecology of Mind.*

13. The harmony of our own nature, of human body and soul, with the nature of the universe is certainly intrinsic to the Socratic ideal. (See Werner Jaeger, *Paideia, The Ideals of Greek Culture.*) And it traces back still further, in unbroken lineage, to Homeric arete, man's perfection, emulating the gods, in physical prowess and breadth of soul. As social critic, Gregory's constant concern was our loss of this large taproot in favor of the thin, branching roots of technical expertise.

14. The two anthropologists had first met at Christmas 1932, in New Guinea, where she too was working. Their years together were a picture in contrast: the small American, a quick-witted Lilliputian who, in immediate coherence and clarity, towered over her tall, introverted Gulliver. Margaret remained his lifelong friend and later, in her autobiography,

paid an ambiguous tribute to his intellectual style. He liked "to generate small stretches of data...not in themselves priceless...that can be discarded when the thinking they were meant to underpin [was] done." Do we hear a note of her feeling discarded herself? His own view, in his seventies, was: "Had we had more quarrels...we might have stayed together."

15. Implicit in the first metalogue, this idea comes into its own three years later in the book, *Communication.*

16. From the third Metalogue: "About Games and Being Serious."

17. The same virtuous disorder is in the most controlled art. Classical French drama, an acme of tidiness, maintains unities of time, place, action, and rhymed alexandrines. But it also keeps, as Corneille said, "unity of danger." And Novalis, celebrating Mozart's music, wrote of it: "Chaos shimmers through the adornment of order." (Quoted by Alfred Brendel, in *Musical Thoughts and Afterthoughts.*)

18. The original has "You are," not "You're." For the sake of style, I've edited in this minor way here and a few other places.

19. In "The Logical Categories of Learning and Communication," *Steps to an Ecology of Mind.*

20. From "Double Bind, 1969," in *Steps to an Ecology of Mind.*

21. Like many research discoveries, this goal was not anticipated. The trainer was just interested in demonstrating the dolphin's response to diverse operant conditioning. And, manipulative as it is, this learning sequence isn't something Gregory would himself ever have *devised.* But as a *fait accompli,* his mind relished it. Then he suggested a second experiment of the same kind, which had the same success.

22. The idea permeates his mature thought, but he only spoke about it publicly twenty-six years after "Why a Swan?" in a talk, "The Eternal Verities," given at the C. G. Jung Institute, San Francisco, during the last months of his life.

23. From *Isaiah,* 40:6.

24. Kant's categories, however, are concerned just with the life we know: space, time, and causality as *human* modes of

perception. (*The Critique of Pure Reason.*) Gregory excludes from "mind" only the inorganic world of forces and impacts, which is not internally self-regulating.

It is his sense of the-mind-as-a-network which led to the rather cryptic phrase in his title, "Ecology of Mind."

25. The 7th Metalogue, "What is an Instinct?" probes this question in a fragmentary way. It's clear, however, that Gregory finds the concept unsatisfactory. "Instinct" is supposed to be unlearned behavior; but it traces to chromosomes, and we don't know, in the first place, if chromosomes can learn. In any case, his preferred view is of *patterns,* as with his definition of mind, and not of *entities,* to which instinct refers.

26. My discussion about mental process and stochastic process is culled from *Mind and Nature.*

27. My essay was completed before the publication of *Angels Fear,* Mary Catherine Bateson's reworking of Gregory's final notes, with additional essays by her. The book does not go beyond the scope of *Mind and Nature,* but is a sparkling commentary on it. In one of her own imagined dialogues with her father, Mary Catherine, herself a professor of anthropology, comments, "You know, you never gave me the good lines when you were writing the Metalogues." In my reading of the Metalogues I haven't agreed with this, but in any case she gives herself a good line here! And throughout her book she keeps pace with him, while faithfully reporting his concern with "the lonely skeleton of truth." As always, this skeleton looks to him Socratic. It bespeaks investigative questions, such as "[W]hat characteristic [will] you want built into a machine to agree that that machine is schizophrenic?" It rouses moral ones, like "How shall we interpret the responsibility of those who deal with living systems?" The book's own morality is its fidelity to the questions, so that, as Mary Catherine concludes, we may recover lost information, or "identify missing pieces" from the web of life.

A still more recent collection of Gregory's essays has appeared, *Sacred Unity,* edited by a devoted follower, Rodney E. Donaldson. Except for a few short pieces, these papers were all previously published in diverse books and journals, and reaffirm Gregory's thought, rather than add to it. His own published books, especially *Steps to an Ecology of Mind* and *Mind and Nature*, remain the best starting place for his ideas.

28. From "Form, Substance, and Difference," the Nineteenth Annual Korzybski Memorial Lecture, January 9, 1970.

29. This idea of a prevailing social system parallels to a degree 20th century theory in physics, which includes the observer and observed into a single system. But, as Gregory emphasized, a living system probes, learns, modifies its behavior, and keeps its own counsel as the inorganic world does not; so that Alice's game of croquet with flamingo mallets and hedgehog balls is far more unpredictable to anyone than, say, tomorrow's weather is to a meteorologist.

30. The metalogues, with all their associated ideas, provide the infrastructure on which Gregory's system insights rest. As we've seen, he himself looks to systems beyond the human, and to human systems beyond the clinical. But my discussion of him, as with the other men in this book, will focus chiefly on his value for therapists.

31. From *The Family and Individual Development.*

32. From his book, *The Psychiatric Interview.*

33. Some new developments in psychoanalytic thinking accord with systems theory. Thus: "Psychoanalysis is...a science of the intersubjective, focused on the interplay between the differently organized subjective worlds of the observer and the observed. The observational stance is always one within, rather than outside, the intersubjective field...being observed." (George Atwood and Robert Stolorow, *Structures of Subjectivity: Explorations in Psychoanalytic Phenomenology.*) Coming a generation after Bateson's work and the climate of opinion it evoked, this new approach in psychoanalysis seems like an offspring of his.

34. From *Shamans, Mystics, and Doctors.*

35. Adapted from a case report by Michele Ritterman.

36. From *Mind and Nature.*

37. From "Jerusalem."

38. As we've seen, the double bind intrigued Gregory as positive learning for dolphins, and as the path to unconditioned human learning. With his usual doubt about therapists' motives, its directive use in psychotherapy interested him less.

39. From "The Use of Symptoms as an Integral Part of Hypnotherapy," in Erickson's *Advanced Techniques of Hypnosis and Therapy,* Jay Haley, ed.

40. I heard this story from him in person.

40. From "Andrea del Sarto." Browning's second line, in case Gregory's has wiped out remembrance, is:

Or what's a heaven for?

CHAPTER 8

1. From *Talk in Ojai, June 25, 1944.*

2. From *Commentaries on Living, First Series.*

3. My account of Krishnamurti's life, and quotations (except as cited from other sources), are based on Mary Lutyens' two volumes, *Krishnamurti, The Years of Awakening,* and *Krishnamurti, The Years of Fulfillment.*

4. At the same time, from 1912-1914 a bitter court battle over Krishnamurti's and Nitya's custody was waged by their father. He had brought them into Theosophy, but it was now proving to be at the expense of their Hinduism. Going abroad, they would break caste rules. He further accused Leadbeater of sexual misconduct with the boys, though they denied this. The court finally settled in Mrs. Besant's favor. As young men, in 1922, Krishnamurti and Nitya attempted to reconcile with their father, but his outrage was beyond recall. For Krishnamurti, the family rupture was sad, but not tragic. He felt himself to be Mrs. Besant's son.

5. From his poem, "The Path."

6. From his novel, *Geneviève.*

7. From Coleridge's "Dejection: An Ode."

8. This refers to the Buddha's first sermon after his enlightenment, as recorded in the Sutras.

9. From *Krishnamurti's Notebook.* (Unless otherwise noted, all the quotations in this section belong to *Freedom from the Known.*)

10. From his *Confessions.*

11. From *Religio Medici.*

12. From *A Gift for God, Prayers and Meditations.*

13. From "For the Time Being, a Christmas Oratorio."

14. I'm aware that I've been presenting the Augustinean version of Christianity, not the gnostic, and the primitive teachings of Buddhism, not, for instance, its complex Tibetan thought which describes man, even a yogi, as often trapped in unenlightenment. But, historically, Christian original sin and Buddhist perfectability stand in the vivid contrast I give them.

15. It is scattered throughout his *Notebook.*

16. From his letter to his brothers George and Thomas, December 21, 1817. In *The Selected Letters of John Keats,* Lionel Trilling, ed.

17. Quoted in *The Viking Book of Aphorisms.*

18. Krishnamrti's talk of unity, between observer and observed, that is not identification, exactly parallels Buber's on creative communion in art, and in the *I-Thou* within mankind and toward God. See chapter V, pages 106-109. To my knowledge, neither man was aware of the other's thought.

19. On the inconsequence of person in the traditions of the East, see Chapter VI, page 125.

20. From *The First and Last Freedom.*

21. From Schiller, *Naive and Sentimental Poetry.*

22. His "explosiveness" is another difference in the *timbre* of his thought from Buddhist "onlooking equanimity." The latter has more the ring of Freud's "even-hovering attention."

23. From "A Weary Hour," in *Stories of Three Decades*.

24. Krishnamurti, of course, was a pacifist. As a young man in England, during World War I, he had wanted to wear a uniform and work in a hospital, but Mrs. Besant asked him to stay with his studies. By the time of World War II, as an international religious teacher, he was opposed to war as to all other cultivations of conflict and defense. In public talks at the time, he insisted on the importance, rather, of attending to "the war within." Needless to say, he was unpopular.

25. My information about Krishnamurti in Washington comes from talks with Dr. Weininger. Confirming views of Sullivan are scattered in his writing, notably the paper, "The Illusion of Personal Individuality," in the journal *Psychiatry*, 1950, Volume 13.

26. His emphasis matches, too, the sense of transformation in the moment, which Gestalt therapy had introduced in this country in the 1950s.

27. From Oliver Sacks, "Sublime Idiot Geniuses," *The New York Review of Books*, February 28, 1985.

28. From his sermon, "Blessed Are the Poor in Spirit."

29. Number 60 of Kafka's "Reflections."

30. Number 51 of Kafka's "Reflections."

31. The wit of this passage stands, though it reveals the books that Krishnamurti may have "very carefully" neglected to read. Emerson wrote, "The act of seeing and the thing seen,...the subject and the object are one." (From his essay, "The Over-Soul.") Coleridge's similar phrase, in *Biographia Literaria*, is "the coincidence or coalescence of an object with a subject" in the act of knowing. Krishnamurti's originality, of course, doesn't depend at all on his being the first person to say a thing, but, to paraphrase him, on his being himself at one with what he says.

32. Verbal report from William Quinn.

A new book, *Lives in the Shadow with Krishnamurti*, has just been published, which must not be ignored in a personal appraisal of the man. The author, Radha Sloss, is the daughter of Rajagopal, Krishnamurti's business manager and editor, 1926-*circa* 1960. Her title comes from T. S. Eliot's "The Hollow Men," and gives the thrust of her text. After the luminous hero of Mary Lutyens' biography, photographed, so to speak, from aerial views, we are shown here, up close, a figure of blight.

The trump card of this exposé is Krishnamurti's love affair, beginning in 1932 and continuing for the next 25 years, with Radha's mother Rosalind, whose husband, on his part, had ended their sexual relationship with the birth of their daughter, the year before the affair began. Krishnamurti always kept the affair secret – it appears to have been the single sexual love of his life – while he continued to encourage his public image as a religious ascetic. He kept it also from the husband, after telling Rosalind that he would confide it to him, and then letting her believe that he had done so. Much later, when Rajagopal did know of it from his wife and no longer wished to work for Krishnamurti, the latter tried, through a lawsuit, to take from Rajagopal all his copyrights of Krishnamurti's writings, and perhaps too papers that might allude to the affair.

The author's revelations about the trio come from her mother, though even as a child she could have written her own Jamesian "What Radha Knew."

But, to give the situation some second thoughts: Just what *should* Krishnamurti have made, publicly, of his private life? His teachings speak not of celibacy but of creative love and going one's own way. He seems in fact to have conducted his love affair at a high level of tenderness, not to speak of romance (he wouldn't smell first the rose that he regularly brought to his beloved's room, so as to take nothing away from the gift). And how announce "a love affair with my business manager's wife," without provoking a scandal, to the unfair denigration of his teachings? But also, he was afraid. He had walked away from the Theosophy Kingdom; but it was something else to have to, perhaps, abdicate the later kingdom of his own making. And, probably, to lose the constant help of Rajagopal, on whom he depended; why risk it, when evasion of the truth with him, and thereby, Rosalind's deception, were easier? No! He held out for the status quo, his image of unreal purity; in that respect, he didn't himself venture to be "free from the known." And gets his comeuppance in this book, with a sort of ironic Greek fatality.

The trio presented is really a quartet which includes the author. One senses that she would have forgiven Krishnamurti a great deal if he hadn't fought her father, in their old age, out of what seems like a quite paranoid fear of treachery; there was no evidence for it. Her anger at him is quite understandable. So is her bewilderment, as she recalls his loving presence throughout her childhood and his intense nonverbal self: seeing clearly, without judgment, and so helping others. How is it, indeed, that fear and vanity so often walk arm in arm with transcendent powers and understandings? But they do. And granting that, one can understand too his guarding his teachings, like inspired and endangered children.

33. Among the "Proverbs in Prose," in *The Permanent Goethe*, Thomas Mann, ed. Number 50, "Maximen und Reflexionen," *Goethes Werke*, Band XII, C. H. Beck.

34. I have taken this image from the end of Tolstoy's folk tale, "Hadji Murád."

34. With his usual complexity, Krishnamurti was himself no stranger to the ongoing love affair between a public speaker and his audience. In her book, Radha Sloss quotes him in his old age telling her candidly: "I speak to live...[I]f there were no more talks I would die."

35. See Artur Schnabel, *My Life and Music.*

36. From Hudson Strode, "Isak Dinesen at Home," in *Isak Dinesen, A Memorial.*

37. In psychoanalytic terms, he has made the case too for *negative* transference and countertransference in psychotherapy. Therapist and client, after their pull to be "all-in-all" to one another, must discover, with dismay and resentment, that this really cannot be.

38. From Keats, "On Melancholy."

39. From Asit Chandmal, "J. Krishnamurti: The Last Walk," in *Bombay*, March 7-21, 1986.

CHAPTER 9

1. Students of philosophy will recognize in this primacy assigned to values a parallel with Plato's Idea of Good, from which all sound values derive. For Plato, nurture applies in this connection too: the idea of Good is the nurturant source of the values.

2. The plot compounds, of course, when a therapist uses his own power to maintain a patient's dependence, and to block self-nurture.

I'm aware, too, that I'm ignoring financial constraints to long-term therapy — which introduces the large question of social injustice in affordable treatment. On the other hand, I have seen patients with limited incomes maintain private psychotherapy for years, if on an intermittent basis, when they knew its importance to themselves.

3. Unconscious data, like a dream, and interpretation of the dream, are of course two different things. But we do not have a way of separating the meaning of the unconscious from an interpretation of it. Is my dream a warning, a memory, a prophecy, a wish, literal truth, symbolic truth, the sleeping version of waking thought, and so on? Since interpretation is unavoidable, one handles it best with modesty: something *may* be true; etc.

4. See Chapter II, page 36.

5. I am indebted to the meditation teacher Jack Kornfield for this pleasant correlation.

6. I am assuming that *the therapist*, as teacher, had better "be aware of" what is happening in the contact. For instance, is the client, with the therapist, projecting an old assumption learned from parents about closeness, in submissive goodwill or in flirtation? Or is there a new development of free contact? These insights are important for the therapist to share. But I am holding out, on the client's behalf, for the *primary* importance of contact; and on the therapist's part, this shows in the *manner* of his sharing his awareness, openly, with compassion, without judgment — attitudes difficult of access for the client by

virtue of his problems. In a word, the therapist's *attitude* says to the client: *Thou*. And it sets the tone for how the client can be nourished by his own self-insights; he comes to treat himself with the forbearance and acceptingness of Thou.

And because of the relation between awareness and quality of contact, the latter is always permeated with value. For example, to speak of *I-Thou* at all is to speak of values of depth and fullness in relationship which are not present in just getting information from another, or exchanging gossip. So it is that "the primacy of contact in psychotherapy" connects with the theme of values central to this book.

7. From Blake "If the fool would persist in his folly he would become wise."

8. This image is not orthodox Buber. To him, *Thou* means a real other; it is never equivalent to self-respect and self-acceptance. But the "otherness" of the mirror-reflection pleads the case. Consider all the substantiating witnesses from *Alice Through the Looking Glass*.

9. Like the ox in the Zen oxherding pictures, the bull here is a symbol of the psyche, transcending gender.

10. But therapy doesn't always go so well. Some people don't find my warmth warming, but instead an irritant, or intrusion, or a deprivation of their independence, and they leave treatment soon after they begin it. Some of them have recurrences of depression which the drug Prozac relieves more effectively than I can. What course is right for the person in front of me? Patients, like life, often leave one guessing.

CHAPTER 10

1. Harry Stack Sullivan, "The Illusion of Personal Individuality," *Psychiatry*, Volume 13, 1950.

2. A Johnsonian-style *bon mot*, unkind but not undeserved, which I've heard against Dr. Johnson's lengthier comments:

"Longitude and platitude." But at its best, of course, his wit had the soul of brevity: "Being in a ship is being in a jail, with the chance of being drowned."

3. From John Perry, *The Roots of Renewal in Myth and Madness.*

4. See Don Jackson, Paul Watzlawick, Janet Bavelas, *Pragmatics of Human Communication*; Jay Hayley, *Strategies of Psychotherapy*; Virginia Satir, *Conjoint Family Therapy.*

5. From Janet Malcolm, "A Reporter At Large, The One-Way Mirror," *The New Yorker*, May 15, 1978; about the work of Minuchin.

6. See Viktor Frankl, *Man's Search for Meaning.*

7. W.R. Bion, *Experiences in Groups and Other Papers.*

8. From his *Notes on Sarobia Discussions*, Eddington, Pennsylvania, 1940; reprinted in *Collected Works*, Volume 3.

9. From Shakespeare, *The Tempest.*

10. I heard this tale in conversation with Erickson. The same story is told a little differently in *A Teaching Seminar with Milton H. Erickson*, Jeffrey K. Zeig, ed.

11. The virtuosity which has led me to quote Erickson so often in this book. For this depth of contact is where the Tao flows.

12. From his letter to John Taylor, February 27, 1818.

13. From his Letter to George and Thomas Keats, December 21, 1817.

14. From No. 76 of the "Reflections."

15. John Donne, *Devotions Upon Emergent Occasions*; from the 6th Meditation.

16. This charming quotation occurs as I quote it, in *The Viking Book of Aphorisms.* But it's only fair to Sir William, a high-minded physician, to point out that his meaning in context is precisely the reverse; for his sentence continues, "...to which no discreet nurse will lend her talents." (From William Osler, *Aequanimias and Other Addresses to Medical Students, and Practitioners of Medicine*).

17. See Isaac Rosenfeld, "Neural Darwinism: A New Approach to Memory and Perception," *The New York Review of Books,* October 9, 1986, about the work of Gerald Edelman.

18. And observant Bateson once noted: "I always suspect that patients in psychotherapy exaggerate their traumatic histories...by a factor of about three; and that this is good for them." That is, it reinforces how seriously they should take their problems. (From Gregory Bateson, "Symptoms, Syndromes, and Systems," *The Esalen Catalogue, October-December, 1978.*)

19. From Ludwig Wittgenstein, *Tractatus Logico-Philosophicus.*

BIBLIOGRAPHY

An Aquinas Reader. (Mary T. Clark, editor). 1972. Garden City, NY: Image Books, Doubleday.

The Arabian Nights' Entertainments (Richard Burton, translator). 1932. New York: The Modern Library.

Atwood, George E., and Stolorow, Robert D. 1984. *Structures of Subjectivity: Explorations in Psychoanalytic Phenomenology*. Hillsdale, NJ: The Analytic Press.

Auden, W.H. 1945. *Collected Poetry*. New York: Random House.

Auden, W.H., and Kronenberger, Louis (editors). 1966. *The Viking Book of Aphorisms: A Personal Selection*. New York: The Viking Press.

Augustine, Saint. 1952. *The City of God*. Great Books of the Western Auden, W.H., and Pearson, Norman Holmes (editors). 1950. *Poets of the English Language, Vol. 2, Marlowe to Marvell*. New York: The Viking Press.

World, Volume 19. Chicago: Encyclopaedia Britannica.

Baron, Joseph L. (editor). 1985. *The Treasury of Jewish Quotations*. Highmount, NY: Aronson Publishing.

Barthes, Roland. 1978. *A Lover's Discourse*. New York: Hill and Wang.

Barthes, Roland. 1986. *The Responsibility of Forms*. New York: Hill and Wang.

Bateson, Gregory. 1958b. *Naven*. Palo Alto, CA: Stanford University Press.

Bateson, Gregory. 1972. *Steps to an Ecology of Mind*. San Francisco: Chandler Publishing.

Bateson, Gregory. 1978. "Symptoms, Syndromes, and Systems." *The Esalen Catalogue, October-December, 1978*. Big Sur, CA: Esalen Institute.

Bateson, Gregory (Donaldson, Rodney E., editor). 1991. *A Sacred Unity.* New York: Harper Collins Publishers.

Bateson, Gregory. 1958a. *Mind and Nature: A Necessary Unity.* New York: E.P. Dutton.

Bateson, Gregory, and Bateson, Mary Catherine. 1987. *Angels Fear: Towards an Epistemology of the Sacred.* New York: Macmillan.

Bateson, Gregory. 1981, Autumn. "The Eternal Verities," *The Yale Review,* Vol. 71.

Benjamin, Walter. 1969. *Illuminations.* New York: Schocken Books.

Berg, Stephen and Mezy, Robert. 1969. *Naked Poetry.* Indianapolis and New York: Bobbs-Merrill.

Bion, W.R. 1961. *Experiences in Groups and Other Papers.* 1961. New York: Basic Books.

Blackstone, Bernard. 1966. *English Blake.* Hamden, CT: Archon.

Blake, William. 1941. *The Poetical Works of William Blake.* John Sampson, editor. London: Humphrey Milford, Oxford University Press.

Bloom, Harold. 1963. *Blake's Apocalypse.* Garden City, NY: Doubleday.

Boswell, James. 1983. *The Life of Samuel Johnson.* New York: Oxford University Press.

Bowra, C.M. 1943. *The Heritage of Symbolism.* London: Macmillan.

Brendel, Alfred. 1976. *Musical Thoughts and Afterthoughts.* Princeton, NJ: Princeton University Press.

Brewster, Sir David. 1965. *Memoirs of the Life, Writings, and Discourses of Sir Isaac Newton.* New York: Johnson Reprint.

Broch, Hermann. 1983. *The Death of Virgil.* San Francisco: North Point Press.

Brontë, Emily. 1971. *Wuthering Heights.* Harmondsworth, Middlesex, England: Penguin Books.

Browne, Sir Thomas. Undated. *Religio Medici and Hydriotaphia (Urn-Burial).* Glasgow: Blackie and Son Limited.

Buber, Martin. 1958. *I and Thou.* New York: Charles Scribner's Sons.

Buber, Martin. 1962. *Good and Evil. Two Interpretations.* New York: Scribner Paperbacks.

Buber, Martin. 1965a. *Daniel.* New York: McGraw-Hill Book Company.

Buber, Martin. 1965b. *The Eclipse of God.* New York: Harper Torchbooks, Harper and Row.

Buber, Martin. 1965c. *The Knowledge of Man.* New York: Harper Torchbooks, Harper and Row.

Buber, Martin. 1967. *A Believing Humanism: Gleanings.* New York: Simon and Schuster.

Buber, Martin. 1971. *Between Man and Man.* New York: Macmillan.

Buber, Martin. 1974. *Pointing the Way.* New York: Schocken Books.

Butler, E.M. 1946. *Rainer Maria Rilke.* England: Cambridge University Press.

Camus, Albert. 1955. *The Myth of Sisyphus and Other Essays.* New York: Vintage Books, Random House.

Canetti, Elias. 1982. *Kafka's Other Trial.* New York: Penguin Books.

Chekhov, Anton. 1982. *Lady with Lapdog and Other Stories.* New York: Penguin Books.

The Cloud of Unknowing. 1961. Baltimore, Md.: Penguin Books.

Coleridge, Samuel Taylor. 1951. *Selected Poetry and Prose.* New York: The Modern Library, Random House.

Collins, Wilkie. 1982. *The Moonstone.* New York: Oxford University Press.

Damon, S. Foster. 1971. *A Blake Dictionary.* New York: E.P. Dutton.

Dante Alighieri. 1954-1970. *The Divine Comedy: The Inferno, The Purgatorio, The Paradiso.* 3 volumes. John Ciardi, translator. New York: The New American Library.

De Quincey, Thomas. 1853. "Essay on Pope," in *Essays on the Poets and Other English Writers.* Boston: Ticknor and Fields.

Dinesen, Isak (*nom de plume* of Karen Blixen). 1934. *Seven Gothic Tales.* New York: The Modern Library, Random House.

Dinesen, Isak (*nom de plume* of Karen Blixen). 1957a. *Last Tales*. New York: Random House.

Dinesen, Isak (*nom de plume* of Karen Blixen). 1957b. *Winter's Tales*. New York: Dell Publishing.

Donne, John. 1960. *Devotions upon Emergent Occasions*. Ann Arbor, MI: University of Michigan Press.

Dostoevsky, Fyodor. Undated. *The Best Short Stories of Dostoevsky*. New York: The Modern Library, Random House, Inc.

Dryden, John. 1950. *The Poetical Works of Dryden*. Boston: Houghton, Mifflin.

Einstein, Albert. 1956. *Out of My Later Years*. Secaucus, NJ: The Citadel Press.

Eliot, T.S. 1943. *Four Quartets*. New York: Harcourt, Brace & World.

Elytis, Odysseus. 1980. *Sema Tologion*. Athens: Ermeias.

Emerson, Ralph Waldo. 1951. *Essays*. New York: Thomas Y. Crowell.

Erickson, Milton H. 1967. *Advanced Techniques of Hypnosis and Therapy*. New York: Grune and Stratton.

Frankl, Viktor E. 1963. *Man's Search for Meaning: An Introduction to Logotherapy*. New York: Pocket Books.

Freud, Sigmund. 1950. *Collected Papers,* Volumes 1-4. London: The Hogarth Press and the Institute of Psycho-Analysis.

Freud, Sigmund. 1952. *Collected Papers,* Volume 5. London: The Hogarth Press and the Institute of Psycho-Analysis.

Freud, Sigmund. 1977. *Introductory Lectures on Psychoanalysis*. James Stravey, translator. New York: W.W. Norton.

Freud, Sigmund, and Breuer, Josef. 1936. *Studies in Hysteria*. New York and Washington: Nervous and Mental Disease Publishing Company.

Friedman, Maurice. 1976. *Martin Buber: The Life of Dialogue*. Chicago and London: The University of Chicago Press.

Friedman, Maurice. 1981. *Martin Buber's Life and Works: The Early Years. 1878-1923*. New York: E.P. Dutton, Inc.

Friedman, Maurice. 1983a. *Martin Buber's Life and Works: The Middle Years. 1923-1945*. New York: E.P. Dutton, Inc.

Friedman, Maurice. 1983b. *Martin Buber's Life and Works: The Later Years. 1945-1965.* New York: E.P. Dutton.

Frye, Northrop. 1958. *Fearful Symmetry: A Study of William Blake.* Princeton: Princeton University Press.

Gide, André. 1961. *Dostoevsky.* New York: New Directions.

Gide, André. 1963. *Pretexts: Reflections on Literature and Morality.* London: Secker & Warburg. First published, Meridian Books, Inc.

Gide, André. 1980. *The School for Wives; Robert; Genevieve.* Cambridge, MA: Robert Bentley.

Goethe, Johann Wolfgang von. "Maximen und Reflexionen." *Goethes Werke, Band XII.* München: C.H. Beck.

Goethe, Johann Wolfgang von. 1962. *The Sorrows of Young Werther.* New York: The New American Library of World Literature, Inc.

Goethe's World View presented in His Reflections and Maxims. 1963. New York: Frederick Ungar.

Goethe, Johann Wolfgang von. 1979. *West-Östlicher Divan.* Zweisprachig: Übersetzung ins Englische von J. Whaley. München: Deutscher Taschenbuch Verleg.

Gogol, Nikolai. 1960. *The Diary of a Madman and Other Stories.* New York: The New American Library.

Gogol, Nokolai. *The Government Inspector.* D.J. Campbell, translator. London: Heinemann.

Goldstein, Joseph. 1976. *The Experience of Insight: A Natural Unfolding.* Santa Cruz, CA: Unity Press.

Green, Hannah. 1964. *I Never Promised You a Rose Garden.* New York: Holt, Rinehart, and Winston.

Gross, John (editor). 1983. *The Oxford Book of Aphorisms.* New York: Oxford University Press.

Guntrip, Harry. 1973. *Psychoanalytic Theory, Therapy, and the Self.* New York: Basic Books.

Haley, Jay. 1973. *Uncommon Therapy: The Psychiatric Techniques of Milton H. Erickson, M.D..* New York: W.W. Norton.

Halifax, Joan. 1981. *Shaman: The Wounded Healer.* New York: Crossroad Publishing.

Havel, Václav, 1990. "On Kafka" (a talk in Jerusalem, April, 26, 1990, on receiving an honorary degree), in *The New York Review of Books,* September 27.

Hayman, Ronald. 1982. *Kafka.* New York: Oxford University Press.

Heller, Erich. 1976. *The Poet's Self and the Poem.* London: University of London, The Athlone Press.

Heller, Erich. 1984. *In the Age of Prose.* London: Cambridge University Press.

Housman, A.E. 1959. *The Collected Poems.* New York: Holt, Rinehart, and Winston.

Huxley, Aldous. 1945. *The Perennial Philosophy.* New York: Harper and Brothers.

Isak Dinesen: A Memorial. 1965. Clara Svendsen, editor. New York: Random House.

Jaeger, Werner. 1939. *Paideia: The Ideals of Greek Culture, Volume 1: Archaic Greece: The Mind of Athens.* New York: Oxford University Press.

Jaeger, Werner. 1943. *Paideia: The Ideals of Greek Culture, Volume 2: In Search of the Divine Center.* New York: Oxford University Press.

James, Henry. 1982. *The Tragic Muse.* New York: Penguin Books.

James, William. 1929. *The Varieties of Religious Experience.* New York: The Modern Library, Random House.

James, William. 1950. *The Principles of Psychology, Volumes 1 and 2.* New York: Dover Publications.

Jantsch, Erich, and Waddington, Conrad H. (editors). 1976. *Evolution and Human Consciousness: Human Systems in Transitions.* Reading, MA: Addison-Wesley.

Johnson, Samuel. 1963. *The Idler and The Adventurer.* New Haven and London: Yale University Press.

Jones, Ernest. 1961. *The Life and Work of Sigmund Freud.* New York: Basic Books,.

Jung, C.G. (commentator). 1931. *The Secret of the Golden Flower: A Chinese Book of Life.* New York: Harcourt, Brace, World, Inc.

Jung, C. G. 1960. "The Transcendent Function," *The Structure and Dynamics of the Psyche.* New York: Pantheon Books.

Jung, C.G. 1963. *Memories, Dreams, and Reflections.* New York: Vintage Books, Random House.

Jung, C.G. 1975. *Letters.* (Bollingen Series XCV: 2.) Princeton: Princeton University Press.

Kafka, Franz. 1946. *The Great Wall of China.* New York: Schocken Books.

Kafka, Franz. 1953. "Betrachtungen über Sünde, Leid, Hoffnung, und den Wahren Weg." *Hochzeitsvorbereitungen auf dem Lande.* Frankfurt: S. Fischer.

Kafka, Franz. 1964. *The Trial.* New York: Vintage Books, Random House.

Kafka, Franz. 1966. *Letter to his Father.* New York: Schocken Books.

Kafka, Franz. 1968. *The Diaries of Franz Kafka, 1910-1923,* 2 volumes. Schocken Books.

Kant, Immanuel. 1949. *The Philosophy of Kant.* New York: The Modern Library.

Keats, John. Undated. *The Poems of John Keats.* London: Simpkin, Marshall, Hamilton, Kent.

Keats, John. 1956. *The Selected Letters of John Keats.* Lionel Trilling, editor. Garden City, NY: Doubleday.

Keleman, Stanley. 1976. *Your Body Speaks its Mind.* New York: Pocket Books.

Kierkegaard, Soren. 1941. *Concluding Unscientific Postscript.* Princeton, NJ: Princeton University Press.

Kleist, Heinrich von. Undated. *S◊mtliche Werke.* Munchen: Th. Knaur Nachf. Verlag.

Kohut, Heinz. 1977. *The Restoration of the Self.* New York: International Universities Press.

Kornfield, Jack. 1977. *Living Buddhist Masters.* Santa Cruz, CA: Unity Press.

Krishnamurti, J. *Krishnamurti's Talks,* 1944. Ojai, CA: Krishnamurti Writings.

Krishnamurti, J. *Krishnamurti's Talks,* 1948. Ojai, CA: Krishnamurti Writings.

Krishnamurti, J. *Krishnamurti's Talks,* 1952. Ojai, CA: Krishnamurti Writings.

Krishnamurti, J. 1954. *The First and Last Freedom.* Harper and Brothers.

Krishnamurti, J. 1969. *Freedom from the Known.* New York: Harper and Row.

Krishnamurti, J. 1976. *Notebook.* New York: Harper and Row.

Krishnamurti, J. 1980. *From Darkness to Light: Poems and Parables*. San Francisco: Harper and Row.

Krishnamurti, J. 1981. *Commentaries on Living: Third Series*. Wheaton, IL: The Theosophical Publishing House.

Krishnamurti, J. 1991. *Collected Works*, Vol. 3. Dubuque, IA: Kendall/Hunt.

Lao Tsu. 1972. *Tao Te Ching*. Gia-fu Feng and Jane English, translators. New York: Vintage Books, Random House.

La Rochefoucauld, Francois de. 1959. *The Maxims*. New York: Modern Library, Random House.

Lipset, David. 1980. *Gregory Bateson: The Legacy of a Scientist*. Englewood Cliffs, NJ: Prentice Hall.

Lovejoy, Arthur O. 1964. *The Great Chain of Being*. Cambridge, MA: Harvard University Press.

Lutyens, Mary. 1975. *Krishnamurti: The Years of Awakening*. New York: Farrar, Straus, and Giroux.

Lutyens, Mary. 1983. *Krishnamurti: The Years of Fulfillment*. New York: Farrar, Straus, and Giroux.

Machiavelli, Niccolo. 1910. *The Prince*. Harvard Classics, Vol. 36. New York: P.F. Collier and Son.

Mahler, M., Pine, F., and Bergman, A. 1975. *The Psychological Birth of the Human Infant*. New York: Basic Books.

Malcolm, Janet. May 15, 1978. "The One-Way Mirror" (on the work of Salvador Minuchin), *The New Yorker*.

Mann, Thomas. 1936. *Stories of Three Decades*. New York: The Modern Library, Random House.

Mann, Thomas. 1948. *Doctor Faustus*. New York: Alfred A. Knopf.

Mann, Thomas. 1939. *The Magic Mountain*. New York: Alfred A. Knopf.

Masterson, James F., editor. 1978. *New Perspectives of Psychotherapy on the Borderline Adult*. New York: Brunner/Mazel.

Mead, Margaret. 1972. *Blackberry Winter*. New York: Morrow.

Meister Eckhart (Raymond B. Blakney, translator). 1941. New York: Harper & Row.

Milton, John. 1950. *Complete Poetry and Selected Prose*. New York: The Modern Library.

Mother Teresa of Calcutta. 1975. *A Gift for God: Prayers and Meditations.* New York: Harper & Row.

Nabokov, Vladimir. 1980. *Lectures on Literature.* New York: Harcourt Brace Jovanovich.

Naked Poetry: Recent American Poetry in Open Forms. 1969. Indianapolis and New York: Bobbs-Merrill Company.

Nietzsche, Friedrich. 1956. *The Birth of Tragedy and The Genealogy of Morals.* Garden City, NY: Doubleday.

O'Connor, Flannery. 1979. *Letters of Flannery O'Connor: The Habit of Being.* New York: Vintage Books, Random House.

Osler, Sir William. 1932. *Aequanimitas and Other Addresses to Medical Students, Nurses, and Practitioners of Medicine.* Philadelphia: Blakiston.

Pascal, Blaise. 1958. *Pensées.* New York: E.P. Dutton.

Perls, Frederick. 1976. *The Gestalt Approach & Eye Witness to Therapy.* New York: Bantam Books.

Perls, Frederick, Hefferline, Ralph F., and Goodman, Paul. 1951. *Gestalt Therapy.* New York: Dell Publishing.

Perry, John. 1976. *Roots of Renewal in Myth and Madness.* San Francisco: Jossey-Bass.

Peters, Heinz Frederick. 1962. *My Sister, My Spouse: A Biography of Lou Andreas-Salomé.* New York: Norton.

Plato. 1948. *The Portable Plato* (Benjamin Jowett, translator.) New York: The Viking Press.

Pope, Alexander. 1931. *The Complete Poetical Works of Pope.* Boston: Houghton, Mifflin.

Proust, Marcel. 1932. *Remembrance of Things Past, Two Volumes.* C.K. Scott Moncrieff and Frederick A. Blossom, translators. French title: *A la Recherche du Temps Perdu.* New York: Random House.

Ram Dass, Baba. 1971. *Be Here Now.* New York: Crown Publishing.

Rilke, Rainer Maria. 1936. *Sonnets to Orpheus.* (J.B. Leishman, translator.) London: The Hogarth Press.

Rilke, Rainer Maria. 1938. *Translations from the Poetry of Rainer Maria Rilke.* M.D. Herter Norton, translator. New York: W.W. Norton.

Rilke, Rainer Maria. 1956. *Sämtliche Werke.* Insel Verlag.

Rilke, Rainer Maria. 1962. *Letters to a Young Poet.* New York: W.W. Norton & Company, Inc.

Rilke, Rainer Maria. 1963. *Duino Elegies.* J.B. Leishman and Stephen Spender, translators. New York: W.W. Norton.

Rilke, Rainer Maria. 1984. *The Selected Poetry of Rainer Maria Rilke.* (Stephen Mitchell, translator.) New York: Vintage Books.

Rosenfeld, Israel. October 9, 1986. "Neural Darwinism: A New Approach to Memory and Perception" (on the work of Gerald Edelman), *The New York Review of Books.*

Rostovtzeff, M. 1963. *Greece.* New York: Oxford University Press.

Ruesch, Jurgen, and Bateson, Gregory. 1951. *Communication: The Social Matrix of Psychiatry.* New York: W.W. Norton.

Ruysbroeck, John. 1951. *The Adornment of the Spiritual Marriage.* London: John M. Watkins.

Sacks, Oliver. February 28, 1985. "Sublime Idiot Geniuses," in *The New York Review of Books.*

Saint Augustine. 1958. *The City of God.* New York: Doubleday.

St. John of the Cross. June 1975. "The Birth of Christ" (Art Beck, translator), in *Invisible City.*

Satir, Virginia. 1983. *Conjoint Family Therapy.* Palo Alto, CA: Science and Behavior Books.

Schacter, Zalman (translator). Undated. "The Torah of the Void," #64 from *Likkuta Maharan: The Book of the Teaching of Reb Nahman of Bratzlaw, recorded by his disciple Nathan.* Transcript of a 2-record set. Recorded by Intermedia Productions, Boston, MA.

Schiller, Friedrich von. 1966. *Naive and Sentimental Poetry* and *On the Sublime.* New York: Frederick Ungar.

Schnabel, Artur. 1961. *My Life and Music.* Great Britain: Longmans.

Schutz, William. 1973. *Elements of Encounter.* Big Sur, CA: Joy Press.

Segal, Lynn. 1986. *The Dream of Reality: Heinz von Foerster's Constructivism.* New York: W.W. Norton.

Shakespeare, William. 1947. *Complete Works.* London: Oxford University Press.

Shaw, George Bernard. 1983. "Maxims for Revolutionists"; appendix to *Man and Superman.* Harmondsworth, Middlesex, England: Penguin Books.

Sloss, Radha Rajagopal. 1991. *Lives in the Shadow with J. Krishnamurti.* London: Bloomsbury.

Smith, Huston, 1958. *The Religions of Man.* New York: Harper and Row, Publishers.

Steegmuller, Francis (editor). 1979. *The Letters of Gustave Flaubert, 1830-1857.* Cambridge, MA: Harvard University Press.

Stern, Daniel. 1985. *The Interpersonal World of the Infant.* New York: Basic Books.

Sullivan, Harry Stack. 1957. *The Interpersonal Theory of Psychiatry.* W.W. Norton.

Swedenborg, Emanuel. 1982. *Heaven and Hell.* New York: Swedenborg Foundation.

Thurman, Judith. 1982. *Isak Dinesen: The Life of a Storyteller.* New York: St. Martin's Press.

Tolstoy, Leo. Undated. *War and Peace.* New York: The Modern Library, Random House.

Tolstoy, Leo. *Great Short Works of Leo Tolstoy.* (Louise and Aylmer Maude, translators of "Hadje Murád" hereon.) New York: Harper & Row.

Trobridge, George. 1949. *Swedenborg.* New York: Swedenborg Foundation.

Wagenbach, Klaus. 1984. *Franz Kafka: Pictures of a Life.* New York: Pantheon Books, Random House.

Watts, Alan, and Chung-liang Huang, Al. 1975. *Tao: The Watercourse Way.* New York: Pantheon Books, Random House.

Watzlawick, Paul, Bavelas, Janet Beavin; and Jackson, Don D. 1967. *Pragmatics of Human Communication.* New York: W.W. Norton.

Whitehead, Alfred North. 1962. *Science and the Modern World.* New York: New American Library.

Whitehead, Alfred North. 1964. *The Concept of Nature.* Cambridge, England: Cambridge University Press.

Whitehead, Afred North, and Russell, Bertrand. 1910. *Principia Mathematica, Volume 1.* Cambridge, England: Cambridge University Press.

Whitman, Walt. Undated. *Leaves of Grass.* New York: The Modern Library.

Wilber, Ken. 1980. *The Atman Project.* Wheaton, IL: The Theosophical Publishing House.

Wittgenstein, Ludwig. 1961. *Tractatus Logico-Philosophicus.* London: Routledge & Kegan Paul.

Wolff, Kurt. 1991. *A Portrait in Essays and Letters.* Chicago, University of Chicago Press.

Wydenbruck, Nora. 1972. *Rilke: Man and Poet.* Westport, CT: Greenwood Press.

Yeats, W.B. 1974. *Collected Poems.* New York: Macmillan.

Young, Arthur M. 1984. *The Reflexiv Universe.* Mill Valley, CA: Robert Briggs Associates.

Yourcenar, Marguerite. 1987. *Mishima: A Vision of the Void.* New York: Farrar, Straus, and Giroux.

Yutang, Lin (editor). 1942. *The Wisdom of China and India.* New York: Random House.

Yutang, Lin (editor). 1948. *The Wisdom of Laotse.* New York: The Modern Library.

Zeig, Jeffrey K. (editor). 1980. *A Teaching Seminar with Milton H. Erickson.* New York: Brunner/Mazel.

NAME INDEX

Andreas: 263
Arendt: 17
Aristotle: 27, 247, 248
Atwood: 276
Auden: 41, 192, 260, 261
Augustine: 126, 190
Austen: 31

Bach: 124
Barthes: 257, 262, 273
Bateson: 8, 17-19, 86, 87, 145, 146, 153, 155, 157, 158, 180, 187, 191, 197, 202, 211, 213, 229, 243, 245, 248, 249, 251, 252, 254, 266, 272, 275, 276, 285
Bavelas: 20, 257, 284
Becker: 50
Benjamin: 21
Besant: 181-183, 185, 277, 279
Binswanger: 262
Bion: 246, 253, 284
Blake: 8, 17-19, 23-44, 52, 58, 73, 85, 91, 104, 117, 122, 151, 154, 157, 166, 171, 175, 187, 193, 211, 214, 230, 233, 234, 248, 251, 252, 254, 259, 260, 283
Blixen: 11, 15, 18, 20, 49, 96, 208
Boehme: 93
Broch: 14, 15
Brod: 72, 76
Brontë: 43
Browne: 190
Browning: 174, 277
Buber: 8, 9, 14, 17-19, 91-119, 121, 122, 126, 131, 147, 157, 187, 207, 211, 212, 223, 239, 240, 247, 248, 251, 252, 254, 266-270, 272, 278, 283
Buddha: 13, 106, 124, 125, 131, 140-142, 180-182, 184, 186, 192, 206, 278
Butler: 54, 82

Camus: 82, 83, 87
Capra: 127
Carroll: 146, 158
Chuang-tzu: 130
Coleridge: 14, 186, 194, 278, 279
Confucius: 13, 128, 129
Conrad: 258
Cummings: 167

Dickinson: 17, 43
Dodge: 182
Donne: 19, 77, 254, 284
Dryden: 35, 36
Duse: 67

Edelman: 255, 285
Eliot: 17, 258, 279
Elytis: 43
Emerson: 16, 271, 279
Erickson: 11, 37, 38, 85, 141, 172, 173, 250, 252, 257, 260, 277, 284

Flaubert: 15, 16, 117
Foerster: 36, 260
Forster: 86
Fra Angelico: 270
Frankl: 81, 284
Freud: 9, 20, 36, 40, 44, 63, 64, 66, 78, 83, 86, 113, 153, 255, 263, 264, 266, 278
Friedman: 98, 117, 266

Gide: 16, 185, 258
Ginsberg: 10, 11
Goethe: 14, 16, 20, 56, 63, 93, 96, 100, 102, 118, 139, 191, 200, 207, 258, 267, 269, 281
Gogol: 74, 265
Goodman: 257
Gregor Smith: 267

Haley: 151, 243, 260, 271, 277
Halifax: 258
Havel: 144, 271
Hefferline: 257
Hegel: 105
Hesse: 56
Hildegard of Bingen: 17
Hitler: 39
Horney: 202
Housman: 146, 269
Hulewicz: 52
Huxley: 187

Jaeger: 273
James: 9, 27, 52, 56, 143, 168, 183, 270, 271
Jantsch: 270
John: 13, 14, 42, 77, 109, 124, 151, 241, 264, 278, 284
Johnson: 34, 241, 248, 259, 283
Joyce: 9, 270
Jung: 9, 36, 63, 114, 128, 217, 224, 263, 269, 274

Kafka: 8, 17-19, 66, 69-89, 91, 94, 96, 98, 108, 122, 140, 157, 187, 199, 205, 211, 214, 222, 248, 249, 251, 252, 254, 264, 265--267, 272, 273, 279
Kakar: 169
Kant: 274
Kappus: 53-58, 60, 63, 68, 96, 261, 262
Kaufman: 267
Keats: 88, 194, 209, 252, 254, 266, 278, 281, 284
Kerouac: 10, 11
Key, Ellen: 53, 55
King: 32, 36, 136, 138, 139, 143
Kipling: 146, 176
Kleist: 44, 45, 260
Krishnamurti: 8, 9, 17-19, 179-185, 187-189, 191-194, 196, 197, 198, 199, 201-207, 209, 211, 217, 220, 223, 242, 248, 252, 254, 277-281

La Rochefoucauld: 39, 41
Lady Murasaki: 17
Lao-Tzu: 8, 15, 17, 18, 121-140, 142-144, 157, 158, 175, 187, 189, 201, 222, 237, 248, 249, 251, 252, 254, 255, 270, 271, 272
Lawrence: 60
Leadbeater: 181, 183, 277
Lipset: 272
Locke: 25
Lutyens: 182, 187, 203, 206, 277, 280

Machiavelli: 132
Mahler: 267, 268
Malcolm: 284
Malinowski: 147
Mann: 9, 56, 200, 257, 258, 267, 269, 281
Marcus Aurelius: 72
Marvell: 106
Masterson: 143, 271
May, Rollo: 262
Mead: 158
Meister Eckhart: 72, 108, 205, 270
Mendel: 146
Milton: 10, 11, 29, 37, 85, 141, 172, 250, 257, 260, 271, 284

Minuchin: 244, 245, 250, 253, 284
Montaigne: 77

Murasaki: 17

Nabokov: 15, 16, 65
Napoleon: 104, 221
Newton: 29, 36, 37, 259
Nicholas of Cusa: 93
Novalis: 274

O'Connor: 111, 268
Orwell: 13
Osler: 254, 284

Pascal: 76
Paul: 88, 243, 257, 284
Perls: 257
Perry: 241, 284
Peters: 263
Phillips: 30
Picasso: 101
Plato: 16, 157, 247, 248, 282
Proust: 255, 262

Radcliffe-Brown: 147, 148
Rajagopal: 279, 280
Ram Dass: 11
Reynolds: 25, 31, 259
Rilke: 8, 17-19, 47-50, 52-68, 70, 73, 77, 81, 86, 91, 96, 100, 122, 187, 194, 211, 220, 248, 249, 251, 252, 254, 261, 262, 263, 264, 266
Rimbaud: 10
Rioch: 116, 201
Ritterman: 276
Rodin: 50
Rogers: 113, 117, 202, 269
Rosenfeld: 285
Rostovtzeff: 138
Ruesch: 153, 155
Russell: 147, 149, 150, 154, 155, 249, 272
Ruysbroeck: 15

Sacks: 204, 279
Sai Baba: 174
Satir: 243, 284
Schiller: 199, 200, 207, 278
Schnabel: 208, 281
Schutz: 257
Segal: 260
Selver: 64
Shainberg: 201
Shakespeare: 14, 88, 194, 240, 271, 284
Sloss: 279, 281
Smith: 203, 267
Stern: 268
Stolorow: 276
Sullivan: 86, 142, 169, 201, 202, 229, 241, 266, 279, 283
Suzuki Roshi: 125
Swedenborg: 23, 24, 28, 29

T'ai Chi: 225, 270
Tolstoy: 16, 49, 67, 191, 247, 248, 281

Van Gogh: 72
Virgil: 14, 15, 56-58, 63, 68

Watzlawick: 20, 243, 257, 284
Weakland: 151
Weigert: 201
Weil: 17
Weininger: 201, 279
Westhoff: 47, 50
Whitaker: 85
Whitehead: 17, 117, 155, 249, 272
Whitman: 84, 99, 101, 267
Wiener: 53, 148-150
Winkler: 93
Winnicott: 168
Wolff: 261
Yeats: 82

SUBJECT INDEX

Active Imagination: 217
Autonomous psyche: 245, 253

Beyond words: 82, 180
Biology: 131
Brief: 19, 48, 63, 106, 211, 212, 225
Buddhism: 124-126, 192, 226, 227, 237, 278

Christianity: 124, 125, 191, 222, 278
Conditioned: 161, 199, 200, 203, 207
Contradiction: 51-54, 58, 63, 66, 73, 104, 108, 180
Contraries: 28, 29, 31, 43, 52, 73, 166
Cybernetics: 149, 171

Dialogue: 95, 100, 111, 116, 158, 161, 166, 167, 203, 269
Double bind: 86, 145, 151, 162, 170, 171, 173, 191, 243, 266, 273, 274, 277
Dream: 14, 36, 73, 74, 167, 168, 182, 185, 201, 202, 220, 260, 282; interpretation 201, 202; symbols 201; work 167; Dream message 220

Eastern: 63, 93, 127, 241, 270
Existence: 7, 17, 28, 35, 52, 54, 61, 62, 66, 67, 84, 102, 114, 117, 124, 130, 131, 144, 147, 165, 212, 213, 244, 247, 248, 266

Faith: 24, 43, 44, 47, 63, 64, 66, 68, 85, 98, 145, 166, 190, 191, 193, 203, 207, 211, 224, 245, 249, 256
Freedom: and Bateson 163, 165, 166; and Blake 42, 43; and Buber 94, 100, 115; and Buddha 124; and character 243; and Kafka 84; and Krishnamurti 184, 187-189, 191, 192, 194, 195, 199, 202, 205, 207, 208, 254; and Lao-tzu 132, 136; and Rilke 52, 53, 61; and the family 245; meaning of to "Beat" generation of 1950's 10, 11; of the client 118; of the therapist 85; v.s. discipline 87; v.s. order 160, 162

Gestalt: 10, 16, 19, 37, 38, 44, 64, 65, 97, 128, 137, 202, 213, 221, 223, 248, 255, 257, 258, 272, 279

I-It: 93, 100, 109, 110, 240, 268
I-Thou: 93, 100, 106, 107, 109-111, 113, 118, 119, 121, 211, 212, 213, 229, 237, 239, 240, 247, 267, 278, 283
Idealized: 39, 122
Individual: 19, 24, 54, 61, 62, 65, 91, 102, 104, 144, 147, 148, 167, 170, 177, 179, 186, 208, 224, 239-241, 243, 245, 246, 247, 248, 252, 253, 276
Insight: 207, 241-243, 250, 257

Interpersonal: 10, 37, 117, 202, 239-241, 250, 266, 268
Interplay: 12, 59, 104, 139, 170, 239, 276

Jungian: 43, 64, 217, 241, 242, 244, 253

Lao-tzu: 8, 15, 17, 18, 121-140, 142-144, 157, 158, 175, 187, 189, 201, 222, 237, 248, 249, 251, 252, 254, 255, 270, 271, 272
Learning: 37, 93, 97, 99, 115, 126, 137, 149, 150, 154, 160, 161, 162, 163, 165, 166, 168, 171, 173, 188, 191, 202, 241, 245, 257, 274, 277
Logical types: 149-151, 154, 249
Love: and Bateson 150, 168, 171-174; and Blake 25, 28, 32-34, 36, 43, 251; and Buber 92, 93, 95, 102-106, 111; and Contextual therapy 211; and Goethe 14; and Kafka 83, 85, 89; and Kohut 143; and Krishnamurti 181-185, 189, 191, 195, 203-205, 208, 280; and Lao-tzu 135, 139, 140; and meditation 245; and Rilke 47-49, 52, 54, 55, 57, 60-65, 66, 249, 254; and schizophrenia 272, 273; as a state of being 18; as communication

Meta: 157, 158, 167, 174
Metaphor: 105, 142, 157, 164, 167, 174
Mind: and Bateson 145, 157, 158, 165-167, 170, 171, 175, 176, 252; and Blake 24, 25, 29, 34, 36, 43, 44; and Buber 106; and Buddha 192; and Krishnamurti 184, 189, 194, 195 - 197, 199, 203, 206; and meditation 197, 198; and Rilke 59, 60; and Therapeutic nurture 214; and writing 14; "cure" of William James 27; expanders of 10; in therapy 7; innocent 195
Mysticism: 60, 109, 270, 271

Negative Capability: 194, 254, 256
Nurture: 37, 211, 214, 217, 232, 234, 282

Obscurity: 49, 129, 255
Order: 13, 28, 29, 31, 32, 35, 99, 128, 130, 131, 133, 145, 150, 156, 159, 160, 167, 169, 175, 176, 182, 186
Original sin: 191, 192, 278
Original virtue: 192

Paradox: 11, 20, 21, 73, 74, 76-78, 87-89, 108, 140, 142, 143, 155, 163, 168, 187, 254, 256
Passion: 34, 40, 104, 124, 186, 195, 196, 198, 261, 270
Personal freedom: 85, 245
Personal problems: 40, 85
Physical: and fullness of being 35; and mental, unity of 60; and spiritual 61; context, and the Theory of Logical Types 150; environment, and awareness 223; metabolism, and Bateson's theories 153; movement, and the subjective 36; mysticism of Rilke 60; nature, and man 108; oriented psychotherapies 64; pain, and Lao-tzu 132; science 127; structure, and Lao-tzu

128; threats, and fear 193; v.s. psychic 35; weakness 38
Plato: 16, 157, 247, 248, 282
Presence: 29, 34, 63, 92-95, 97, 100, 101, 110-112, 176, 183, 199, 211, 223, 224, 267, 281
Primary Words: 14, 93, 109, 119, 270; and Buber 93, 109, 110, 112, 119, 270; as acts of fundamental creation 14
Psyche: 9, 35, 36, 39, 61, 63, 86, 240, 242, 244, 245, 253, 283
Psychoanalytic: 243, 265, 268, 276, 281
Psychotherapy: 7-12, 19, 35, 91, 97, 98, 112, 128, 140, 153, 161, 171-173, 202, 208, 229, 271, 277, 281-285; and Bateson 171-173; and Blake 35; and Buber 91, 97, 98, 112; and Krishnamurti 202; and learning 161; and self-discovery 12; and the therapist's use of self 229; and values 7-9; and wu-wei 140; different approaches to 19; dissatisfaction with 10; in Gestalt therapy 128; Indian religious thought and 11; problems with 208

Reason: 28, 29, 39-41, 43, 52, 54, 58, 70, 83, 147, 195, 241, 254, 275
Refractory: life v.s. idealized life 66
Relationship: 12, 38, 54, 55, 62, 91, 94, 96, 102, 107112, 121, 147, 154, 157, 161163, 179, 195, 202, 205, 220, 248, 251, 267, 280, 283

Sacrament: 94, 157, 164
Sacred: 18, 110, 117, 136, 166, 167, 180, 184, 275
Sage: 15, 49, 54, 87, 125, 128, 131, 132, 135, 137, 138, 142, 143, 248, 254, 270
Schizophrenia: 25, 86, 145, 154, 191, 243
Selflove: and Kafka 85
Sexuality: 63, 86
Simplicity: 24, 30, 79, 117, 137, 142, 143
Solitude: 43, 50, 54, 57, 58, 62, 63, 65, 66, 88, 100, 233, 248, 249
Spiritual: 8, 23, 29, 43, 49, 61, 64, 66, 77, 79, 80, 82, 94, 114, 116, 174, 176, 181, 199, 205, 207, 208, 237, 251, 252
Spontaneity: 94, 116, 199
Stochastic: 156, 165, 275
Strategic: 11, 251, 272
Systematic: 97, 98

T'ai Chi: 225, 270
Tao: and Bateson 161; and Buber 121; and formlessness 139; and fulfillment 132; and Gestalt therapists 128; and God 125; and good and evil 124; and Jung 128; and Krishnamurti 205, 207; and Lao-tzu 122, 123, 126, 129, 251, 252; and law or social virtue 135; and morality 140; and personality 143; and physics 128; and power 133; and psychotherapy 142; and the political ruler 138; and the unity of all life 127; and timelessness 139; and wu-wei 136, 137, 140, 144; and yeilding 132; and yin-yang 133; as a "How-to-be" book 132; as source 131;

enigma of 129, 130, 132; pursuit of 126
Tao Te Ching: 18, 19, 121, 123, 125, 126, 133, 139, 269, 271
Taoism: and Gestalt therapy 128; v.s. Buddhism 125
Taoist: and Bateson 146, 156, 161, 163, 176, 180; and Buber 122, 126; and Contextual psychotherapy 211; and the political ruler 139; and wuwei 142; spontenaity and I-Thou 94; will of Buber 94
Te: and Contextual Psychotherapy 211; and the Tao 134; and wu-wei 136; power of 133
The psyche: 9, 36, 39, 63, 86, 240, 242, 244, 245, 253, 283
The sage of Lao-tzu: 142
Time: and Bateson 170, 171; and Blake 32-34; and Buber 99, 103, 105; and causality 100; and Krishnamurti 194, 206; and Lao-tzu 131; and relativity theory 127; and Rilke 58; and the cycles of nature 30
Timeless: and "the unconcious" of Freud 36; and Krishnamurti 194, 201

Unconditioned: 161, 179, 186, 193, 197, 199, 203, 207, 277

Values: 7-9, 12, 105, 148, 170, 185, 191, 211, 221, 282, 283
Verbal: 109, 207, 268, 279

Western: communicational speech patterns, and Bateson 150; cosmology, Chain of Being in 126; culture, and free will v.s. fatalism 247; culture, and shamanism 250; God v.s. the Tao 125; Hasidic tale 111; industrial worker, and Pavlovian behavior 149; life, and schismogenic balance 148; myth, and language 13; religious tradition 15; thought, and Lao-tzu 124, 127, 129; thought, and Lao-tzu and Jung 128; view of individuality 249; visual art - and passion 124; writers, and the individual and destiny 248